Sustainable Luxury

Managing Social and Environmental Performance in Iconic Brands

Sustainable Luxury

MANAGING SOCIAL AND ENVIRONMENTAL PERFORMANCE IN ICONIC BRANDS

EDITED BY MIGUEL ANGEL GARDETTI AND
ANA LAURA TORRES

Routledge
Taylor & Francis Group
LONDON AND NEW YORK

First published 2015 by Greenleaf Publishing Limited

Published 2017 by Routledge
4 Park Square, Milton Park, Abingdon, Oxon OX14 4RN

and by Routledge
605 Third Avenue, New York, NY 10158

Routledge is an imprint of the Taylor & Francis Group, an informa business

British Library Cataloguing in Publication Data:
A catalogue record for this book is available from the British Library.

ISBN-13: 978-1-783530-61-8 (hbk)

Contents

Foreword

María Eugenia Girón
IE Premium and Prestige Observatory, Madrid, Spain

It was 2010 when I received the first email from Miguel Angel Gardetti. We have kept in touch ever since. At the time, he invited me to be part of the jury of the first awards in sustainable luxury, taking place in Buenos Aires on 30 October 2010. I had just published *Secretos de Lujo* (*Inside Luxury*), which included a chapter about eco-luxury. I had identified sustainability as one of the new meanings of luxury for savvy, well-educated and demanding luxury clients. Miguel Angel had read it, was interested, and made some insightful remarks. He was ready to take action and launch the first sustainable luxury awards. He was inviting me to be part of the action.

Miguel Angel Gardetti is a textile engineer with extensive experience of working with fashion companies—an industrial sector of great importance for the global economy. He was made aware of the negative impacts of the industry in terms of water consumption and waste, as well as negative social aspects derived from the fierce competition. I can imagine Miguel Angel embracing the challenge to expand his academic focus from the textile industry. He decided to take a more global approach and become an expert in corporate sustainability.

For two decades Miguel Angel has built a body of knowledge around the subject. He told me that one day he realised changes needed to be made beyond researching and lecturing. It was then that he thought about awards to recognise those companies and initiatives that had taken steps to address challenging and difficult issues, first traceability-related and then sustainability-related. Due to his previous involvement with textiles and fashion he had been exposed to the fascination that luxury can elicit in people. He concluded that it was time to inspire rather than punish.

I travelled to Buenos Aires to attend the ceremony of the first edition of the Sustainable Luxury Awards in October 2010. Miguel Angel and Gloria, his wife, were waiting for me at the airport. The bouquet of flowers they were holding for me was big, colourful and welcoming. I was overwhelmed by this reception, so warm and affectionate. I discovered later that this was the way Miguel Angel would approach all of his endeavours—with care and thoughtfulness, as if it was a family matter.

This was the beginning of a long adventure. We soon realised that honouring prestigious luxury companies was going to be a tough matter as there were only a handful of them taking action in this direction, and also because brand executives might be reluctant to receive an award with no history.

However, we discovered that, while dialogue with established brands was not an easy one, there were many entrepreneurs eager to participate—pioneers who launch new premium and luxury brands guided by the desire to integrate sustainable value into the meaning of luxury. The annual Sustainable Luxury Awards evolved to become a celebration of entrepreneurship and recognition of those who start with this point of view. Additionally, we soon realised that giving these honorary awards would provide visibility for these ventures. This was a very useful way of supporting these entrepreneurs.

As I said, Miguel Angel makes a family matter of his work. Since the first time we met we have held lively lunches and dinners with candidates, supporters, friends and members of his team. I soon met Ana Laura, who worked closely with him at the Center for Study of Corporate Sustainability. She also leads the Sustainable Textile Center. Thoughtful and experienced, Ana Laura has for many years been a support to the award and to the work of Miguel Angel.

After three presentations of the awards in Buenos Aires, the Center for Studies on Sustainable Luxury, founded by Miguel Angel and IE Business School (also home to the Premium and Luxury Research Center that I founded) have decided to bring the awards to Europe and expand its scope to have an international appeal. The fourth presentation of the IE Awards for Sustainability in the Premium and Luxury Sectors took place in Madrid at IE Business School in July 2014 in the emblematic Paper Pavilion built by Pritzer-honoured architect Shigeru Ban. There will be an award for a Latin American focused project. These awards are now established as the world reference in this category.

When Miguel Angel asked me to write a Foreword to this book, I was hesitant. On the one hand it was difficult to add any more information to the issue of sustainable luxury explored and developed by this book with such depth and academic discipline. On the other, I could not resist the temptation of using the opportunity to thank, on behalf of many, both Miguel Angel and Ana Laura for their work. It is also an opportunity to express my gratitude for all the good times in Buenos Aires, the learning, the feeling of sharing a common goal, and the chance to take action together. I am especially grateful to Miguel Angel for his vision and trust to initiate a new phase together with IE Business School. Lastly, I want to truly thank him for his first email to me, almost five years ago.

María Eugenia Girón
Madrid, 20 April 2014

Introduction

Miguel Angel Gardetti
Center for Studies on Sustainable Luxury, Buenos Aires, Argentina

Ana Laura Torres
The Sustainable Textile Center, Buenos Aires, Argentina

Luxury and sustainability

Seen as a whole, the 'luxury industry' is important for the global economy since, measured in terms of income, it has a volume of sales of approximately €740 billion. Only considering so-called 'personal' luxury, which includes fashion and accessories, cosmetics and fragrance, jewellery and watches, amounted to €217 million in 2013.[1]

However, given the complexities existing in the industry of luxury, its evolution nowadays, and the importance of our social connection with it, it seems appropriate to explain some issues.

What is sustainable development?

One of the most widely accepted definitions of sustainable development is the one proposed by the World Commission on Environment and Development (WCED 1987) in *Our Common Future*, also known as the Brundtland Report, which defines sustainable development as the development model that allows us to meet present needs without compromising the ability of future generations to meet their own needs. According to the Brundtland Report, the three pillars of sustainability are 'people, profit and planet'. The main objective of this development model is to raise quality of life by maximising the productive potential of the ecosystem in the long term through appropriate technologies. The Brundtland Report can be considered

1 Fundazione Altagamma, www.altagamma.it, accessed 15 November 2013.

as the starting point of the debate on sustainable development, thus constituting an important political change (Mebratu 1998). Yet at the World Summit on Sustainable Development in Johannesburg in 2002, this evolved into 'people, planet and prosperity' where prosperity is broader than profit.

Bansal and Howard (1997) argue that sustainable development can also be described as a process to carry out development in an equitable, connected, safe and prudent way. Connectivity includes ecological, social and economic interdependence. Equality suggests justice, within and across generations and species. Prudence means the duty of care for life in the technological, scientific and political sense. Security involves the mitigation of chronic threats and damage (Warhurst 2001). To some extent, sustainable development is about social and environmental justice. Meanwhile, Ruggero Schleicher-Tappeser (2001) argues that sustainable development is not only a new concept, but also a new paradigm which requires looking at things in a different way. It is a notion of the world deeply different from the one that dominates our current thinking and includes satisfying basic human needs such as justice, freedom and dignity (Ehrenfeld 1999). It is the vision through which we can build a way of being.[2] Also, Suzuki and Dressel (2002) define sustainability, at the individual level, as the assessment of all human behaviours with the vision of reformulating those that contradict the development of a sustainable future.

According to Penny Allen, Christophe Bonazzi and David Gee (2001) sustainable development is a complex expression, whose meaning few people agree on. It is a 'conservative' notion, transversal through social, environmental and economic considerations. These authors state that anyone can take the term and 'reinvent' it according to his or her own needs.

What is luxury?

Coco Chanel once defined luxury as '. . . a necessity that begins when necessity ends' (quoted in Okonkwo 2007: 7). Along the same lines, Klaus Heine (2011) defines luxury as something desirable and more than a necessity. These definitions, though relative depending on the cultural, economic or regional contexts which transform luxury into an ambiguous concept (Low 2010), show the absurd aspect of this industry (Scheibel 2010). However, luxury has been a sign of prosperity, power and social status since ancient times (Kapferer and Basten 2010). Thus, luxury is a matter of seeing and being seen. 'Seeing' as a search of the latest distinctive signifiers that can be used to 'be seen' in different distinctive group processes (Mortelmans 2005). Also, according to Ricca and Robins (2012), luxury is a source of inspiration, controversy, admiration and considerable economic success.

2 J.R. Ehrenfeld (2002) *Sustainability by Choice*, unpublished.

Christopher L. Berry (1994) in *The Idea of Luxury*—one of the most interesting and comprehensive pieces on the concept of luxury, particularly its intellectual history—establishes that luxury has changed throughout time and that it reflects social norms and aspirations. This transformation of the idea of luxury was necessary to adapt to global changes (Shamina 2011). Luxury is the intimate perception and experience of things that turns them from not necessary into indispensable. True elements of (authentic) luxury rely on the search for beauty, refinement, innovation, purity, the well-made, what remains, the essence of things, the ultimate best (Girón 2012). However, this luxury has given way to the *new luxury* through its democratisation (massification?) that occurred when family and artisanal luxury companies sagged against the large conglomerates which had a strong focus on economic aspects.

Dana Thomas (2007: 13) in her work *Deluxe: How Luxury Lost Its Luster* is very clear about the consequences of this process: '[T]he luxury industry ... has sacrificed its integrity, undermined its products, stained its history and deceived its customers'. It is that the image, neither the reputation nor the legitimacy, was the way and the marketing the function. Caroline Weber (2007) from *The New York Times* in her article 'The Devil Sells Prada', published on 26 August 2007, synthesised this idea very well: '[L]uxury brands were guarantors of value and integrity, they are now markers that point toward nothing, guiding the consumer on a road to nowhere'. But back in 1999, Robert H. Frank observed in his book *Luxury Fever: Weighing the Cost of Excess* the need to minimise the culture of 'excess' to restore the true values of life.[3] William Howard Adams (2012: 7) synthesised this phenomenon by saying that luxury 'has lost its original record as to its meaning'.

Sustainable luxury: evolution and definition

While Magnus Macfarlane, Anne Tallontire and Adrienne Martin (2003) from the Natural Resources Institute of the University of Greenwich at Medway presented their work *Towards an Ethical Jewellery Business*, the relationship between luxury and sustainability began to deepen strongly after some facts. Towards the end of 2007, an in-depth documentary by RAI 3 entitled 'Slaves of Luxury' showed the supply chain of Italian luxury fashion brands. The documentary showed cases of Chinese illegal immigration in Italy making accessories for Dolce & Gabbana and Prada. The audience was estimated at four million people and the RAI's Internet forum collapsed (Ilari and Zargani 2007).

In 2007, Roberto Saviano published *Gomorra* which described how a white suit worn by one of the world's most famous women, Angelina Jolie, on the red carpet

3 This debate is not new. Edward J. Urick, when writing *Luxury and Waste of Life* in 1908, a book that investigates the luxury industry, reflects (and questions) if the money spent on this type of products and services wouldn't be better 'invested' in projects focused on communities, as well as for reasons related to the consumption of luxury.

at the Oscars, was made by someone employed by organised criminals accused of multiple murders (Saviano 2007). Although Saviano did not mention the brand of the dress, it was known by some bloggers such as BabelMed that it was Dolce & Gabbana (Cornet 2007).

The 2007 bestseller by Dana Thomas, *Deluxe: How Luxury Lost Its Luster*, which has been translated into almost every language, gave some warning signs. The report *Deeper Luxury*, published in November 2007 by WWF-UK, points out that consumers of luxury products and services are influenced by aspirations and these can encompass deep values such as environmental and social issues (Bendell and Kleanthous 2007). Luxury, according to Kleanthous (2011), is becoming less exclusive and less wasteful and more about helping people to express their deepest values.

By following these guidelines, the two most important conferences of this sector in 2009 addressed these issues and focused their discussions on the assessment of these changes in the consumer and the new concept of success for achieving 'sustainable luxury'. One of them, organised by the *International Herald Tribune* in New Delhi (India) was called the Sustainable Luxury Conference. The other, promoted by the *Financial Times* in Monaco and attended by Prince Albert, was entitled Business and Luxury Summit—Beyond Green: Economics, Ethics and Enticement.

It is important to note that the legitimacy of luxury becomes more complicated in situations of extreme inequality and poverty. If sustainability integrates a principle of justice and social equity, and some consider luxury to be an excess, then it may not be moral while there is poverty. In 2009 the worlds of luxury and poverty collided when the *Slumdog Millionaire* child actors from the slums of Mumbai led a parade of fashion in New Delhi almost simultaneously with the *International Herald Tribune* Sustainable Luxury Conference. The success of the film and the parade raised a great debate on the relationship of poverty with luxury brands.

Sustainable luxury is the concept of returning to the essence of luxury with its traditional focus on thoughtful purchasing and artisanal manufacturing, to the beauty of quality materials and to respect for social and environmental issues. This deeper approach requires, and will require, a relentless search for knowledge, discovery and understanding. Thus, the luxury consumer will be identified as one who has both the means and the motivation to ensure care for the environment and for other people to improve their quality of life (Bendell and Kleanthous 2007).

Subsequent to the above, additional relevant facts solidify and promote the notion of sustainable luxury. Some of them are set out in the book *Inside Luxury* by María Eugenia Girón (2009), which presents a documented study of luxury and its future and how sustainability influences it. Another fact was the realisation, also in 2009, of the conference Redefining Sustainability in the International Agenda—Inspiring Greater Engagement in Biodiversity Issues, organised by UN Conference on Trade and Development (UNCTAD) together with Green2Greener, in which several luxury brands participated.

In early 2010, the Center for Studies on Sustainable Luxury was established with the aim of assisting companies in the luxury sector to transition towards sustainability, thus encouraging sustainable business practices across all areas of the organisation and its supply chain. To this end, academic learning and research will become vital and current for future sustainable leaders. This means taking a broader picture to ensure that social and environmental issues are completely integrated in the decision-making process.[4] Not least were the impacts of the report *Uplifting the Earth: The Ethical Performance of Luxury Brands* by Ian Doyle and Jem Bendell (2011), *Raconteur on Sustainable Luxury* developed jointly by Raconteur Media and the WWF (2011) and *Style Over Substance: Why Ethics Are Not in Fashion for Designer Labels* developed by Bryony Moore for the Ethical Consumer Research Association (Moore 2011) in which 20 luxury brands are assessed under a series of criteria such as environment, testing on animals, furs, gold and diamonds, rights of workers, activity in politics, among others.

In 2012 María Eugenia Girón develops and publishes the *Diccionario LID Sobre Lujo y Responsabilidad* (*LID Dictionary on Luxury and Responsibility*; Girón 2012) with a multidisciplinary team of eight experts in the field. The dictionary has 2,000 entries defined and translated into English. In August Jem Bendell (2012) publishes the report *Elegant Disruption: How Luxury and Society Can Change Each Other for Good*. This shows how creative destruction is typical in most industry sectors, including luxury, and how disruptive innovation by entrepreneurs is key to that process. At the end of 2013, *The Journal of Corporate Citizenship* dedicated its entire issue (December 2013) to sustainable luxury, with the guest editors being Miguel Angel Gardetti from the Center for Studies on Sustainable Luxury, Argentina, and Ana Laura Torres from the Sustainable Textile Center, Argentina (Gardetti and Torres 2013).[5] A book entitled *Sustainable Luxury and Social Entrepreneurship: Stories From the Pioneers*, edited by Miguel Angel Gardetti and María Eugenia Girón (Executive Director for IE Business School Premium and Prestige Business Observatory, Spain), was presented in Madrid, at IE Business School, on July 2nd, 2014.[6] It describes the work of sustainable pioneers in the luxury sector putting in practice their knowledge and intuition in many different ways, to make a significant change in society. (Fig. 1)

4 www.lujosustentable.org and www.awardinsustainableluxury.org

5 www.ctextilsustentable.org.ar

6 http://www.ie.edu/ie-luxury-awards-es/

Figure 1 **The evolution of sustainable luxury**

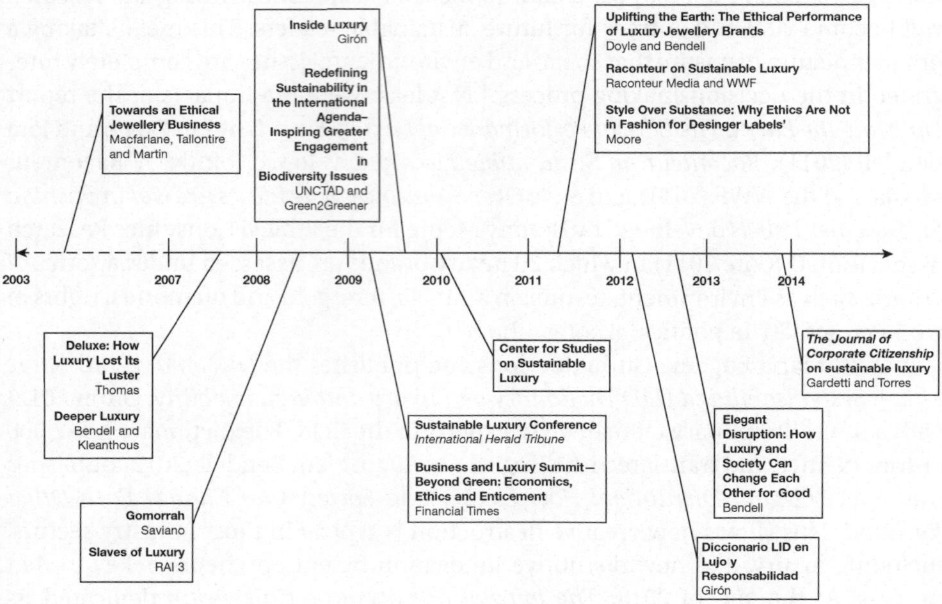

The book

This book complements the December 2013 special issue of *The Journal of Corporate Citizenship* on sustainable luxury. As with the special issue, this book intends to explore the different dimensions of the luxury industry in relation to sustainability. The call for papers for this book attracted 20 submissions, 13 of which were invited to the second round for full manuscript review. Finally, and with the help of the review panel throughout this process, 11 top quality papers were selected which deal with essential aspects in the luxury sector.

For a better understanding, the book is divided into three parts:

- Part I: Luxury, sustainability, fashion and value chain in textiles
- Part II: Luxury, sustainability and consumption
- Part III: Luxury and sustainability in relation to various topics and areas

Part I begins with a chapter by Frédéric Godart and Sorah Seong called 'Is sustainable luxury fashion possible?'. This chapter unfolds the challenges and opportunities specifically faced by luxury fashion brands in pursuing an eco-sustainability agenda by taking a theory-informed, action-oriented approach towards the six core principles of fashion. In light of the principle-based investigation of how both consumers and producers can take advantage of each principle in favour of practising eco-sustainable fashion at the individual and brand levels, the authors suggest that the institutionalisation of eco-sustainability paradigms in luxury fashion can be realised without negating the core principles of fashion. The next chapter, 'Fake remake: the role of the luxury fashion market in driving sustainable fashion practices' by Angela Finn and Kim Fraser, identifies and analyses the merits of the successful 'make do and mend' practices that were introduced during the 1940s' wartime campaign to address textile shortages. The aim of this research is to draw attention to the emergence of the insidious practice of 'fake remake'. The authors argue that the faking of the remaking process by mass market fashion brands should be considered highly detrimental, and further contributes to the problem of textile waste. A high-end refashion model, taken by designers within the luxury market, such as Martin Margiela, provides the best opportunity for a bottom-up, consumer desire-driven approach that utilises genuine 'remake' processes to reduce textile waste. Completing Part I, Catarina Holmsten-Carrizo and Cecilia Mark-Herbert present the chapter 'Luxury marketing strategies related to ethical sourcing'. This chapter addresses the topic of responsible sourcing in the cotton value chains through a comparative case study of a Swedish and a Finnish home textile retailer. Given the extent of ethical challenges that cotton production implies, most of the production would qualify as luxury. The authors argue that the careful selection of production methods is one way to minimise undesired environmental and social effects.

Part II begins with 'Redefining luxury in the 21st century: where was yours made? A case study of Made in San Francisco' by Connie Ulasewicz. Expanding the perception towards what has traditionally been considered luxury (i.e. quality), this paper explores, through research conducted among designers from the city of San Francisco, another element of growing consumer support—the 'local made' label as part of the new criteria for defining luxury. Following this, Gjoko Muratovski with the chapter 'Sustainable consumption: luxury branding as a catalyst for social change' examines how we can promote sustainable consumption through appeals related to subjective wellbeing and self-fulfilment—elements that can be found in luxury branding. The author argues that a social change of this nature can be achieved if sustainable consumption is introduced as a preferred lifestyle. The sixth chapter, written by Ana Carolina De Pierro Bruno and Edgard Barki, bears the title 'Luxury versus conscious consumption: are they really paradoxical? A study of Brazilian and Portuguese luxury consumer behaviour'. This exploratory research describes the purchasing behaviour of Brazilian and Portuguese luxury consumers and their attitudes towards conscious consumption. The study provides an important empirical advance over previous work on conscious and luxury consumption behaviour, accomplishing to connect both concepts in order to understand consumption in a period of growing awareness about sustainability issues. Closing Part II, 'Are luxury purchasers really insensitive to sustainable development? New insights from research' by Jean-Noël Kapferer and Anne Michaut-Denizeau, challenges the widely shared belief that consumers do not feel concerned by sustainable development when they buy a luxury object. This research is based on two consecutive surveys, in 2012 and 2013, of actual luxury buyers. The authors argue that, today, sustainable development is certainly not a salient purchasing criterion for most luxury buyers, but it can become a rejection factor if specific negative information are released about the brands. In addition, luxury buyers are aware of a latent contradiction between luxury and some facets of sustainable development.

Part III of the book deals with luxury and sustainability in relation to various topics and areas. The first chapter in Part III is a case study written by Martin Perry, 'Luxury Lodges New Zealand and prospects for elegant disruption', in which the author explores how far New Zealand's luxury lodges' engagement with sustainability is consistent with the possibility of luxury enterprises generating an 'elegant disruption' in favour of sustainable business models. The following chapter, entitled 'Diversity of human capital as a driver for corporate responsibility engagement: the case of the luxury industry', by Catarina Pessanha Gomes and Masaru Yarime, analyses the corporate responsibility (CR) strategy and diversity management strategy of 17 companies in the luxury sector. Findings reveal that the level of strategic commitment to CR is correlated with the inclusiveness of organisational culture. The chapter discusses the potential of organisational culture and human capital for the adoption of creative and innovative CR strategies in the luxury sector. Completing the book, Xenya Cherny-Scanlon presents a chapter called 'The wild side of luxury: can nature continue to sustain the luxury industry?', which includes case studies on CITES (Convention on International Trade in Endangered Species of Wild Fauna and Flora)-regulated (with varying degrees of success) species used in the luxury industry. She also provides insights into how the industry can contribute towards ensuring the sustainability of wildlife trade, arguing for defining the limits of sustainable supply, ensuring transparency and traceability, involving local communities and engaging consumers.

It is important to highlight that these diverse contributions represent a great step forward in expanding the knowledge base and understanding of this nascent relationship (luxury and sustainability): it is certainly the most comprehensive collection of writing on the subject to date. Note that this initiative has received a large international response and we hope it will continue to stimulate further debate.

Acknowledgement

Our special thanks go to the review panel for their outstanding work. This special issue would not have been possible without their dedication and commitment.

Bibliography

Adams, W.H. (2012) *On Luxury: A Short History of the Perils of Excess from Ancient Times to the Beginning of the Modern Era* (Washington, DC: Potomac Books).

Allen, P., C. Bonazzi and D. Gee (2001) 'Sustainable Development', in P. Allen, C. Bonazzi and D. Gee (eds.), *Metaphors for Change: Partnership, Tools and Civic Action for Sustainability* (Sheffield, UK: Greenleaf): 2-3.

Bansal, P., and E. Howard (eds.) (1997) *Business and the Natural Environment* (Oxford, UK: Butterworth Heinemann).

Bendell, J. (2012) *Elegant Disruption: How Luxury and Society Can Change Each Other for Good* (Queensland, Australia: Griffith University).

Bendell, J., and A. Kleanthous (2007) *Deeper Luxury* (London: WWF-UK).

Berry, C.J. (1994) *The Idea of Luxury: A Conceptual and Historical Investigation* (New York: Cambridge University Press).

Cornet, C. (2007) 'Gomorrah and Camorra', BabelMed (22 June 2007; http://eng.babelmed.net/letteratura/245-italia/450-gomorrah-and-camorra.html, accessed 4 December 2012).

Doyle, I., and J. Bendell (2011) *Uplifting the Earth: The Ethical Performance of Luxury Jewellery Brands* (Geneva: Lifeworth Consulting and Fair Jewelry Action; www.lifeworth.com/consult/2011/06/uplifting/, accessed 6 December 2012).

Ehrenfeld, J.R. (1999) 'Cultural Structure and the Challenge of Sustainability', in K. Sexton, A.A. Marcus, K.W. Easter and T.D. Burckhardt (eds.) *Better Environmental Decisions: Strategies for Governments, Businesses, and Communities* (Washington, DC: Island Press).

Frank, R.H. (1999) *Luxury Fever: Weighing the Cost of Excess* (Princeton, NJ: Princeton University Press).

Gardetti, M.A., and A.L. Torres (2013) 'Sustainable Luxury', *The Journal of Corporate Citizenship* 52 (December 2013).

Gardetti, M.A., and M.E. Girón (2014) Sustainable Luxury and Social Entrepreneurship: Stories from the Pioneers (Sheffield, UK: Greenleaf Publishing).

Girón, M.E. (2009) *Inside Luxury* (Madrid: Editorial LID).

Girón, M.E. (2012) *Diccionario LID Sobre Lujo y Responsabilidad* (Madrid: Editorial LID).

Heine, K. (2011) *The Concept of Luxury Brands* (Berlin: Department of Marketing, Technische Universität Berlin).

Ilari, A., and L. Zargani (2007) 'Italian Television Program Alleges Fashion Misconduct', *WWDTUESDAY Ready-to-Wear/Textiles*, 4 December 2007: 2.

Kapferer, J.N., and V. Basten (2010) *The Luxury Strategy: Break the Rules of Marketing to Build Luxury Brands* (London: Kogan Page).

Kleanthous, A. (2011) 'Simple the Best is No Longer Simple' Raconteur on Sustainable Luxury (July 2011; http://theraconteur.co.uk/category/sustainability/sustainable-luxury/, accessed 7 December 2012).

Low, T. (2010) *Sustainable Luxury: A Case of Strange Bedfellows* (Luton, UK: Institute for Tourism Research, University of Bedfordshire).

Macfarlane, M., A. Tallontire and A. Martin (2003) *Towards an Ethical Jewellery Business* (Kent, UK: Natural Resources Institute, University of Greenwich at Medway).

Mebratu, D. (1998) 'Sustainable and Sustainable Development: Historical and Conceptual Review', *Environmental Impact Assessment Review* 18.6: 493-520.

Moore, B. (2011) *Style Over Substance: Why Ethics Are Not in Fashion for Designer Labels*, Ethical Consumer Research Association (www.ethicalconsumer.org/buyersguides/clothing/designerclothing.aspx accessed 13 December 2012).

Mortelmans D. (2005) 'Sign Values in Processes of Distinction: The Concept of Luxury', *Semiotica* 157.1/4: 497-520.

Okonkwo, U. (2007) *Luxury Fashion Branding: Trends, Tactics, and Techniques* (New York: Palgrave Macmillan).

Raconteur Media and WWF (2011) *Raconteur on Sustainable Luxury* (http://theraconteur.co.uk/category/sustainability/sustainable-luxury/, accessed 13 December 2012).

Ricca, M., and R. Robins (2012) *Meta-Luxury: Brands and the Culture of Excellence* (New York: Palgrave Macmillan).

Saviano, R. (2007) *Gomorra* (Barcelona: Random House Mondadoni SA).

Scheibel, S. (2010) *Ethical Luxury: Myth or Trend? Essay* (London: London School of Economics and Political Science).

Shamina, Y. (2011) 'A Review of the Main Concepts of Luxury Consumer Behavior and Contemporary Meaning of luxury', paper presented on the *2ème Colloque Franco-tchèque Trends in International Business*, Prague, 30 June 2011.

Schleicher-Tapperser, R. (2001) 'Assessing Sustainable Development in the European Union: The Sustainable Quality Management® Approach in the Context of Structural Funds', *Greener Management International Journal* 36: 51-66.

Suzuki, D., and H. Dressel (2002) *Good News For A Change: How Everyday People Are Helping the Planet* (Toronto: Stoddart Publishing Co.).

Thomas, D. (2007) *Deluxe: How Luxury Lost its Luster* (New York: Penguin Books).

Urik, E.J. (1908) *Luxury and Waste of Life* (London: J.M. Dent & Co).

Warhurst, A. (2001) 'Corporate Citizenship and Corporate Social Investment: Drivers of Tri-sector Partnership', *The Journal of Corporate Citizenship*, Spring 2001, 57-73.

WCED (World Commission on Environment and Development) (1987) *Our Common Future* (Oxford, UK: Oxford University Press).

Weber, C. (2007) 'The Devil Sells Prada', *The New York Times* (26 August 2007; www.nytimes.com/2007/08/26/books/review/Weber-t.html?adxnnl=1&adxnnlx=1374667433-b8wWiT9lWxPq+lu7FYYc5g, accessed 20 June 2011).

Miguel Angel Gardetti holds a PhD in environmental management (Pacific Western University, CA). He was founder of the Center for Studies on Sustainable Luxury, which he has directed since its beginnings. He is also the head of the Instituto de Estudios para la Sustentabilidad Corporativa (Center for Study of Corporate Sustainability).
Email: mag@lujosustentable.org

Ana Laura Torres holds a BSc in ecology, granted by Universidad Nacional de La Plata, specialising in corporate sustainability at the Center for Study of Corporate Sustainability. She collaborated in the creation and development of the Sustainable Textile Center, which she has co-ordinated since its beginning. She has worked as an environmental consultant for the German Institute of Investment and Development (DEG) in Cologne, Germany, and has conducted research and teaching activities at Universidad Nacional de La Plata (Argentina).
Email: alt@ctextilsustentable.org.ar

Part I

1

Is sustainable luxury fashion possible?

Frédéric Godart and Sorah Seong
INSEAD, Fontainebleau, France

Introduction

Since the 1980s there has been increasing awareness towards ethical fashion both from the producer and the consumer sides, particularly with regards to ethical sourcing and apparel production (Shen *et al.* 2012). Ethical fashion, to use a definition suggested by Joergens (2006: 361), is 'fashionable clothes that incorporate fair trade principles with sweatshop-free labour conditions while not harming the environment or workers by using biodegradable and organic cotton'. Based on the notion that ethical fashion can be achieved on both social and environmental dimensions, we divide the concepts into two highly interrelated categories: Eco-sustainable fashion and socially responsible fashion. This conceptual categorisation is in line with the so-called 3P (people–planet–profit) or triple bottom line (TBL) approach (Elkington 1998). The TBL approach posits that a 'corporation's ultimate success or health can and should be measured not just by the traditional financial bottom line, but also by its social/ethical and environmental performance' (Norman and MacDonald 2004: 243).

Eco-sustainable fashion engages in environment-related practices with the specific aim of reducing environmental damage during and after the production process. One example of this is producing longer lasting products. On the other hand, socially responsible fashion focuses on improving issues related to communities, working conditions or salaries. It should be noted that, although eco-sustainable and socially responsible fashion can be distinguished at the conceptual level, the distinction is often tricky in practice. The sustainability effort is driven by, and aims to achieve, the goal of benefiting both people and planet. Thus, while the focus of this paper is on eco-sustainable luxury fashion, the discussion can also be relevant to the social component of TBL.

Such mounting interest in ethical fashion is accompanied by the question of whether eco-sustainable fashion is compatible with the very definition of fashion. Fashion, in itself, can be a confusing term, as there are usually two meanings attached to the word: fashion as change and fashion as dress (Kawamura 2011). In the empirical setting of the fashion industry, the distinction between these two meanings is not very useful, as fashion can be defined as a process of 'recurrent change' (Aspers and Godart 2013) in dress. That fashion is 'a passing trend, something transient and superficial' (Gardetti and Torres 2012: 7) involves the unnecessary replacement of still useable fashion items, such as clothing and fashion accessories. The renewal cycle for fast fashion collections can be less than two weeks.

On the other hand, eco-sustainable fashion is the type of fashion that can last long enough to reduce negative environmental externalities. In the industry's retail markets, the introduction of fast fashion as a new business model has increased the rate of premature product replacement and fashion outmodedness (Kozlowski *et al.* 2012). Does this mean that fashion cannot stand hand in hand with the pursuit of sustainability? This incompatibility issue can be even more pronounced in the fashion industry's luxury segments, where change is systematically driven and maintained by bi-annual fashion seasons. While change can be slow at the bottom of the 'fashion pyramid' (e.g. commodity and fashion basics) (Doeringer and Crean 2006), and probably slowed down in the mass market segments, slow change may not work for the higher bound of the pyramid (i.e. haute couture and designer collections), because the luxury identity of these segments is based on change. In the next sections, we will examine the concept of luxury, and luxury fashion in particular, and discuss the specific sustainability opportunities and challenges faced by the luxury fashion industry.

Luxury: what are we talking about?

What is luxury? As pointed out by Kapferer and Bastien (2008), there is a lot of confusion surrounding the definition of this concept. In standard economics, luxury goods are defined 'as those whose income elasticity of demand is greater than one' (Kemp 1998: 592) or, in other words, goods for which demand increases as income rises. However, this definition does not give a fully satisfying answer to what defines the core attributes of luxury goods, other than consumers' responses at different income levels. Outside the mainstream economic model, Veblen (1899) was one of the first to undertake an analysis of luxury in the context of a comprehensive theory of social class dynamics. With a renewed interest in the subject matter in the 1990s, Allérès (1997) defined luxury by building a three-level hierarchy, each representing a different degree of accessibility: 'inaccessible luxury', corresponding to exclusive models (e.g. in fashion, haute couture); 'intermediary luxury', corresponding to expensive replicas of individual models (e.g. specially tailored dresses that are full or partial duplicates of haute couture models); and 'accessible luxury', corresponding to products made in larger series (e.g. luxury brand's ready-to-wear lines). Berry (1994: 24) undertook a philosophical approach towards the conceptualisation of luxury based on the needs/wants distinction and, following Sombart (1913), highlighted the idea that luxury is 'an expenditure that goes beyond what is necessary'. There is no scholarly consensus regarding the definition of luxury to date, but the complex nature of luxury has been discussed widely by scholars of different disciplinary origins.

In *The Republic*, the Greek philosopher Plato (ca. 380 BCE) discusses luxury as something that is scarce, highly desirable and indicative of individual social success. He argues that its scarcity is the root cause for wars and conflicts, and therefore luxury should be banned. This first European theory of luxury set the tone for subsequent debates on luxury and its intellectual development, at least within the European philosophical tradition (Godart 2011). Luxury stems from the desires of powerful, high status consumers who want to assert their status and power. These consumers converge on scarce products or services to assert their identity and, as a result, scarcity becomes consubstantial to luxury. Due to its link with status and power, luxury has often been at the centre of a moral debate. On the positive side, we have scholars such as French philosopher Voltaire (1736) who sees luxury as a source of Earthly joys and of economic development. On the negative side, philosophers and moralists such as French philosopher Rousseau (1750–1755) consider luxury morally reprehensible, not only because it causes conflicts over the acquisition of scarce resources, such as gold (i.e. the Platonician argument), but also because it is an activity that turns people away from engaging in more valuable endeavours, such as studying philosophy or leading a moral political life.

From this negative perspective, luxury is seen as feeding itself on scarce resources and continuously triggering or stirring conflicts. This particular view on luxury has been popularised in movies such as *Blood Diamond* (Edward Zwick, 2006), which triggered consumer awareness on where their jewellery comes from, or the story behind it. Consequently, luxury jewellery brands are now gearing the jewellery industry in the direction of responsible practices, such as responsible sourcing of gemstones and precious metals (Doyle and Bendell 2011). Luxury may not be 100% exempt from the criticism that individuals' desire for luxury generates conflicts, as our history has witnessed. However, as we can see from the cases of luxury jewellery brands, there are numerous ways in which the luxury industry can bring positive changes to the process of luxury creation in the first place.

Furthermore, unlike commoditised markets, luxury can offer a unique opportunity for creating sustainable business environments due to its two central features that set it apart from other market segments or industries. First, luxury is (oftentimes) characterised by craftsmanship based on unique skills. This allows luxury to provide high quality and rewarding business conditions. Second, luxury is characterised by its particular relationship with time, for its value is inscribed in the long term. This allows luxury to offer a sustainable business model for resource management and high quality product development, just to name a few relevant elements of sustainable luxury.

When it comes to starting a conversation about the opportunities and challenges of luxury industries' sustainability efforts, trying to narrow down definitions of luxury may not be the most pragmatic approach. The reason is that luxury is a highly diversified construct, and there is a lack of general consensus among scholars regarding the definition of luxury. Rather than conceptualising luxury, Chevalier and Mazzalovo (2008) start out by building different segments of luxury in order to define what luxury really is. These segments include: exclusive ready-to-wear and fashion accessories; luxury jewellery and watches; selective perfumes and cosmetics; some wines and spirits; luxury automobiles; hotels; tourism; and private banking. Based on Chevalier and Mazzalovo's segmentation of luxury, this chapter focuses on one specific segment: luxury fashion (that is to say, exclusive ready-to-wear and fashion accessories).

The relationship between luxury and fashion is quite an ambiguous one, as fashion does not fully belong to the luxury world as it once did up until the turn of the 19th century, but overlaps with luxury in its most expensive and exclusive segments. Both luxury and fashion share the common need for social differentiation, but they differ in two major aspects: first, whereas luxury is timeless, fashion is ephemeral (relationship to time); and, whereas luxury is for self-reward, fashion is not (relationship to self) (Kapferer 2012). Thus, luxury fashion seems to be a contradiction in terms—as luxury it is supposed to last, but as fashion it is supposed to change frequently. However, since the essence of fashion is change, luxury fashion gives exclusive access to enforced change. Luxury fashion is recurrent change at its highest level, and it is distinguished from other luxury segments by its constant pressure for change.

Luxury fashion: how is it different from lower-end fashion?

The centrality of waste and change

Several scholars have studied ways of representing the fashion industry as a collection of different segments. A useful representation introduced by Doeringer and Crean (2006) sees fashion as a pyramid: luxury fashion, such as haute couture and designer collections, is placed at the top of the pyramid, while commodity and fashion basics, such as socks and underwear, sit at the bottom. Luxury fashion goods are produced by high status fashion houses, which organise bi-annual fashion shows.[1] A limited number of fashion brands are able and allowed to display their know-how and creativity at these fashion shows, which in turn maintains their high status. Haute couture fashion shows are largely a remnant of a former era when couturiers dominated the industry and catered to a wealthy clientele. Thus, such shows now represent an important investment for the participating fashion houses and are seen as a marketing expense by many. Today, luxury fashion is comprised mostly of designer labels belonging to major international fashion and luxury business groups, such as LVMH, Kering (formerly known as PPR) or Puig (Barkey and Godart 2013).

In pursuing eco-sustainability, luxury fashion is faced with additional challenges that do not necessarily exist in other luxury segments, such as luxury jewellery and watches. In luxury fashion, change itself embodies a form of luxury. Unlike in other luxury segments where products are made to last (e.g. luxury watches and cars), luxury fashion serves the need of consumers to signal their luxury affiliation not only by purchasing the 'right' luxury goods, but also by following constant changes in fashion style driven by the industry's fashion cycles (e.g. spring/summer and autumn/winter seasons). Status and power are asserted through consumers' ability to discard products that are still useable, and this prompts, and maintains, recurrent change—a consubstantial element of the luxury fashion industry. This need for change in luxury trumps its patrimonial dimension in which people purchase, for example, jewellery or watches to make an investment as these products have a long life on secondary markets. This is even more salient in dress where the market for collectibles is not well developed (Crane 2012). In this sense, luxury fashion may be one of the most formulaic examples of Veblen's (1899) conspicuous consumption characterised by recurrent change and waste.

In sum, luxury fashion presents a specific challenge to the eco-sustainability agenda. While it shares some of the challenges of the luxury industries in general, such as how to manage scarce resources and conflicts, it is also subject to the constant pressure for change inherent in the fashion industry. The cyclical mechanism of fashion seasons shapes, and is shaped by, the luxury fashion segment's rigorous adherence to stylistic evolution each season, triggering consumers to replace still functional fashion goods with new goods that are more in line with the season's 'in fashion' style. Since luxury fashion consumers are most sensitive to such cyclical changes in style, luxury fashion faces the problem of how to pursue eco-sustainability when it distinguishes itself from the lower segments of the fashion industry by driving the mechanism of systematic, recurrent change.

1 More recently, many brands have introduced additional collections, but the main collections are still spring/summer and autumn/winter.

The conditions of sustainable luxury fashion

Some scholars have tried to tackle the sustainability challenges faced by mass market fashion segments. For example, Kozlowski *et al.* (2012) elaborate on the challenges of fast fashion, which is driven by the fierce international competitive environment constantly pushing for rapid cycles and low costs, and which results in negative environmental implications for both production and transportation processes. The authors propose a life-cycle assessment (LCA) approach that encompasses entire product value chains and suggests solutions for each stage of the cycles. Now, our challenge is to adjust the existing sustainability paradigms and to develop new ones that fit with the very nature of the luxury fashion industry.

In order to tackle this challenge, it is important that we are aware of the eco-sustainability challenges that are specific to firms in the fashion industry, and luxury fashion in particular. It is equally, if not more, important to identify the types of opportunities these fashion brands have, by virtue of operating in the fashion industry, of adding eco-sustainable dimensions to their core business strategy. As Porter and Kramer (2006) argue, firms should be able to identify opportunities where they can pursue corporate social responsibility (CSR), not in generic ways but in ways that are most appropriate for their business strategies. In this way, they can effectively create values for both society and their own competitiveness. In the next section, we take a look at six principles of fashion, as suggested by Godart (2012), and the unique sustainability challenges and opportunities associated with each principle, which we summarise in Table 1.1.

Table 1.1 **Luxury fashion's limitations and opportunities for sustainability**

Principle	Limitations for sustainability	Opportunities for sustainability
1 Affirmation	Consumers' desire to assert their individuality and social affiliation by being 'in fashion', which prompts regular changes of clothes. This leads to, and is reinforced by, inflated production cycles	Institutionalising the practice of sustainable fashion by changing consumers' perception of buying sustainable fashion items as a socially accepted or 'in fashion' practice
2 Convergence	Local styles converge with dominant fashion design trends that are formulated, updated and disseminated by big fashion capitals. These dominant designs are not always compatible with local climates	Increasing consumers' preference for purchasing sustainable fashion items (principle 1: affirmation) in order to prompt the convergence of producers around producing sustainable fashion

➔

Principle	Limitations for sustainability	Opportunities for sustainability
3 Autonomy	The fashion industry maintains its autonomy when it comes to the choice of fashion styles and designs. This autonomy makes it difficult for third party actors to push the sustainability agenda in the production process	Encouraging actors within the fashion industry to develop aesthetically appealing designs that are also high on the eco-sustainability agenda
4 Personalisation	Market audiences share their belief in individual fashion designers' creative autonomy. This makes it difficult for third party actors to push the sustainability agenda in the production process	Encouraging each designer to use his/her autonomous influence to set a pro-sustainability trend and let it spill over from the fashion industry to other social spheres
5 Symbolisation	Fashion brands symbolise a power engine behind a stylistic trend change in the fashion industry. This may not go hand-in-hand with the notion of sustainability	Encouraging each fashion brand to leverage on, and reshape, its existing identity to include a proactive message on environmental issues
6 Imperialisation	Business groups play a major role in the industry. The sheer size and power centrality of these business groups can make adoption of changes in favour of sustainability difficult	Using the power of business groups to influence individual fashion brands and even other luxury segments via ripple effects to adopt and implement a large-scale sustainability agenda

The principles of fashion

When thinking about the sustainability challenges and opportunities of luxury fashion, we should not forget that the primary role of luxury fashion, and fashion in general, is to bring beauty and creativity to the world through a process of constant change. In this sense, in fashion, there is no stability in beauty. Compromising this aesthetic aspect of fashion in the name of an environmental agenda would mean the death of fashion, and the end of this major cultural and economic endeavour—after all, fashion is an economic activity that stands at the crossroads of art and commerce and exerts an immense influence over the world (Godart 2012). By the early 21st century, it was estimated that the clothing industry's output was topping US$1 trillion annually and employing approximately 26.5 million people (Cooperrider and Fry 2012: 3). More recent estimates from 2010 show that the fashion industry, defined in the largest sense, is worth more than US$1.5 trillion annually and represents about 6% of total global output (Godart 2012).

Luxury fashion's role as a potential harbinger of eco-sustainability is particularly promising, as it can leverage on its status-based influence to play a diffusion mechanism towards the other segments. In other words, luxury fashion's practice of sustainable fashion can get diffused across segments in a top-down manner. We build on Godart's (2012) six main principles of fashion to assess how each principle corresponds to luxury fashion's sustainability opportunities and challenges. These principles are, in order of historical appearance: affirmation; convergence; autonomy; personalisation; symbolisation; and imperialisation. Based on this assessment, we then offer principle-based action points for fashion brands and their stakeholders, or 'any group or individual who can affect or is affected by the achievement of the organization's objectives' (Freeman 1984: 46). Within the literature on stakeholder theory, there have been studies on how to identify the types of opportunities and threats posed by major stakeholder groups under moral management (Carroll 1991), and how to assemble stakeholder networks to systematically bring together knowledge and resources in implementing social change (Svendsen and Laberge 2005). A strategy of stakeholder engagement is arguably effective in transforming the ways in which firms approach their ethical issues in business, and in enhancing public perceptions of these firms (Smith *et al.* 2011). Building on these studies, this paper examines how the fashion industry's key stakeholders, and in particular producers (fashion brands and individual designers) and consumers, can jointly push for eco-sustainable fashion without negating the core principles of the field.

The first principle of fashion is *affirmation*. Driven by the desire to assert one's identity, individuals use fashion as identity signals to express their individuality and social affiliations. If 'being in fashion' implies changing clothes regularly, producers and consumers will inevitably end up pushing for artificially inflated production cycles, making the principle of affirmation a major hurdle to achieving sustainability. This can be tackled, however, by satisfying that same individual desire for identity affirmation: Persuading consumers that purchasing fashion items with pro-eco-sustainability nametags is a fashionable thing to do and that it will let them tell a story about themselves and where they fit—the core function of fashion in the first place. Successful persuasion would require eco-sustainable fashion not to compromise on the style factor. As one fashion designer said during an interview for news channel Euronews (2013): '[Green fashion] should never look as though the clothes are ethical. It should always be the surprise fact behind them'. Once an increasing number of consumers start perceiving the act of buying sustainable fashion items as a socially accepted practice, and even an 'in fashion' practice, it will be institutionalised over time as something desirable for both consumers and producers.

The second principle of fashion is *convergence*. In today's world, fashion is characterised by global trends. Styles may have multiple local origins, but the production of styles in the form of design takes place in big fashion capitals, such as Paris, New York, Milan and London. There, design trends are formulated and updated regularly, which then spread out to the rest of the world. These fashion designs, however, are not always compatible with local climates, both in a literal (weather) and figurative (cultural) sense. For example, Western suits are not very conducive to operating in the hot summer of Japan, which prompted the government to start a state-sponsored campaign ('Cool Biz') promoting people to wear local clothing items such as Okinawa kariyushi. One big goal of the campaign was to save energy and protect the environment by reducing air conditioning usage (BBC News 2011). The convergence principle complements the first principle of affirmation by enabling key industry stakeholders to converge around consumers' interest in purchasing eco-sustainable fashion items.

The third principle of fashion is *autonomy*. This principle concerns the creative dynamics of the fashion industry, where the creative choice for styles and designs maintains its autonomy against external factors. This autonomy makes it difficult for third party actors, such as policy makers, to penetrate the industry and push for the sustainability agenda in the production process. Such difficulty is magnified by the common notion that eco-sustainable fashion advocates for slower fashion trend cycles to reduce waste, and that therefore it impedes fashion designers' creativity efforts. However, sustainability does not always have to equate to a diminishing of creativity. Several high-end fashion houses have already been engaged in mobilising exceptional creativity across the fashion industry in order to develop aesthetically appealing designs that are also high on the eco-sustainability agenda (e.g. cutting down on the amount of fabric used or using eco-friendly materials) (Euronews 2013).

The fourth principle of fashion, *personalisation*, brings individual designers centre stage. Instead of arguing that individual designers have absolute autonomy in their creative choices, this principle captures the market audience's shared belief that individual designers indeed possess creative autonomy. While such perceived autonomy of individual designers may hinder outsiders from coming in with a sustainability agenda, this belief can be used by each designer to influence a pro-sustainability trend and let it spill over from the fashion industry to other social spheres. For example, German-born, Paris-based Karl Lagerfeld has recently shown that he could use his personal influence to convince French drivers to wear presumably unfashionable yellow safety jackets (LEXPRESS.fr 2008). Such influence of individual designers can be actively utilised for mobilising a sustainability drive.

The fifth principle of fashion, *symbolisation*, is about the power of brands and the importance of meanings in fashion. The power of brands, and of luxury brands in particular, lies in their time-proven tradition and stylistic adaptation to bi-annual fashion seasons. Brands symbolise a power engine that drives a stylistic trend change in the fashion industry. While it is true that such symbolisation may not go hand-in-hand with the notion of sustainability, each fashion brand can also leverage, and reshape, its existing symbolic power to include a proactive message on environmental issues. When each brand's symbolic power is aggregated, there could be an industry-wide discourse infused in the practice of fashion based on the portrait of mutually 'inclusive' fashion and sustainability.

Additionally, the 'citizen sector', or those 'groups established and run by mission-minded individuals across the globe who are attempting to address critical social needs' by providing strong insights into consumers and communities (Drayton and Budinich 2010: 58). These citizen sector organisations (CSO) can play an integral role in semantically and cognitively reframing fashion as a stylish and ethical consumption that does not necessarily have to follow fast trend cycles. When fashion brands collaborate with CSOs, or engage in what Drayton and Budinich (2010), term a 'hybrid value chain' to draw on each side's complementary strengths in tackling large-scale problems, they can more effectively enhance consumer perceptions of sustainable fashion while leveraging the symbolic power of their brand names.

The sixth and last principle, *imperialisation*, could be a major leeway for sustainability. This principle is about the major role played by business groups in the fashion industry, and also about how fashion has come to stand at the core of many other industries, such as high technology and automobile manufacture. Although scholars have suggested varying definitions of business groups, we take on Granovetter's conceptualisation of business groups as 'legally separate firms bound together in persistent formal and/or informal ways' (Granovetter 1994: 429). The sheer size and power centrality of these business groups can make the adoption of changes in favour of sustainability difficult, but when they do adopt changes, the impact can be powerful. They can leverage their power in the fashion and luxury industry to influence affiliated individual fashion brands to adopt and implement large-scale sustainability agenda. For example, in 2012, the luxury brands group formerly known as PPR (Kering as of June 2013) launched a five-year plan to implement a series of core environmental targets across its brands, which include reducing water use, waste and carbon emissions, eco-sustainable sourcing of raw materials and eliminating hazardous chemicals. The plan will be complemented by an environmental profit & loss account (EP&L) as a measurement tool to calculate, and subsequently compare, environmental performance across the group's product categories and business units (Niculae 2013). Furthermore, business groups can also make use of the ripple effects to spread the practice of sustainable fashion across other luxury segments, and even industries.

From the analysis above, we can conclude that pursuing eco-sustainability does not have to mean a threat to the luxury fashion industry, despite some hurdles. Implementing a new sustainable paradigm may require some adaptation to the existing industry structure, but it does not negate the core principles of fashion. In fact, we have seen that various stakeholders can actively use these principles in favour of propelling eco-sustainable development, with mutual support coming from both producers and consumers. As Smith (2003: 68) wrote: 'In figuring out a CSR strategy, stakeholder engagement must be at the core'.

We will now introduce three possible scenarios in which the various stakeholders of the fashion industry can proactively take on an eco-sustainability agenda. While these three scenarios might already be, to some extent, in place, we believe they are, for the most part, still to be implemented. Each of the three scenarios demonstrates different ways of developing and implementing market-based solutions to eco-sustainability, though they can also occur simultaneously. In Table 1.2 we summarise the three scenarios: institutional change through slow luxury fashion; innovative luxury fashion; and upgrading luxury fashion through regulation.

Table 1.2 **Three sustainable fashion scenarios**

Scenario	**Most relevant principle(s)**	**Summary**
Institutional change through slow fashion	Affirmation Convergence	Sustainability goal: efficient management of scarce resources Implications: modification of current institutional dynamics based on fast trend cycles or 'seasons' to slower seasons 'Degrowth' strategy: slow fashion motivates producers to focus on designs with lasting appeal and consumers to keep their clothes for a longer period of time Requirement: institutional level change Challenge: turnover reductions for producers due to reduced purchasing cycles
Innovative fashion	Symbolisation Imperialisation	Sustainability goal: efficient management of scarce resources and reducing waste Implications: fashion cycles remain as they are, but innovative solutions make fashion items both creative and sustainable. Three possible innovative solutions: • Use materials that have a lower impact on the environment (e.g. organic fabric) • Reduce waste at each step of the production process • Increase recycling of discarded clothes Requirement: investments, collective efforts to redirect creative talents in the field, and some support from advocacy groups and governmental bodies Producers drive innovative fashion, but consumers complement the effort
Upgrading luxury fashion through regulation	Autonomy Personalisation	Sustainability goal: establishment of sustainability enforcement Implications: industry-wide regulations are developed. External considerations (e.g. legal frameworks, norms and traditions) determine formal versus informal stance of these regulations Challenge: regulations may prompt price increase, which then reduces consumer purchasing Requirement: the entire fashion industry has to shift upwards to the premium segments, where the practice of producing less with better (and more expensive) techniques is the norm Both producers and consumers play pivotal roles with the strong support of public authorities

Scenarios for sustainable luxury fashion

Scenario 1: Institutional change through slow luxury fashion

What are the conditions that are essential for sustainable fashion? The efficient management of scarce resources is crucial for pursuing sustainable fashion and therefore we hereby suggest a 'slow fashion' scenario. Slow fashion can be adopted in many creative ways, but it would in most cases imply modifying the current institutional dynamics of fast trend cycles or seasons to slower seasons. In other words, both producers and consumers would favour fashion designs and items that last longer. This suggestion corresponds to a 'degrowth' strategy, as it motivates producers to focus their creative energy on 'stylish designs with lasting appeal [such as] trench coats and quiet handbags, camel coats and classic trouser shapes' (Fox and Chilvers 2010), and consumers to keep their clothes for a longer period of time. This strategy does not negate the core principles of fashion, but would modify some of their features—eco-sustainability would become central to the affirmation principle, and convergence would happen at a different pace. The 'slow fashion' scenario requires an institutional change with key stakeholders taking an active part in organising and implementing the change. One possible challenge of this scenario would be turnover reductions for producers due to the slowing down of consumers' purchasing cycles.

Scenario 2: Innovative luxury fashion

Another scenario is to keep the current institutional dynamics of seasonal fashion cycles as they are, but come up with innovative solutions for producing fashion items that are both creative and sustainable. Three possible solutions can be suggested: First, use materials that have a lower impact on the environment, such as organic fabric. Second, reduce waste at each step of the production process. Third, increase recycling of discarded clothes. This last solution is supported by the observation that 1 kg of used clothing collected can reduce as much as 3.6 kg of CO_2 emissions (Schuetze 2012). The innovative fashion scenario requires investments and collective efforts to redirect the industry's creative talents and energy: the imperialisation principle can be used to mutualise investments, and symbolisation to shape perceptions by costumers of innovative eco-sustainable fashion. Support from advocacy groups and governmental bodies are important as well. Although producers have the primary role in realising this scenario, it would be important for fashion brands to communicate clearly about the effort to consumers.

Scenario 3: Upgrading luxury fashion through regulation

The last scenario is to develop industry-wide regulations, which could take a formal or informal stance depending on the country-specific external factors, such as legal frameworks, customs and norms regarding public action. For example, the

Sustainable Apparel Coalition has created the Higg Index 1.0 to coordinate and help industry actors measure the social and environmental performance of their apparel products across various stages of the supply chain (Euronews 2013). More recently, in December 2013, Higg Index 2.0 was released as a follow-up to the original version, adding footwear to the target product category and social/labour performance dimensions to the existing sustainability topic.[2]

Having regulations in action may prompt a price increase and reduction in consumer purchase: the autonomy principle can be preserved through leveraging the personalisation principle, and by relying on individual industry stalwarts who would internalise regulatory principles. Consequently, this scenario requires the entire fashion industry to be 'upgraded'. When both low- and high-end segments are shifted upwards into premium segments, the practice of producing less, locally, and with better (and more expensive) techniques is accepted as the norm. Both producers and consumers are expected to play a pivotal role in this scenario.

Conclusion and discussion

As the goal and practice of eco-sustainability stretch beyond individual countries to the global community, it is crucial that the luxury fashion industry stakeholders collaborate in ethical fashion movements towards making a tangible impact on the environment. Taking an active stance in global responsibilities can also benefit companies in return (Smith 2003), as being ethical, and being seen to be engaged in concrete actions, can protect and promote a company's brand in light of changing social expectations. By addressing the environmental dimension of TBL, companies can save costs through reductions in waste and raw materials usage. They can also drive up financial performance by finding a niche market within the industry where their eco-friendly agenda will give them competitive advantage over others. The notion of eco-sustainable businesses serving as a new profit-driving engine for companies, however, can get thorny when it is applied to the fashion industry, and luxury fashion in particular.

For certain fashion consumers, keeping clothes from past seasons may mean being unfashionable or out of fashion. Some mitigate the risk of falling out of fashion by exploring new venues in vintage clothing, given the cyclical nature of fashion styles, or mixing vintage with contemporary. At the systemic level, however, the luxury segment of the fashion industry runs on seasonal change, which then drives the rest of the industry to adopt the changes with differing levels of social accessibility and speed (e.g. fast fashion in retail markets). Against such an institutional force that has been continuing since the birth of fashion, how can consumers and producers work together to reduce the use of resources and thereby achieve

2 www.apparelcoalition.org/higgindex/, accessed 18 June 2014.

eco-sustainability at the individual and collective levels? What does eco-sustainable luxury fashion mean for producers and consumers? How can both sides work together in realising sustainable luxury fashion without negating the core principles of fashion?

In this chapter, we used the six core principles of fashion to examine the eco-sustainability opportunities and challenges specifically faced by luxury fashion. We conclude that both consumers and producers can play an integral role in facilitating the practice of eco-sustainable fashion, while upholding what fashion means to both sides. The core principles of fashion do not have to be undermined in order to achieve ethical fashion. Rather, we suggest that these principles can be actively used by luxury fashion brands to invent and reinvent eco-sustainability paradigms in creative ways. This coupling of eco-sustainability and creativity could lead to an institutional-level uplifting of fashion as a leading industry of ethical business, where the mechanical embodiment of functionality, style and creativity lasts for a long time. Long lasting beauty is our global responsibility.

Acknowledgement

We thank Christine Driscoll-Goulay for her comments and suggestions.

Bibliography

Allérès, D. (1997) *Luxe... Stratégies, Marketing* (Paris: Economica).

Aspers, P., and F. Godart (2013) 'Sociology of Fashion: Order and Change', *Annual Review of Sociology* 39: 171-92.

Barkey, K., and F. Godart (2013) 'Empires, Federated Arrangements, and Kingdoms: Using Political Models of Governance to Understand Firms' Creative Performance', *Organization Studies* 34.1: 79-104.

BBC News (2011) 'Japan Promotes "Super Cool Biz" Energy Saving Campaign' (1 June 2011; www.bbc.co.uk/news/business-13620900, accessed 18 June 2014).

Berry, C.J. (1994) *The Idea of Luxury: A Conceptual and Historical Investigation* (Cambridge, UK: Cambridge University Press).

Carroll, A.B. (1991) 'The Pyramid of Corporate Social Responsibility: Toward the Moral Management of Organizational Stakeholders', *Business Horizons* 34.4: 39-48.

Chevalier, M., and G. Mazzalovo (2008) *Luxury Brand Management: A World of Privilege* (Singapore: Wiley).

Cooperrider, D., and R. Fry (2012) 'Editorial: Tied Into a Single Garment of Destiny', *The Journal of Corporate Citizenship* 45: 3-4.

Crane, D. (2012) 'Auction Prices of Fashion Collectibles: What Do They Mean?', in E. Tseëlon, A.M. González and S. Kaiser (eds.), *Critical Studies in Fashion and Beauty Volume One* (Bristol, UK: Intellect Books).

Doeringer, P.B., and S. Crean (2006) 'Can Fast Fashion Save the US Apparel Industry?' *Socio-Economic Review* 4.3: 353-77.

Doyle, I., and J. Bendell (2011) *Uplifting The Earth: The Ethical Performance of Luxury Jewellery Brands* (Geneva: Lifeworth Consulting and Fair Jewelry Action).

Drayton, B., and V. Budinich (2010) 'A New Alliance for Global Change', *Harvard Business Review* 88.9: 56-64.

Elkington, J. (1998) *Cannibals With Forks: The Triple Bottom Line of 21st Century Business* (Stony Creek, CT: New Society Publishers).

Euronews (2013) 'Eco Fashion, Smart Fashion' (19 February 2013; http://www.euronews.com/2013/02/19/eco-fashion-smart-fashion/, accessed 18 June 2014).

Fox, I., and S. Chilvers (2010) 'Slow Fashion: Forever Yours', *The Guardian* (7 July 2010; www.guardian.co.uk/lifeandstyle/2010/jul/07/slow-fashion-high-street, accessed 18 June 2014).

Freeman, E. (1984) *Strategic Management: A Stakeholder Approach* (Cambridge, UK: Cambridge University Press).

Gardetti, M.A., and A.L. Torres (2012) 'Introduction', *The Journal of Corporate Citizenship* 45: 5-15.

Godart, F. (2011) *Penser la Mode* (Paris: Institut Français de la Mode/Editions du Regard).

Godart, F. (2012) *Unveiling Fashion: Business, Culture, and Identity in the Most Glamorous Industry* (London: Palgrave-Macmillan).

Granovetter, M. (1994) 'Business Groups', in N. Smelser and R. Swedberg (eds.), *Handbook of Economic Sociology* (Princeton, NJ: Princeton University Press).

Joergens, C. (2006) 'Ethical Fashion: Myth or Future Trend?', *Journal of Fashion Marketing and Management* 10.3: 360-71.

Kapferer, J.-N. (2012) *The Luxury Strategy: Break the Rules of Marketing to Build Luxury Brands* (London: Kogan Page).

Kapferer, J.-N., and V. Bastien (2008) *The Luxury Strategy: Break the Rules of Marketing to Build Luxury Brands* (London: Kogan Page).

Kawamura, Y. (2011) *Doing Research in Fashion and Dress: An Introduction to Qualitative Methods* (New York: Berg).

Kemp, S. (1998) 'Perceiving Luxury and Necessity', *Journal of Economic Psychology* 19.5: 591-606.

Kozlowski, A., M. Bardecki and C. Searcy (2012) 'Environmental Impacts in the Fashion Industry: A Life Cycle and Stakeholder Framework', *The Journal of Corporate Citizenship* 45: 17-36.

LEXPRESS.fr (2008) 'Lagerfeld Défend le Gilet Jaune', *L'Express* (19 June 2008; www.lexpress.fr/actualite/societe/lagerfeld-defend-le-gilet-jaune_513642.html, accessed 18 June 2014).

Niculae, E. (2013) 'Kering Director: Sustainability is Non-Negotiable', *Worldwatch Institute Europe* (29 May 2013; www.worldwatch-europe.org/node/185, accessed 18 June 2014).

Norman, W., and C. MacDonald (2004) 'Getting to the Bottom of "Triple Bottom Line" ', *Business Ethics Quarterly* 14.2: 243-62.

Plato (ca. 380 BCE) *The Republic* (New York: Penguin Classics, 2007).

Porter, M.E., and M.R. Kramer (2006) 'The Link Between Competitive Advantage and Corporate Social Responsibility', *Harvard Business Review* 11 (December 2006): 78-92.

Rousseau, J.-J. (1750–1755) *'The Discourses' and Other Early Political Writings* (Cambridge, UK: Cambridge University Press, 1997).

Schuetze, C.F. (2012) 'Sustainable Innovation: Reducing Fashion's Carbon Footprint', *International Herald Tribune* (20 August 2012; http://rendezvous.blogs.nytimes.com/2012/08/20/sustainable-innovation-reducing-fashions-carbon-footprint/, accessed 18 June 2014).

Shen, B., Y. Wang, C.K. Lo and M. Shum (2012) 'The Impact of Ethical Fashion on Consumer Purchase Behavior', *Journal of Fashion Marketing and Management* 16.2: 234-45.

Smith, C. (2003) 'Corporate Social Responsibility: Whether or How?' *California Management Review* 45 (Summer 2003): 52-76.

Smith, N.C., S. Ansett and L. Erez (2011) 'How Gap Inc. Engaged With Its Stakeholders', *MIT Sloan Management Review* 52.4: 69-76.

Sombart, W. (1913) *Luxus und Kapitalismus* (Munich: Duncker & Humblot).

Svendsen, A.C., and M. Laberge (2005) 'Convening Stakeholder Networks: A New Way of Thinking, Being and Engaging', *The Journal of Corporate Citizenship* 19 (Autumn 2005): 91-104.

Veblen, T. (1899) *The Theory of the Leisure Class: An Economic Study of Institutions* (New York: Dover Thrift).

Voltaire (1736) *Le Mondain* (Ferney-Voltaire, France: Centre International d'Étude du XVIIIe Siècle, 2002).

Frédéric Godart is Assistant Professor of organisational behaviour at INSEAD, France. He holds an MPhil in social and political sciences from Cambridge University and a PhD in sociology from Columbia University. He is the author of *Unveiling Fashion: Business, Culture, Identity in the Most Glamorous Industry* (London: Palgrave-Macmillan, 2012). Email: frederic.godart@insead.edu

Sorah Seong is a PhD student in management at INSEAD, France. She holds a BA in sociology from Harvard University and an MSc in theory and history of international relations from LSE. She currently specialises in organisational behaviour from a macro-interdisciplinary perspective. Email: sorah.seong@insead.edu

2

Fake remake

The role of the luxury fashion market in driving sustainable fashion practices

Angela Finn and Kim Fraser
Auckland University of Technology (AUT), Aotearoa New Zealand

Introduction

A main concern for researchers in the contemporary academic debate surrounding the development of more sustainable fashion design practices is to address the problems of consumerism and consumer behaviour. This chapter draws attention to the emergence of the faking of the remaking process by mainstream fashion brands to highlight how these damaging behaviours prolong and uphold unsustainable practices in the international fashion industry. Consumerism, the mass phenomenon of the 20th century, is a product of long-term historical changes and transformations and Fordism, according to Gabriel and Lang (2006), which embraced both production and consumption, and transformed consumerism from the elite to the masses. Furthermore, in the early 1900s, new department stores developed *planned obsolescence* strategies to encourage consumers to *replace* goods in order to stimulate and perpetuate consumption (Sturken and Cartwright 2001). Within the new era of mass consumption and urbanisation, goods came in throwaway bottles, boxes, bags and cans, encouraging a cultural shift away from the virtues of thrift to the conveniences of consumerism.

After World War II, business strategies to boost growth included a more aggressive attitude to obsolescence to encourage consumption, create demand and increase production. Businesses competed by cutting costs along the supply chain, enabling them to retail fashion garments at competitively low prices. Brands are forced to place high minimum orders to secure low manufacturing costs, which can result in over-production (Farrer and Fraser 2009; Fraser 2011, 2013). While in the early stages this model provided Westernised countries with access to a wide selection of cheap goods, the aggressive expansion required to maintain growth and profit has led to the current 'pile it high/sell it cheap' and 'fast fashion' culture that remains dominant in the current fashion and clothing marketplace in the UK, Australia and New Zealand.[1] The mainstream fashion sector provides diffusion of designer fashion to the mass market reliant on this over-production/over-consumption model.

A solution to this problem has been to extend the life-cycle of garments which are being sent to landfill prior to the end of the usefulness of the textiles themselves. This chapter looks specifically at the process of fashion 'remake', which uses no longer desirable garments to create new fashion items. This approach is an authentic method of textiles reuse which has resulted in an aesthetic that can be similarly identified as 'remake/refashion'. The characteristics of this aesthetic, although tacit in nature, include a sense of vintage or retro textiles; mismatched patterns, colours or prints by mixing various textiles, patchwork components or vintage lace or appliqué embroidery elements. An increased and general awareness within the market of sustainable design is often associated with these design aesthetics which have been established at the higher end of the market by designers/labels engaging with remake as a sustainable design process. The problem that the authors identify is that the success of the high-end fashion look has been adopted by the mainstream, but without the authentic remake processes, thus limiting a solution for more sustainable fashion manufacturing processes through design.

The commercialisation of the aesthetic, or the diffusion of the look utilising unsustainable manufacturing methods, plays on consumers' desire to 'do the right thing' in making purchasing decisions based on their knowledge of the consequences of unsustainable fashion production. The UK, Australia and New Zealand share a common past in terms of demonstrating this desire to change buying behaviour to extend the life of fashion garments and textiles. During World War II (1939–45), these Allied countries participated in the 'make do and mend' wartime campaigns to extend the life of textiles in support of the war effort. This chapter examines some of the methods of this campaign in relation to authentic remake processes and identifies the importance of communicating transparent production processes alongside transparent supply chain models to end consumers. The aim is to highlight the importance of authentic production processes, and of making these processes transparent, particularly in respect of an emerging practice of duplicating an authentic remake aesthetic without adopting an authentic process.

1 The UK, Australia and New Zealand were specified for this study because of their shared history surrounding the 'make do and mend' ideology which resulted from their participation in the Allied war effort between 1939 and 1945.

Research design and methodology

This research identifies and analyses the merits of the successful make do and mend practices that were introduced during the 1940s' wartime campaign to address textile shortages, contextualised through a comparative analysis of consumer behaviour towards preserving fashion textiles during this campaign, historically and within the context of the contemporary marketplace. New Zealand is used as an example to discuss key aspects of the study, which draws on research from the UK, Australia and New Zealand. The fashion market in Australia and New Zealand is similar to that of the UK: both of which had retained strong ties as a result of their relative recent status as British colonies. The make do and mend (1939–45) strategies are compared with contemporary approaches to sustainable fashion and textiles to identify a gap in current practices which could be exploited to encourage more sustainable fashion production. A contextual review of recent fashion collections (spring/summer 2014) reveals a continuing trend of the remake aesthetic. The review of existing company literature reveals that this aesthetic is not supported by any transparency surrounding the supply chain or production processes which support the existence of an authentic remake process. This chapter is the result of ongoing practice-based research which focuses on sustainable design practices. The main methods used in this study were action research, reflective practice, contextual review and comparative analysis. This chapter discusses an aspect of this ongoing research to provide a better understanding of the role of the consumer, and the importance of consumer awareness, in developing more sustainable fashion practices.

Textile waste and New Zealand

The mass market model combined with fast changing trends, reduced price and diminished intrinsic value, encourage consumers to replace and dispose of products before their real life-cycle has ended (Birtwistle and Moore 2007). As a result consumers perceive garments as being disposable, with recent research indicating that clothing discarded to landfill has escalated in the last decade (Allwood *et al.* 2006; Oakdene Hollins *et al.* 2006; Fletcher 2008; DEFRA 2009). Clothing in the waste stream contributes to a range of unsustainable environmental problems for landfills, of which the issues and consequences are well documented (Allwood *et al.* 2006; Oakdene Hollins *et al.* 2006; Fletcher 2008; DEFRA 2009). Research in the UK suggests that a high proportion of useable quality clothing is being binned: contributing to the one million plus tonnes of textiles sent to landfill each year (Allwood *et al.* 2006). Notwithstanding a more informed public awareness of sustainable practices, emergent theory of sustainable textiles continues to advocate educating the consumer to ensure these useable quality items are returned to the secondary market for reuse and upcycling. A wide variety of sustainable practices in fashion/textiles have been identified and tested through research (Fletcher 2008; Gwilt and

Rissanen 2011). While the feasibility of these practices might work in smaller-scale operations, in general the profit-driven mass market—having not recognised the consequences—continues with 'business as usual' and persists with unsustainable practices. Most literature suggests both manufacturers and the general public are under-informed of the harmful effects of discarding clothing to landfill (Birtwistle and Moore 2007; Draper *et al.* 2007; Fletcher 2008; Hethorn and Ulasewicz 2008). While the spotlight remains focused at the end of the pipeline (e.g. landfill) the real problems are not being addressed. It is the unsustainable practices within the fashion and textiles industries that are developing unsustainable products which are consequently predestined for landfill.

Consumer desire to 'do the right thing'

Recent research in the UK links an increase in public awareness with a consumer desire to 'do the right thing'. In the last five years statistical confirmation of a change in consumer behaviour, in terms of disposing of no longer wanted clothing and textiles, was recorded. In 2007, the Department for Environment, Food & Rural Affairs (DEFRA) reported 47% of end-of-life garments were sent to landfill and recommended a national campaign to improve on the low percentage collected for reuse and recycling (at the time just 24%). As a result, the Donate Don't Waste campaign was launched in February 2010, urging people to donate all their unwanted clothes to the 5,000 participating charity shops and 'leave nothing to landfill'.[2] Since the campaign, a recent UK Waste & Resources Action Programme (WRAP) report confirmed a 17% drop (from 47% to around 30%) in end-of-life garments being sent to landfill (WRAP 2012: 48). The report states:

> Much unwanted clothing is donated to charity shops or discarded using other appropriate routes, but clothing is often binned because people consider it too damaged or heavily worn. People would be most likely to separate more clothing for re-use or recycling if made aware that such items have value.

Indications are that consumers are confused with the value or real worth of garments. The huge reduction in the price of clothing serves to confound the consumer, who then fails to comprehend the value of the time and effort required in making textile products. For example, in the UK, the Make Do and Mend organisation draws attention to the apparent futility of repairing a t-shirt when a brand new one can be purchased for £3.[3] Similarly, in New Zealand, a $10 t-shirt compares to little more than the cost of two loaves of bread (Fraser 2013).

2 www.charityshops.org.uk/donate.html, accessed 18 January 2013.

3 See paragraph three of www.make-do-and-mend.org/make_do_mend.html, accessed 25 June 2009.

Using the bread benchmark, we might begin to understand the dilemma for the average consumer, who probably has enough general knowledge to assign a measurable value based on the time and materials required to bake a loaf of bread. However, the same does not apply for the textile product, whereby the average consumer has little knowledge of the expert labour, time or processes involved in making textiles and garments. In this case, the loaf of bread benchmark becomes the measurable value and the $10 textile product is treated like a consumable. Within the behavioural changes of the past century, the status of textiles has changed to a point of being just another disposable material within a ready-made product, no longer prized for its own worth in terms of raw materials and labour.

New Zealand has a long history of valuing textiles—colloquial stories around the turn of the century reminisce the days of mail order textiles, which would see avid dressmakers waiting at the docks for the ship to come in. Although affected by international trends in terms of fast fashion, in contemporary terms, New Zealanders are currently performing sustainable actions and behaviours. A report by the Ministry for the Environment (2008: 20) substantiates a general sustainable behaviour, with many respondents reporting '… that they engaged in such actions because it is "good for them"'. The 2008 study of New Zealanders' sustainable actions/behaviours found that 90% of the 30–39 age group used clothing bins, which reflects their better understanding of the value of textiles than the consumers described in the UK WRAP report. In terms of sustainability, interrupting the cycle of disposing of unwanted garments to landfill is an internationally desired habit (Fraser 2013).

Overcoming the perception of cheap garments as throw-away is an important aspect of addressing the problem of post-consumer textiles waste. The problem of over-consumption in New Zealand is also far more recent than in Australia and the UK. Throughout the 1960s, 1970s and 1980s the local market was insulated from cheap imports for a variety of reasons, including government protections, geographical isolation and a relatively small population (reaching three million c. 1980). At the beginning of the 1990s, locally available products, including clothing, were still relatively expensive. In 2002, for example, there remained a 19% import duty on fashion garments (Blomfield 2002: 49) meaning that consumers bought fewer clothes as they were more expensive. There was still a strong culture of dressmaking alongside an industry which expanded under tariff reductions in the early 1990s (Hamon 2007: 259). As a result, the disconnection between the labour involved in producing garments and the value of the textiles themselves was not as acute. A key observation of these factors is that, where elsewhere in the world the value of textiles had diminished as a result of over-consumption, the comparative rarity of textiles in New Zealand led to the ingrained continuation of desirable behaviour. This included such practices as 'hand-me-downs' for clothing, to distributing unwanted clothing to Salvation Army, hospice, thrift shops and recycle boutiques. These sustainable practices have emerged as a result of necessity rather than as a guilt-free way to dispose of unwanted garments.

Luxury fashion and the remake aesthetic

In the context of sustainable fashion design, the emergence of a remake aesthetic has gained popularity in line with the development of an ethical and sustainable fashion movement. The look can be argued to have emerged in the late 1990s from designers such as Martin Margiela whose collections challenged ideas of quality and finish by being couture without the documented requirement of high quality 'finish' (Gill 1998: 27):

> Margiela sells linings extracted from recovered 'vintage' dresses, giving these linings a chance of a new-old life 'on the outside', that is, as lining dresses in their own right ... His dresses are made from mis-matched fabrics, lining-silks with jerseys, and one can see the inside mechanics of the dress structure—darts, facings, and zippers. Or old jackets have been re-cut, tacked, sewn and re-detailed, their seams and darts reversed and exposed to the outside.

The result was fashion that was exciting, it broke the rules but, at the same time, unleashed a new dimension in couture fashion from which other designers were soon to draw inspiration. The use of existing or 'vintage' couture garments within a fashion context was most notably seen in the case of vintage Valentino worn by Julia Roberts on the red carpet at the Oscars in 2001 (Michault 2004). The interest in vintage has prevailed and, in the decade since, has disseminated from the high-end to the ready-to-wear (RTW) market, with contemporary menswear fashion for autumn 2013 retaining a strong handmade/craft/vintage look and feel (e.g. Dsquared^2).[4] At the same time, designer Thom Brown evoked a definite remake/refashion/reuse aesthetic through the direct use of patched details at the knee.[5]

A key observation is that this remake aesthetic tacitly infers the resultant product has been created using authentic, sustainable, remake fashion processes; but this is not necessarily the case. While these looks are at the high end of the market there is reduced impact of the social, environment and economic considerations for unsustainable design and manufacturing processes. As these looks filter down to the lower end of the mainstream fashion market there will be a greater impact in the context of mass production. Spanish label Desigual,[6] which retails men's jackets from £150, is an example of a label that capitalised on a remake aesthetic by creating new remake garments[7] through a standard cut-and-sew manufacture process without the reuse of textiles and components.

4 www.style.com/fashionshows/complete/F2013MEN-DSQUARE, accessed 24 February 2013.

5 www.style.com/fashionshows/complete/slideshow/F2013MEN-TBROWNE/#37, accessed 24 February 2013.

6 www.desigual.com, accessed 27 February 2013.

7 www.flickr.com/photos/desigual-barcelona/6025607520/in/photostream/, accessed 27 February 2013.

The brand position of this label draws heavily on sustainable and ethical fashion aesthetics which are not the result of a sustainable design process but rather related to a fashion trend. The name of the label strengthens this perception: 'desigual' translates as meaning 'unequal', which could be interpreted as the company providing social opportunities or 'not the same' which infers some ethical point of difference given the strong fashion remake aesthetic. This is especially relevant in combination with the desire of consumers to 'do the right thing' in support of what they perceive to be refashion brands. The connection between labels like Desigual and sustainable design is not a claim made by the brands themselves but something which is tacitly promised through the aesthetics of the garments.

The mainstream fashion market in New Zealand is open to taking direction from the runways of what Entwistle (2009: 139) describes as the key 'fashion cities', and the local industry has evolved from the practice of copying looks from the catwalk and re-interpreting them in a New Zealand context. Indeed, the practice of looking to international catwalks is well documented (Schwimmer 1949; Sterling 1991; Blomfield 2002). This model of reinterpreting another designer's work, normally seen as a somewhat unethical practice, has emerged as commonplace in the local industry taking the form of direct copying (unacknowledged) as well as through the adoption of a licensee model. Although these practices were initially as a result of isolation and distance, they have continued to be an important aspect of design for an industry in a country where the population is estimated at some four and a half million people.[8]

The interest in New Zealand fashion, which arose during the late 1990s and early 2000s, is largely the result of emergent designers experimenting with developing a New Zealand aesthetic. This was at the same time as creativity in other fields, in particular the acclaim received by quintessential New Zealand films such as *The Piano*,[9] portrayed New Zealand as 'dark and edgy' and 'intellectual' in terms of fashion, film and art (Molloy 2004). The result is a microcosmic representation of the influence of high-end fashion on the mainstream fashion market, with the bulk of fashion following the northern hemispheric runway and the high-end section of the market best described as niche and 'eclectic' or 'eccentric' depending on the individual's point of view.

Despite this proclivity for taking looks from the overseas runway, in New Zealand the popularity of fashion remake as a 'look' has been connected to an authentic remaking process. This could be attributed to a cultural paradigm of 'waste not want not' combined with local optimism involving being able to make anything from No. 8 wire! A most well-known example is the work of local label

8 www.stats.govt.nz/tools_and_services/tools/population_clock.aspx, accessed 13 May 2014.

9 www.imdb.com/title/tt0107822/?ref_=sr_1, accessed 26 February 2013.

Nom*D. designer, Margarita Robertson, known to have interpreted Margiela's deconstructed jackets by sourcing high quality tailored pieces and deconstructing them.[10] This is in opposition to other parts of the world where a remade aesthetic has become fashionable but is disconnected from a genuine remake process. Reflecting on this point of difference has resulted in a discussion about why there is such a connection between fashion consumers and fashion objects. The authors theorise that it may be the result of the popular make do and mend campaigns during the 1940s and 1950s which still have a continuing resonance with New Zealanders more than 60 years later. What is it that makes these campaigns so successful?

World War II and the make do and mend campaigns

The World War II is often identified as a turning point for fashion in New Zealand, and there is little argument about its immense influence on the economic and social fabric of the national identity. For most of the 1940s, the war effort was the central focus of life for families in New Zealand. From the perspective of New Zealand fashion researcher Jan Hamon (2007: 156):

> By December 1941, thirty per cent of the male population aged between eighteen and forty-five was in the armed services. At this time, the total population of New Zealand was about one million, six hundred and thirty thousand.

In addition, the war front—particularly the Japanese expansion in the Pacific—had a direct effect on trade by limiting non-essential transport during the period. At the same time there was an increased need for essential wartime materials including textiles (particularly wool and silk). Between 1942 and 1947 a rationing system, similar to the systems introduced in Australia and the UK, was introduced to help manage these shortages.

These rationing systems were not conducted in isolation but formed a part of a larger campaign generally known as Make Do and Mend. At the time of these measures during the 1940s, New Zealanders were already quite adept at minimising waste—the period leading up to the declaration of war by New Zealand was one of recovery in the 1930s from the effects of the Great Depression, and 'making ends meet' was 'deeply ingrained' (Hamon 2007: 158).[11]

10 In winter 2002 Nom*D 'used vintage 1940s' men's suiting, breaking it down and reassembling it to create a singular look'. See www.generalcucumber.com/designer.php?designer=5, accessed 9 September 2008.

11 Jan Hamon gives a more detailed account of the effects of World War II and rationing within the context of the important role of the dressmaker in New Zealand in contributing

However, part of the success of the campaign was the formalisation of many inherent household practices. The literature and advertising material developed for the campaign was disseminated across the globe along with the war effort (campaigns were run in the UK, Australia, New Zealand and the US). Analysis identifies some key aspects which could be useful in creating awareness and potentially developing a culture around sustainable fashion practices for consumers. The key aspects of Make Do and Mend are compared to sustainable design practices and interventions with the aim of shedding new light on an ongoing issue.

In association with the more direct methods of limiting consumption, such as rationing, there were two main aspects of the Make Do and Mend campaign—education and community involvement. Both of these aspects seemed to work in combination with each other to create interest and support for the main aim of the campaign, which was to minimise waste for the war effort. The formalisation of best practices around minimising waste constitute a major part of the material that was produced by the Ministry of Trade, originally in the UK, and reused for parallel campaigns around the globe. Information pamphlets such as *Every Woman Her Own Clothes Doctor* and *Hints on Renovating and Recutting* (National Archives 2007) included reasonably detailed instructions on how to eke the most out of a garment, which we now refer to as maximising the garment's life-cycle. These pamphlets were available on a wide variety of topics from saving cooking oil to resoling footwear. The pamphlets were supported by magazine and newspaper advertisements which directed consumers to obtain materials from the campaign or to 'join a make do and mend class' (Board of Trade 1943). The programme became one of participation as well as practice, with social events aimed at making everyday New Zealanders directly involved in supporting their troops through their practices on 'the home front'. These community events were supported by a central campaign which provided materials for local distribution. This is especially evident in campaign material such as the Mrs Sew and Sew posters (Fig. 2.1). The co-ordination and branding of these events formalised local efforts and brought the community together.

to fashionability. Her thesis is available via RMIT University Research Repository: http://researchbank.rmit.edu.au/.

Figure 2.1 **Mrs Sew and Sew poster from the Make Do and Mend campaign of the 1940s. Image is reproduced under conditions set out by the National Archives, UK: www.nationalarchives.gov.uk/legal/images.htm**

There are unmistakable links between the Make Do and Mend campaign approaches and activities and more recent approaches which have emerged more organically as a part of the sustainable and ethical fashion movement. The more obvious parallels are shoe and clothing exchange initiatives and a reuse approach such as cutting down grown-up clothes for children. The difference between then and now is the focus of these methods within a fashion context where previously the focus had been on thrifty practices to extend the life of everyday clothing, particularly childrenswear. This may be attributed to the rationing systems allocation of a meagre number of rations for children's clothing compared to the reality of how quickly they outgrew the garments which they were able to purchase through the system. More recent interventions are more focused on the fashion consumer, and particularly on creating a fashion aesthetic and attitude to otherwise unwanted fashion garments. Events such as fashion clothing swaps and photo shoots aim to 're-invent' existing garments as fashion and thus increase their desirability. The social interactive events have been given a facelift by researchers such as Otto Von

Busch and his Hactivism,[12] the emergence of collectives such as The Stitchery[13] and labels such as Junky Styling[14] whose work has become synonymous with refashion looks and, importantly, looks achieved through an authentic refashion process.

Aesthetics versus authentic processes

The focus of discussion here is the emergence of a fake remake that we define as fashion garments which signify a refashion process through an eclectic or 'eccentric' mix of fabrics and colours, or the appearance of being reconstituted from more than one existing garment, or from more tacit indicators where no remake process exists.[15] In other words, mainstream fashion labels that are designed to have a remake aesthetic (for whatever reason) resulting in new garments constructed from new materials yet which appear to have been remade. There is a lack of evidence to suggest that this practice has been intentionally insidious but we argue that the result is harmful to the sustainable fashion movement. In reflecting on the significance of this observation we are able to speculate that a co-ordinated approach is needed, a manifesto or an organised campaign for sustainable design or a very transparent way for consumers to identify authentically produced refashion garments. From the Make Do and Mend campaigns we can see that there was a focus on method rather than end product. This is inspiration for designers who are interested in working in a sustainable way, incorporating materials' reuse, aside from the development of a particular remade aesthetic. The challenge is to develop product which relies on sustainable practices but avoids a resultant and expected remake look.

The move away from the designer dictating the exact detail of a finished piece, but rather designing the methods of creating fashion items, might provide new opportunities for a sustainable design aesthetic. One that—whether we are daring enough to admit it or not—is growing old, which in terms of fashion is impending death. Experimental solutions are being developed through a raft of practice-based research projects (see Gwilt and Rissanen 2011), including our own design research focusing on developing different methods which can be carried through to manufacturing (Finn 2008; Fraser 2009). These interventions could be limited by a lack of engagement with the fashion consumer, particularly from the perspective of interaction or dynamic involvement between the consumer and the product. Interestingly, it appears that history is being repeated, to some extent, with the

12 www.youtube.com/watch?v=miWzqZmKAlw, accessed 3 November 2012.

13 http://thestitcherycollective.org.au, accessed 8 September 2012.

14 www.junkystyling.co.uk, accessed 26 February 2013.

15 For a more in-depth account of what is meant by tacit aesthetic knowledge in fashion see Entwistle (2009).

strong resurgence in home sewing, contemporary craft and community education. There is a definite social aspect evidenced by the emergence of significant online communities such as BurdaStyle,[16] Etsy[17] and Wardrobe Refashion,[18] which are reminiscent of Mrs Sew and Sew in a contemporary context. The desire of many consumers to 'do the right thing' is present but not supported by a clear definition of 'the right thing', a problem that was clearly overcome in the Make Do and Mend campaign.

A final aspect of the 1940s' approach was that the rationing system was a direct means of providing consumers with a method of accountability. The lack of accountability for wasteful practices remains the key issue for unsustainable fashion consumption. This problem extends beyond our own accountability as individual consumers, with different levels of knowledge of how many items of clothing we purchase or dispose of each year, to a national and international level. There seems to be an ad hoc approach to dealing with the problem of post consumer textiles waste. In New Zealand, famously spruced as 100% pure by Tourism New Zealand,[19] there remains a lack of explicit knowledge of post consumer textiles waste. There is a lack of statistics around the extent of the problem of garment textiles going to landfill and ignorance around the realities of the end of garment life-cycle beyond the 'charity' clothing bins scattered around local shopping centres. A characteristic of the Make Do and Mend campaign, which would be worth replicating, was the connection made between the source of the problem and the solution to the same problem. In this case, the textiles shortage was 'solved' by a campaign that focused on saving textiles, with public education and social interaction used to address the key issues. In contrast there is no organised approach to addressing the problems of over-consumption which directly contributes to unsustainable practices in fashion. Mainstream fashion brands and retailers who promote the 'pile it high, sell it cheap' model are disconnected from accountability. As suggested elsewhere, we may have a different situation if the producers of these products became responsible for their eventual disposal.

Conclusions and further research

In conclusion, without an organised approach, sustainable fashion looks to remain a fringe movement, fashionable and topical largely due to consumer desire to 'do the right thing'. This is particularly obvious in places like New Zealand where, as a

16 www.burdastyle.com, accessed 26 February 2013.

17 www.etsy.com, accessed 26 February 2013.

18 http://nikkishell.typepad.com/wardroberefashion, accessed 26 February 2013.

19 www.tourismnewzealand.com/about-us/what-we-do/campaign-and-activity/, accessed 13 May 2014.

result of geographical and historical factors affecting its development, the market acts as a microcosmic representation in terms of what is possible. The consumer mindset of many New Zealanders has remained aligned with frugal ideology of 'making do' and 'waste not want not'. The success of more sustainable design practices, including environmental issues which result from post-consumer textiles waste, can be connected with the success of sustainable fashion within the marketplace. The reliance on a remake fashion aesthetic to communicate a connection with sustainably designed and made product is not sufficient to develop a more widely successful brand. The answer may lie in lessons from the past—focusing on education, social engagement and a clear campaign to help consumers know *how* to do the right thing.

Finally, connecting the source of the problem to the solution could provide real opportunity to move forward. The privileging of textiles as a valuable resource, an understanding that has existed for thousands of years before mass production, could be regained by reconnecting consumers to the design and labour involved in textiles' production. The most pressing area for further research is to gather some quantitative data around the extent of the post-consumer textiles waste problem. In the meantime, the psychological campaign to take advantage of consumers' growing desire for more responsible fashion choices could be supported by considering key aspects of the 1940s' Make Do and Mend campaign—essentially wartime propaganda—which has previously been considered rather obsolete. Even in New Zealand, the days of 'use it up, wear it out, make it do, or do without'[20] are gone, but existing research shows that most people will 'do the right thing' when it is the easiest thing to do.[21] This is increasingly difficult in Westernised markets where the 'right thing' can be commoditised and consumers can be led to believe that they are able to buy more products to remedy the problems of mass consumerism—buying the 'right' kind of fashion becomes the 'easiest thing to do'. Changing behaviour is a lot more difficult.

Bibliography

Allwood, J.M., S. Ellebæk Laursen, C. Malvido de Rodríguez and N.M.P. Bocken (2006) *Well Dressed? The Present and Future Sustainability of Clothing and Textiles in the United Kingdom* (1 November 2006; www.ifm.eng.cam.ac.uk/resources/sustainability/well-dressed/, accessed 15 June 2009).

Birtwistle, G., and C.M. Moore (2007) 'Fashion Clothing: Where Does It All End Up?' *International Journal of Retail & Distribution Management* 35.3: 210-16.

20 Phrase originally presented in a speech by B.K. Packer in 1975. See http://speeches.byu.edu/?act=viewitem&id=1136, accessed 27 February 2013.

21 Setting aside the argument of whether or not donating goods to charity is the best solution for no longer wanted garments, causing any interruption between placing still useful garments into the trash must be a move in the right direction.

Blomfield, P. (2002) *The Designer Fashion Industry in New Zealand: A Scoping Study Commissioned by Industry New Zealand* (Wellington: Industry New Zealand).

Board of Trade (1943) *More Make Do and Mend Ideas* (www.advertisingarchives.co.uk, accessed 27 February 2013).

DEFRA (Department for Environment, Food & Rural Affairs) (2009) *Maximising Reuse and Recycling of UK Clothing and Textiles: Project Summary* (15 December 2009; http://ww2.defra.gov.uk, accessed 12 October 2010).

Draper, S., V. Murray and I. Weissbrod (2007) *Fashioning Sustainability: A Review of Sustainability Impacts of the Clothing Industry*, Forum for the Future (www.forumforthefuture.org/sites/default/files/images/Forum/Documents/Fashionsustain.pdf, accessed 25 June 2009).

Entwistle, J. (2009) *The Aesthetic Economy of Fashion: Markets and Value in Clothing and Modelling* (London: Berg Publishers): 129-48.

Finn, A. (2008) *Fashion Manufacturing in New Zealand: Can Design Contribute to a Sustainable Fashion Industry?* (Auckland: Auckland University of Technology).

Farrer, J., and K. Fraser (2009) 'Conscience Clothing: Polarisation of the Fashion Textile Market', *Textiles: Quarterly Magazine of the Textile Institute* 36.1: 10-13.

Fraser, K. (2009) *ReDress: ReFashion as a Solution for Clothing (Un) Sustainability*, Master of Art and Design thesis, AUT University, Auckland.

Fraser, K. (2011) 'ReFashioning New Zealand: A Practitioner's Reflection on Fast Fashion Implications', *International Journal of Environmental, Cultural Economic & Social Sustainability* 7.3: 275-88.

Fraser, K. (2013) 'Throwaway Fashion: The Real Cost of Cheap Fashion for New Zealand', paper presented at *OnSustainability 2013 Conference*, Hiroshima, Japan, 23–25 January 2013.

Fletcher, K. (2008) *Sustainable Fashion and Textile: Design Journeys* (London: Earthscan).

Gabriel, Y., and T. Lang (2006) *The Unmanageable Consumer* (London: Sage).

Gill, A. (1998) 'Deconstruction Fashion: The Making of Unfinished, Decomposing and Reassembled Clothes', *Fashion Theory: The Journal of Dress, Body & Culture* 2.1: 25-49.

Gwilt, A., and T. Rissanen (2011) *Shaping Sustainable Fashion: Changing the Way We Make and Use Clothes* (London: Earthscan).

Hamon, J. (2007) *New Zealand Dressmaker: Experiences, Practices and Contribution to Fashionability, 1940 to 1980*, PhD thesis, School of Architecture and Design, RMIT University, Melbourne.

Hethorn, J., and C. Ulasewicz (eds.) (2008) *Sustainable Fashion—Why Now?: A Conversation About Issues, Practices and Possibilities* (New York: Fairchild Books).

Michault, J. (2004) 'The Vogue of Vintage: Victim of its Own Success', *The New York Times* (23 March 2004; www.nytimes.com/2004/03/23/style/23iht-fvint_ed3_.html, accessed 27 February 2013).

Ministry for the Environment (2008) *Household Sustainability Benchmark Survey* (4 February 2008; www.researchnz.com/pdf/Household%20Sustainability%20Public%20Report%2004-02-08.PDF, accessed 17 June 2012).

Molloy, M. (2004) 'Cutting Edge Nostalgia: New Zealand Fashion Design at the New Millennium', *Fashion Theory* 8.4: 477-90.

National Archives (2007) *Make Do and Mend: Keeping Family and Home Afloat on War Rations: Reproductions of Official Second World War Instruction Leaflets* (London: Michael O'Mara Books).

Oakdene Hollins Ltd., Salvation Army Trading Company Ltd. and Nonwovens Innovation and Research Institute Ltd. (2006) *Recycling of Low Grade Clothing Waste* (30 September 2006; www.oakdenehollins.co.uk/pdf/defr01_058_low_grade_clothing-public_v2.pdf, accessed 27 April 2009).

Schwimmer, F. (1949) 'The Industrial Fashion Designer', *Design Review* 2.3: 46-49.

Sterling, P. (1991) 'Raiders of the Rack', *Listener* 130: 14-19.
Sturken, M., and L. Cartwright (2001) *Practices of Looking: An Introduction to Visual Culture* (New York: Oxford University Press): 189-235.
WRAP (Waste & Resources Action Programme) (2012) *Valuing Our Clothes* (July 2012; www.wrap.org.uk/content/valuing-our-clothes, accessed 18 January 2013).

Angela Finn is a senior lecturer and researcher in design at AUT University. Her published research focuses on the role of design in creating more sustainable fashion industry practices, craftsmanship and make, and tacit knowledge transfer. Her PhD studies explore the importance of tacit aesthetic knowledge in fashion design practice. Email: afinn@aut.ac.nz

Kim Fraser is a senior lecturer and researcher in design at AUT University. Her fashion design research is practice-led and focuses on sustainable design in relation to addressing post-consumer textiles waste. She has presented her research at international conferences and has organised sustainable fashion workshops, seminars and events. Email: kfraser@aut.ac.nz

3

Luxury marketing strategies related to ethical sourcing

Catarina Holmsten-Carrizo
Department of Economics, Swedish University of Agricultural Sciences, Uppsala, Sweden

Cecilia Mark-Herbert
Department of Economics, Swedish University of Agricultural Sciences, Uppsala, Sweden

Introduction

Ethical challenges related to consumption of fast-moving consumer goods (food and fibre products) have received a lot of attention in the last decades (Gardetti and Torres 2013). Complex value chains in most fibre value chains complicate decision making. In addition, a number of management challenges are related to lack of awareness of all aspects of production, sales and use of the product. In the case of textile production for garments, as well as for home textiles, the predominant material used is cotton. The production of cotton is associated with a number of challenges in the value chain (Fig. 3.1). These challenges can be split in accordance with the 'triple bottom line' (Elkington 2004) of social, environmental and economic threats to sustainable development.

Figure 3.1 **Selection of challenges related to textiles' production in a triple bottom line framework**

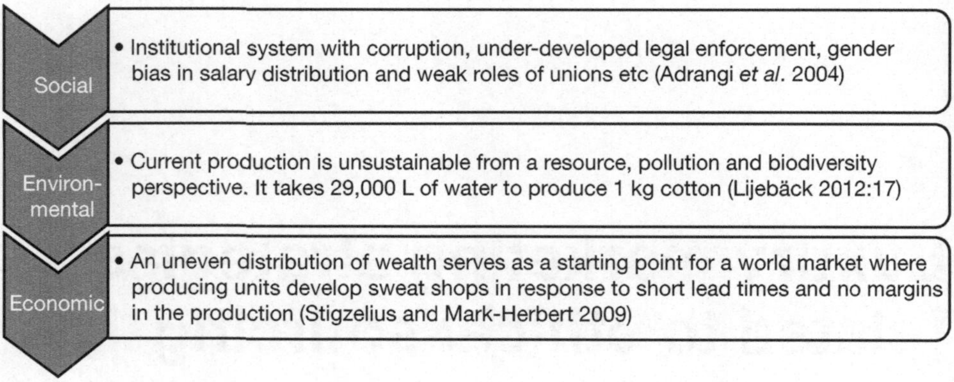

The term 'luxurious' raises the question of when a product is seen as something extravagant. The economics' perspective distinguishes between needs and wants, and considers anything beyond a need to be a luxury (Mortelmans 2005; Sandell *et al.* 2005: 93-110). A more marketing oriented explanation of luxury is tied to the functions of the product in social and cultural contexts related to the consumer's needs and wants (Wiedmann *et al.* 2007). It offers understanding of the importance of a brand (Black 2008). Much of the branding efforts in marketing talk in favour of a definition of luxury as something rare, extravagant and expensive. Branding also implies a risk in cases like these ones of creating a fallacy of 'clean' luxury (Davies *et al.* 2012). Given the extent of the ethical challenges in cotton production, most home textile products, above and beyond that in current use in an average home, would qualify as luxury. Our study concerns the corporate perspective of the value chain in the production of cotton, keeping consumer needs in mind, and how the corporation can enhance its brand by communicating the added value of ethically sourced cotton.

The aim of this chapter is to describe ethical sourcing initiatives in two home textile retail corporations in Sweden and Finland. We are assuming that responsible sourcing in the cotton value chain will limit threats to sustainable development as well as create opportunities in terms of marketing strategies. The overall objective is to increase the understanding of how ethical sourcing is used for strategic branding purposes as well as for market development purposes. Key research questions are related to how corporate responsibility (CR) is perceived within the corporation, which stakeholder groups are prioritised and the use of procurement tools. A mixed method approach (Robson 2011) allows for a combination of data collection methods; in this project a literature review of academic journals, personal interviews with CR officers and an analysis of digital information of what the selected case study companies say about their products on their Web pages and in their responsibility reports.

This chapter is based on a research study of five home textile retailers (Holmsten-Carrizo 2013). Of these five cases, two are particularly interesting with regard to luxury consumption—Ikea and Finlayson. The selection of the case studies is based on the following criteria: a main market in the Nordic countries to ensure similar cultural contexts; and communication efforts from the corporation as an indicator of transparency in their CR efforts. The secondary empirical material relies heavily on what each of these corporations communicates on Web sites and in various reports. The primary empirical data, mainly interviews, serves as sources for understanding motives and attitudes towards ethical sourcing. Throughout the research process efforts were made to ensure validation in several steps (during the interview and sending the transcripts to the interviewees after the interview) as well as in triangulation of data (Eisenhardt 1989).The project addresses responsible sourcing aspects in the cotton value chains for home textile products (such as towels, bedding and curtains). These products account for roughly one-third of the cotton produced in the US, the third largest cotton producer in the world.[1] Despite a large part of the cotton resource use, home textile production receives limited attention, while garment production remains the focus in the political, media and academic spotlights.

The results of the study show that there are similarities in the case companies' strategies and approach to CR, with both using a life-cycle assessment tool. The results also show some differences in communication efforts on ethical sourcing. In this chapter we will present the differences in the companies' sustainable business development strategies in terms of marketing added value of luxury products, starting with presenting a conceptual framework, then the empirical results and lastly the conclusions.

Corporate responsibility and marketing added value: a conceptual framework

CR builds on the idea of responsible conduct—where corporate management takes a 'triple bottom line' (Elkington 2004) to account for a wide set of stakeholders. In the case of a private organisation, CR is not merely defined by profitability but also by the organisation's sense of commitment and responsibility to its internal and external stakeholders. The concept is closely tied to external pressures as: 'CR is about adapting to the ever-changing social reality and about making oneself fit to take societal demands seriously' (Pompe and Korthals 2010: 370). Businesses, regardless of industry and size, are active members of society, which is reflected by context bound visions, social realities and operations in accordance with regulations and other societal expectations.

1 www.cotton.org/pubs/cottoncounts/fieldtofabric/uses.cfm, accessed 28.1.2013

Porter and Kramer (2006: 64) suggest that CR is about creating shared value for society in order to legitimise businesses and create 'a new way to achieve economic success'. Shared value refers to business conduct where business and society are interconnected. As an integrated way to create policies and operating practices that enhance competitive edge and, at the same time, affect the social, environmental and economic conditions for the communities in which a business operates, a shared value lens can be applied to every business decision. The additional value is created by offering sustainable products and services and communicating them in ways that empower and educate consumers, which in turn strengthens the brand and the corporation's reputation (Porter and Kramer 2006; Ottman 2011).

A notion of shared value in a global business environment points to the necessity of rethinking models for stakeholders as well as strategic thinking, questioning to whom the retailers are responsible and accountable on a global market. Rainey (2006: 711) refers to CR work as sustainable business development. He defines stakeholder as 'any individual or group that is directly or indirectly affected by the products, programs, processes, and/or systems, but does not directly benefit as an economic participant such as a customer or supplier'. He emphasises a value network perspective that recognises a context bound and a wide set of stakeholders in his enterprise management model (Fig. 3.2), as a base for sustainable business development.

Figure 3.2 **An enterprise management model (Rainey 2006: 89)**

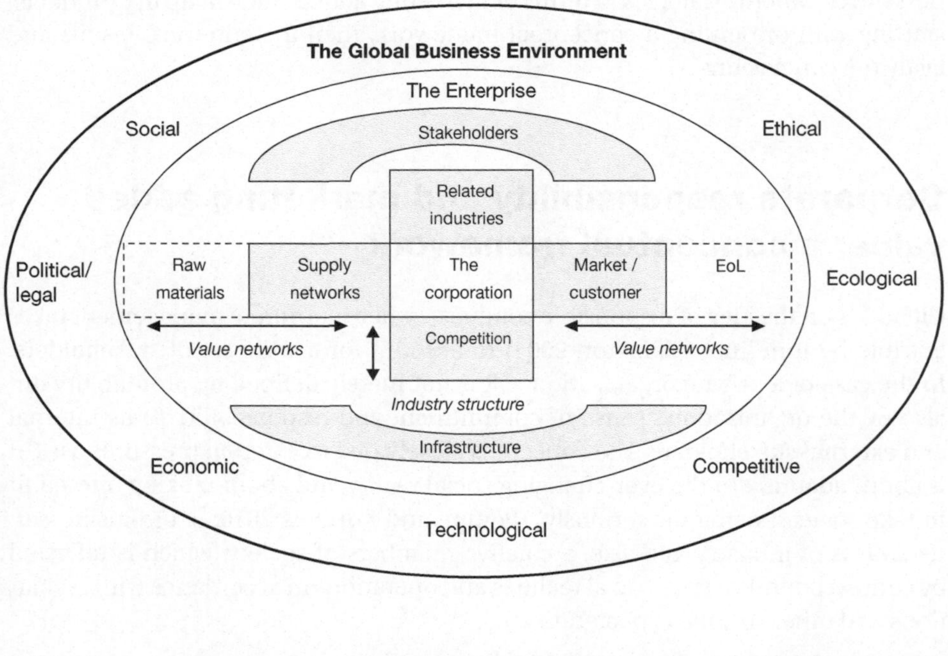

Rainey (2006: 90) argues that the value chain perspective in ethical sourcing is an important part of sustainable business development. It is an extension of Michael

Porter's value system in that it reaches beyond first tier suppliers and it covers the life-cycle of a product (from raw material to end-of-life). Identifying institutional conditions, stakeholder groups and individuals that are connected to a firm's environment with the intention to 'broaden management's vision of its roles and responsibilities beyond the profit maximization function ...' (Mitchell *et al.* 1997: 855) is key in the value chain perspective. It includes stakeholders in value networks upstream as well as downstream (Fig. 3.2). Textile retailers are central in the value chain as a link between farmers, processors and consumers, which enables them to benefit from a powerful position in various decisions.

Decisions made by the integrated producer and retailer network may affect a large number of stakeholders. These decisions may concern conditions in the procurement process that are stipulated by an internal code of conduct or a standard (Larsson and Häversjö 2001). As a labour intense industry, a number of these standards concern local working conditions, reinforcing a weak legal enforcement (Stigzelius and Mark-Herbert 2008). The retailer's role in consumer education refers to efforts in marketing communication (Söderlund and Berg 2012: 74) for consumers in search of branded products with luxurious properties grounded in ethical sourcing processes, which translates well to this research project.

Ethical sourcing initiatives in the home textile retail corporations

In the research project, both case study corporations (Ikea and Finlayson) have dealt with ethical sourcing with support from multi-stakeholder initiatives (membership in networks) and through standards (audits by certification agents). Some facts about each case corporation are offered in Table 3.1, followed by a presentation of the ethical sourcing initiatives in each of these cases.

Table 3.1 **Ethical sourcing initiatives in two home textile corporations (Holmsten-Carrizo 2013)**

Corporation key feature	Ikea[a]	Finlayson[b]
Internal view of value of ethical sourcing	Value in itself to lessen environmental impact[c]	Differentiate from competitors and deliver added value to consumers[d]
Internal corporate social responsibility strategy	Three main change drivers: inspiring and helping customers to live more sustainably at home; striving for resource and energy independence; and taking the lead in creating a better life for people and communities impacted by Ikea's business[e]	One of Finlayson's values is to act responsibly.[d] On its Web page the company communicates respect for nature as well as the connection to Finland and how it wants to contribute to the wellbeing of society[g]
Goal	100% BCI cotton by 2015[c,f]	When it comes to cotton, Finlayson has decided to focus on more responsible cotton for its towel collections. Possibly in the future it will move on to other products once it sees how these are received by customers[d]
Stakeholder engagement in value chain	BCI is a multi-stakeholder initiative that works to improve social and environmental impacts in the conventional chain. BCI follows cotton production to the ginning stage in the supply chain[h]	Cradle to Cradle criteria includes material health, material reutilisation, renewable energy, carbon management, water stewardship and social fairness. Products that adhere to the strong criteria are awarded an eco-label. Companies working with this label get access to other practitioners and best practice information[i] Fairtrade is a label focusing on producers at the beginning of value chain. When products are certified according to the Fairtrade standard, it is the cotton, not the finished garment, that has been ethically traded. In this case it means that the farmer has received a fair price for the cotton[j]
Communicating the ethical sourcing efforts	The Ikea department stores, information on the products, Fairtrade organisation Web page and on its own products[c]	Fairtrade organisation Web page and on its own products[d]

Innovation for sustainability	Weaving technique. Ikea DVALA series is made with a weaving technique using 15% less cotton, which means less material used during production. Also looking at alternative materials such as wood and hemp[c]	Soya towels. Finlayson has towels that contain both soya and cotton. The soya used is a by-product during food production. These towels 'have a more silky and luxury feel'[d]
Luxury approach	Sustainability is not only for luxury products, it applies to everyday products such as home textiles as well[c]	More responsible consumers are willing to pay a higher price for a product with added value and luxurious properties[d]

Notes:

a Ikea has 139,000 co-workers and operates worldwide; www.ikea.com/ms/en_GB/about_ikea/facts_and_figures/facts_figures.html, accessed 6 March 2013.

b Finlayson has about 216 employees and has stores in Finland, Russia and Estonia; http://en.finder.fi/Sisustustekstiilej%C3%A4/Finlayson%20Oy/HELSINKI/economy/522480, accessed 30 March 2013.

c Telephone interview with E. Stål, Sustainability Co-ordinator, Ikea, 15 January 2013.

d Face-to-face interview with L. Suurla, Product Manager, Finlayson, 22 March 2013.

e *People and Planet Positive Sustainability Strategy 2020*: 8, www.ikea.com/ms/en_GB/pdf/people_planet_positive/People_planet_positive.pdf, accessed 7 March 2013.

f *People and Planet Positive Sustainability Strategy 2020*: 9, www.ikea.com/ms/en_GB/pdf/people_planet_positive/People_planet_positive.pdf, accessed 7 March 2013.

g *Finlayson Oy*, www2.finlayson.fi/finlayson-en/finlayson-oy-en, accessed 30 March 2013.

h www.bettercotton.org/files/BCSInfoPack/1_Overview_of_BCS_final_eng_ext.pdf, accessed 7 March 2013.

i http://c2ccertified.org/about/what_is_cradle_to_cradle, accessed 8 April 2013.

j www.fairtrade.net/what_is_fairtrade.html, accessed 8 April 2013.

The vision of the global corporation Ikea is to improve the 'everyday life for the many people'.[2] Ikea's Sustainability Co-ordinator, E. Ståhl, comments: 'Given that we are big and want to continue working towards our vision, it is self-explanatory that what we put on the market has to make as little impact as possible, still keep a low price but good quality'.[3] This is quite the opposite of Finlayson, with Product Manager L. Suurla observing: 'We believe that consumers are educated and more willing to pay a higher price for a product that has an additional [ethical] value, not from being a certain colour but from offering something more and keeping what it promises'.[4] However, even if Finlayson is focusing more on adding the shared value aspect in the eyes of a narrower consumer segment, it is only doing so with one product category, towels, so far. By focusing only on towels the company has been able to extend the 'more responsible' towel collections, instead of trying to work on all product categories with a risk of less to show as a result. At the moment Finlayson has three responsible collections, each with a different focus, which can appeal to consumer segments with varying expectations on sustainable development. One towel collection with a lot of colour carries the Fairtrade label. Another towel collection is made out of a mix of soya and cotton—these towels have other physical properties, a silkier feel to them, and they carry a soya label. Towels in the third collection carry the Cradle to Cradle label and are 100% recyclable, and the colour range is more natural.[5,6]

Compared to Finlayson's approach, the Ikea sustainability strategy seems much bolder, or clearer, in setting a goal of 100% better cotton by 2015. Ikea is a founding member of BCI (Better Cotton Initiative), which works with the conventional cotton chain. As E. Ståhl explains: 'When it comes to cotton, one can choose either ecologically grown cotton or conventionally grown cotton. We tried to take a middle way as there are not such volumes of ecologically grown cotton as we and also others would need'.[7] The criteria are aimed at improving the farming practices in use of water, pesticides and the financial and social situation for farmers. Even though the criteria are not very strict, Ikea has improved the life of a significant number of farmers (100,000 farmers in seven years).[8,9]

> So this spread because, what happened [for the farmers] except for using less chemicals and water and buying fewer chemicals ... was that the sales grew. So it was a positive combination of different parts and then this sort

2 www.ikea.com/ms/en_GB/about_ikea/the_ikea_way/our_business_idea/index.html, accessed 6 March 2013.
3 Personal communication, 15 January 2013.
4 Personal communication, 22 March 2013.
5 Personal communication with L. Suurla, Product Manager, Finlayson, 22 March 2013.
6 *Finlayson Oy*, www2.finlayson.fi/finlayson-en/finlayson-oy-en, accessed 30 March 2013.
7 Personal communication, 15 January 2013.
8 Personal communication with E. Stål, Sustainability Co-ordinator, Ikea, 15 January 2013.
9 *Social & Environmental Responsibility Report 2012*: 33, www.ikea.com/ms/en_GB/pdf/annual_report/ikea_group_sustainability_report_2012.pdf, accessed 7 March 2013.

> of knowledge spread faster: because there was such a great economic advantage. That was a win both for environment, cotton [farmers] and Ikea, as we get a better raw material.[10]

Finlayson, on the other hand, works with Cradle to Cradle, which rests on five criteria tied to aspects of sustainable development (Table 3.1), Finlayson also offer Fairtrade towels, which it hopes appeal to a different consumer segment as this range of towels carry a variety of colours that cannot be produced within the range of the environmental criteria for Cradle to Cradle. According to L. Suurla:

> We have a possibility to offer something different than the competitors with the innovation techniques [Cradle to Cradle and soya towels], other companies also have Fairtrade but at present our Fairtrade towel range is colourful. With the different ranges we brought in slightly different styles to decorate for different sorts of people … Fairtrade is colourful while the soya towels are low-key and luxurious; they are a bit silky to the touch. Cradle to Cradle colours are tied to what is possible due to the criteria; they are therefore beige, dark grey, green, quite natural earthy colours and dark blue.

Differences are also noted in the companies' innovation strategies. Ikea has focused on innovation that will make the production more efficient, which offers possibilities to lower prices given a cost-based price strategy. As E. Ståhl notes: '… by having a new weaving technique we use 15% less material, that is even better, then we can make more out of less'.[11] Finlayson, on the other hand, has focused its research and development efforts towards desired product qualities that give the product a desirable luxury feel to it, with a price strategy that presupposes consumers' understanding of added values.

The common denominator of the corporate strategies is that communicative efforts concerning sustainability are limited to information on some products in the stores.[12,13] Finlayson also markets Fairtrade towels on the Finnish Fairtrade Web page.[14] However, none of these strategies are focused on educating the consumer about the larger scale global business environment. These findings indicate that there is still room for improvement in both case studies when it comes to communicating product life-cycle responsibility efforts to consumers. So far the companies have not invested extensively in educating consumers about the shared values of ethically sourced products.

10 Personal communication with E. Stål, Sustainability Co-ordinator, Ikea, 15 January 2013.
11 Personal communication, 15 January 2013.
12 Personal communication with E. Stål, Sustainability Co-ordinator, Ikea, 15 January 2013.
13 Personal communication with L. Suurla, Product Manager, Finlayson, 22 March 2013.
14 Personal communication with L. Suurla, Product Manager, Finlayson, 22 March 2013.

Ethical sourcing, differentiation and branding of luxury products

Exploring CR through the lens of home textile retailers illustrates how ethical sourcing may serve as a basis for differentiation both at product and corporate level. Products, product lines and entire corporations that are engaged in an ethical sourcing initiative create capacity to communicate added values. However, in order for the consumer to perceive the added value, it has to be communicated, for example through a certification mechanism such as an eco-label or through other consumer educational efforts. So far home textile products and corporations have not made significant efforts to create a more ethically oriented brand, in comparison to the garment textile industry where a brand makes all the difference in the world for the consumer (Black 2008). From a strategic marketing point of view there is a lot of potential in developing the branding capacity (Ottman 2011; Söderlund and Berg 2012) in creating products with added values in the product life-cycle, thereby using ethical sourcing to create a luxurious identity.

The increased understanding of value chain and networks values serves as grounds for strategic differentiation (Rainey 2006; Ottman 2011), but it assumes that consumers attribute value to ethical aspects of production to the overall value of the product. Grounds for the added value, the luxuriousness in product properties, are created in the value network (Rainey 2006; Ottman 2011), but how do these efforts affect consumer perception of a product's luxuriousness? The cases presented here offer insight to how ethical sourcing is communicated, but not how consumers perceive these values. Ethical sourcing may support the value of a branded product, assuming consumers are aware of the network values created in the value chain. The strategic value in ethical sourcing initiatives is hard to assess. It is not clear how consumers may translate ethical sourcing, along with long-lasting quality, to sustainability values (Wiedmann *et al.* 2007; Davies *et al.* 2012).

In the case of Ikea, branding is based on reasoning around making the everyday products luxurious because of their ethical added value property, which is supported in Davies *et al.* (2012) who report positive consumer propensity to consider ethics in commoditised products. This raises the issue of the role of the retailer as not only an ethical sourcing agent but also as an educational resource. Ironically, in traditional luxury products, ethics seems to be an added bonus that does not affect the purchasing decision, while in everyday products ethics is the luxury that makes the difference during the purchase decision (Davies *et al.* 2012). Finlayson has solved this by adding different options in its towel collection to appeal to consumers with different preferences. One of the options is Fairtrade, which is a relatively well known concept for consumers due to marketing and educational efforts (Davies *et al.* 2010). Finlayson has seen an increase in the sale of Fairtrade towels in recent years and its understanding and experience is that this is because of consumers' increased knowledge of the label.[15] Both Finlayson and Ikea could benefit from marketing and extending their educational efforts for the consumer more about the less known initiatives, such as BCI, weaving techniques, soya towels and Cradle to Cradle, as part of their responsible sourcing efforts. Perhaps the future concept of luxury will be associated with a less materialistic view, which will be replaced with a perspective in which ethically sourced everyday products, such as home textiles, are seen as luxuries.

Bibliography

Adrangi, B.K., K.K. Dhanda and R.P. Hill (2004) 'A Model of Consumption and Environmental Degradation: Making the Case for Sustainable Consumer Behavior', *Journal of Human Development* 5.3: 417-32.

Black, S. (2008) *Eco-chic: The Fashion Paradox* (London: Black Dog Publishing).

Davies, I.A., B. Doherty and S. Knox (2010) 'The Rise and Stall of a Fair Trade Pioneer: The Story of Café Direct', *Journal of Business Ethics* 92: 127–47.

Davies, I., Z. Lee and I. Ahonkhai (2012) 'Do Consumers Care About Ethical Luxury?', *Journal of Business Ethics* 106: 37-51.

Eisenhardt, K. (1989) 'Building Theories from Case Study Research', *Academy of Management Review* 14.4: 532-50.

Elkington, J. (2004) 'Enter the Triple Bottom Line', in A. Henriques and J. Richardson (eds.), *The Triple Bottom Line: Does It All Add Up?* (London: Earthscan): 1-16.

Gardetti, M.A., and L.A. Torres (2013) *Sustainability in Fashion and Textiles: Values, Design, Production and Consumption* (Sheffield, UK: Greenleaf Publishing).

Holmsten-Carrizo, C. (2013) *Responsible Sourcing and Transparency in the Home Textile Industry: The Case of Cotton* (Uppsala, Sweden: Swedish University of Agricultural Sciences).

Larsson, B., and T. Häversjö (2001) 'Management by Standards: Real Benefits from Fashion', *Scandinavian Journal of Management* 17: 457-80.

Liljebäck, L-E. (2012) 'Billigare Kläder, Dyrt för Miljön', *Naturvetare* 6: 12-17.

Mitchell, R.K., B.R. Agle and D.J. Wood (1997) 'Toward a Theory of Stakeholder Identification and Salience: Defining Principle of Who and What Really Counts', *Academy of Management Review* 22.4: 853-86.

Mortelmans, D. (2005) 'Sign Value in Process of Distinction: The Concept of Luxury', *Semiotica* 157.1/4: 497-520.

Ottman, J.A. (2011) *The New Rules of Green Marketing: Strategies, Tools and Inspiration for Sustainable Branding* (Sheffield, UK: Greenleaf Publishing).

Pompe, V., and M. Korthals (2010) 'Ethical Room for Manoeuvre: Playground for the Food Business', *Business and Society Review* 115.3: 367-91.

Porter, M., and M. Kramer (2011) 'Creating Shared Value', *Harvard Business Review*, January/February 2011: 62-77.

Rainey, D.L. (2006) *Sustainable Business Development* (Cambridge, UK: Cambridge University Press).

Robson, C. (2011) *Real World Research* (Chichester, UK: John Wiley, 3rd edn).

15 Personal communication with L. Suurla, Product Manager, Finlayson, 22 March 2013.

Sandell K., J. Öhman and L. Östman (2005) *Education for Sustainable Development: Nature, School and Democracy* (Lund, Sweden: Studentlitteratur).

Stigzelius, I., and C. Mark-Herbert (2009) 'Tailoring Corporate Responsibility to Suppliers: Managing SA8000 in Indian Garment Manufacturing', *Scandinavian Journal of Management* 25.1: 46-56.

Söderlund, M., and H. Berg (2012) 'Customer Retail Chain Satisfaction Rubs Off on Purchase Intentions for Other Retail Chains', in J. Hakberg, U. Holmberg, M. Sundström and L. Walter (eds.), *Nordic Retail Research: Emerging Diversity* (Göteborg, Sweden: BAS Publishers): 65-78.

Wiedmann, K., N. Hennings and A. Siebels (2007) 'Measuring Consumers' Luxury Value Perception: A Cross Cultural Framework', *Academy of Marketing Science Review* 7: 1-21.

Catarina Holmsten-Carrizo has a BSc in business administration and MSc in environmental management and economics. Her Master's thesis focused on global supply chain and managerial tools for communicating corporate social responsibility work in the textile industry. Email: catarina.holmsten@gmail.com

Cecilia Mark-Herbert is an Associate Professor at the Department of Economics at the Swedish University of Agricultural Sciences. She works as a researcher and lecturer in marketing. Her specialisation is in corporate responsibility and most of her research is related to economic, environmental, social and ethical aspects of marketing management. Email: cecilia.mark-herbert@slu.se

Part II

4

Redefining luxury in the 21st century: where was yours made?

A case study of Made in San Francisco

Connie Ulasewicz
San Francisco State University, California, USA

Introduction

Luxury is constantly on the move and in our 21st century global society a shift in what defines a product's luxury, or how it is defined, is in motion (Kapferer *et al.* 2012). A garment or product is frequently identified as luxurious in the fashion industry because of its high quality or extravagant materials and trims, limited production or availability, designer name and associated social status (Ma *et al.* 2012); all are essential, yet a new component has emerged. The perception of a brand's luxury is increasingly determined by the designer-made product-related choices for country, state or city of origin for each component and method of production, and the transparency of these choices for the brand's identity as fashionable luxury.

San Francisco is host to a growing number of designer names or brands which are part of this transformation in the garment industry, and these designers and manufacturers are the source of this research study. Collectively, their objective is not to be classified by the term 'luxury' because of a name, label or pre-determined category price point, which brings prestige to the end wearer (Heine 2012) or that will position them as an upscale brand in the market (Dubois *et al.* 2005). Rather, their focus is based on a decision to manufacture their products in San Francisco, where they design (Roberts 2013), because of the brand identity value that local production or manufacturing brings to their product. A brief historical synopsis offers background and the roots to the phenomenon of luxury in dress and apparel, followed by an analysis of the new luxury emerging today from designer names or brands in the San Francisco market.

Brief context of what defines luxury in apparel

In the late 19th century, Charles Frederick Worth designed fashionable dresses with opulent fabrics and trims, chosen by his clients before being tailor-made in his workshop to their exact fit and desired proportions (Krick 2004). His talents for the design of entire collections of sumptuous dresses earned him the title of 'the first couturier' (Stegemeyer 1996: 2) a label associated with the intrinsic value of the designer or brand name that established a reputation for quality, style and status (Mulvey and Richards 1998). Perceived luxury rested on the understanding that a designer product equalled excellence in the quality of design and aesthetics, was of a high cost, and would not be mass produced (Heine 2012). Paris was the centre for design houses such as Poiret, Vionnet and Chanel, who flourished through two world wars and into the 20th century (Bigelow 1979). American designers or manufacturers were born in the 20th century when the Western world was cut off from Europe in the 1940s due to World War II, and Manhattan New York's Seventh Avenue was chosen as the site for the autumn opening of the first America-only fashion showings (Anon 1940).

The unsatisfied US demand for luxury Parisian fashions fostered both legal and illegal design imitations, manufactured in the US at a much reduced cost (Welters 2008). The market for ready-to-wear clothing, mass produced in standardised sizes and sold in finished condition without the need for significant alteration,[1] was first introduced by the US retailer Bergdorf Goodman early in the 20th century. As the international demand for affordable fashion increased, the growing global economy allowed for a decreased cost of goods when components or production were outsourced to countries and cities with lower labour costs. The impact on consumers' decision to purchase both luxury and ready-to-wear designer names or brands based on where or how a product was made was unclear. Western luxury brands were unwilling to concede how much of their production was manufactured in China (Masidlover 2013).

1 B. Farfan 'Ready-to-Wear', *About.com Retail Industry*, http://retailindustry.about.com/od/glossary/g/readytowearclot.htm, accessed 30 July 2013.

In the 21st century, the social and environmental meaning of how, why and where products are designed and produced has gained momentum (Binkley 2010). The conscious choice of country, state or city of origin for each component and method of production are a descriptive litany of a designer or brand's identity and values (Hethorn and Ulasewicz 2008). The awareness that 'no resource ought to be considered dispensable' (McDonough and Braungart 2013: xv) has encouraged and supported more responsible production and consumption practices. A designer name or brand may be considered luxury because of the higher cost required for the chosen design and production practices, and the higher retail value. The term 'demi-couture', meaning 'high end side of ready-to-wear' (Mistry 2011), was recently coined to represent product created by known or up-and-coming couture-like designers who incorporate luxury practices, producing what is special and unique from exquisite fabrics and trims, in small quantity, selling at a high cost. Concurrently in San Francisco, the terms 'local manufacturing', 'locally made' or 'SF made' are referenced (Roberts 2013), sought out by consumers and may also be considered a new form of luxury. This new luxury aesthetic resonates the resourcefulness required (Ioakimedes 2011) to manufacture in and around the city by the bay—San Francisco.

Brief context of the history of Made in San Francisco

The San Francisco Bay area, the geographic region in Northern California defined as the ten county's surrounding the San Francisco Bay, has a rich history of product design houses and companies dating back to the 1920s. This region was the original west coast hub of the production of millinery, fur, leisurewear and suiting for men and women. At its peak, from about 1937 to 1962, San Francisco attracted buyers from major department stores headquartered in New York, Chicago and Los Angeles to attend seasonal industry fashion weeks (Anon. 1943). Beginning in the 1970s, the international trade policies and globalisation of the apparel industry decimated the local manufacturing industry, as it was increasingly less expensive to produce products in other regions of the word (Lai and Jeung 2008).

Despite the highest labour costs in the US, \$10.55/hour (Woolfolk 2013), the San Francisco Bay area, the third largest garment industry location in the US behind New York and Los Angeles, is growing (Ioakimedes 2011). Apparel and accessory manufacturing companies represent 40% of the San Francisco manufacturing sector, with an increase in design companies since 2009 (City and County of San Francisco 2012). The reasons for this growth are varied. However, recent developments suggest that higher costs of offshore production and the consumer desire and support for 'locally' designed and manufactured products are key sources (Tilley 2012).

Purpose

The purpose of this study was to investigate those who are designing and manufacturing in the San Francisco Bay area, both how and why, while also identifying their challenges, concerns and aspirations. The research intent was not an investigation of luxury brands; rather, it was through the interview process and analysis of the data that this component of the new luxury erupted.

This research was framed by three questions:

- What is the message or mission of your product or company?
- What are the most challenging variables that impact your sustainability?
- What is the future of being able to design and manufacture in San Francisco?

It was anticipated that the data gathered in this project would reveal insights about what has contributed to the sustainability of the garment industry in San Francisco, and shed light on what assets the industry has, what threats it faces and what professionals in the business believe about the local community's ability to be competitive in a global market.

Method/procedure

Given the complexity of choices and manufacturing decisions that designers make on a continual basis, dialogue, a qualitative methodology, was considered the most appropriate for this research (Forney *et al.* 1990). The desire was to gather data in the interviews that would directly speak to the research questions and reveal discrete information from an 'insider's' perspective. A single page interview instrument was developed. Four of the questions were demographic in nature, with the remainder more general and open ended. The proposition was to offer the designer an opportunity to share their responses, with the awareness that their individual and collective content was the primary source of analysis.

Sample

Beginning in July 2012, potential participants known to the researcher through industry connections or recommendations were asked to participate in the study via an email invitation. Criteria for respondent selection included:

- The design 'headquarters' was located in the San Francisco area
- The representative was the designer, owner or key decision-maker on how and where products were created and produced
- All or part of the product(s) were made, or had been recently made, in the San Francisco area

A total of 83 companies were contacted, with 50 responding. Appointments were scheduled on days and times that were convenient to them throughout August to December 2012. The total time commitment for the in-person interview was anticipated to be 20–30 minutes. However, the average was 40 minutes and the longest was 90 minutes, due to the general enthusiasm of the interviewees. Each interview was audio recorded and then the audio files were transcribed verbatim to allow for detailed content analysis. Participants were given the option to remain anonymous in any reporting and representation of the interviews.

Results

Forty-five of the respondents self identified as company owners, co-owners or founders, two as vice presidents, one as a merchandising director, one as a president and one as a designer. Categories of business identified were 43% women, 18% accessories, 14% men and women, 12% men, 6% other (including alterations, men, women and children, toys). As identified in the literature review, and supported by these respondents, the San Francisco Bay area has been, and continues to be, a region for garment manufacturing. Half (25) of the respondents replied that the company had been in business for 1–9 years, nine for 11–20 years, 11 for 21–35 years and five for over 36 years. Further, the findings support that the San Francisco Bay area continues to be supportive to start-ups as 18 of the companies are in their first through fifth year of business, with seven in their sixth through tenth year.

What is the message or mission of your product or company?

Interviewees were asked to describe the core mission or emphasis of the company and the label or brand they designed and produced. The product itself, the principles and methods chosen to determine its value, surfaced as being reflective of the company mission and was referred to by 70% of the respondents. Two additional themes emerged throughout the interviews, both being mentioned by 50% of the respondents, relating to what has been termed the company ethics and their focus on the customer. The customer theme that continually emerged in response to this question related specifically to the relationship the company had with the customer, their focus and their awareness of customers' needs and desire for product information. Table 4.1 presents the three themes, the number of interviewees that it denotes and representative responses within each theme.

Table 4.1 **Recurring themes for company and product mission**

Product focus (35)	• Unique, new, innovative products in fabric and feature • Well made products, not catering to trends, products that will last • Keep it local, quick response time to orders. • Well merchandised, fit or create a niche • Design for efficiency, lower labour costs, minimise waste in design and cutting • Continually search for the best, most unique, specialised fabric, trims, and enhancements • Produce excellent and sustainable products, be seasonless, be trendless, and do not add to landfill • Create a brand that is you • Sell a product rather than a collection • Refine fit; take fewer risks with new styles • Reduce margins by simplifying the product, control minimum orders, and utilise the fabric
Company ethics (25)	• Create, sell and ship only what has a proven great fit, that meets your criteria for excellence and quality • Open production house so the customer can walk around and see what is going on • Give people all product information so they feel good about buying the product • Listen and respond to customer requests • Keep product local, Made in San Francisco, Made in California • Stay true to ourselves, be honest, create products with integrity, have incredible ethics • Give as much value as possible to our customers • Social good is intrinsically tied to the product • Develop devoted employees and vendor relationships • Work really hard
Focus on customer (25)	• Get the message out about what distinguishes your product • Work with customers on custom work, understand their requirements • Design for the specific needs of your customer, listen to them, and grow a brand to meet their needs throughout their lives • Customers are interested in ecology, design this into product, the packaging, make the goods in USA or San Francisco • Provide for the customer, develop relationships with them, have contact with them in store and online. Provide a voice for them to listen to through social media • Accommodate for the demographics of your customer; make them feel good about themselves in your garments

What are the most challenging variables that impact your sustainability?

When asked to describe the challenges that impact their ability to design and manufacture in the San Francisco area, the lengthiest and most consistent responses were given. Two recurring themes emerged, with over 80% of the respondents mentioning the actual production process of cutting and sewing the goods, and over 58% mentioning the actual materials and trims required or desired for the design. Table 4.2 presents the two themes, the number of interviewees that it denotes, and representative responses within each theme.

Table 4.2 **Recurring themes for business success sustainability**

Sewing contractors, sewers and cutters (41)	• The cost of sewing here is too high • A lot of contractors have gone out of business, closed down • Little technology, old machinery • Communication problems/language challenges at factories, they do not use email • Cannot find them, they do not have websites or advertise • The inability for sewers to follow a spec sheet, lack of product production as sampled • Lack of sophistication, not a formal business relationship • Average age of sewer is 52, they have more health problems and are slower, do not want to work as hard and are not being replaced • Lack of ability to sew quality garments • Factories say yes, and do not deliver on time • They are jammed with goods from other manufacturers, they can not take orders, they are at full capacity • Minimum wage highest in the country • Very difficult to find seamstresses • There is not a one-stop-shop • When equipment breaks down, there is no one to fix it, or it is so expensive to fix • Only a handful of excellent factories left • We are not seeing another generation of sewers coming up
Raw materials and suppliers (29)	• The high price of fabrics • A lot of support businesses are gone; no sources for finding trims on the fly are gone • Vendors and mills no longer stock fabrics, minimums are too high • Cotton pricing is an issue, domestic and offshore • The US did not invest in fabric technology • Struggle to find US made textiles, used to be here • There's nothing left here, snaps, rivets, grommets, zippers, are all gone • The quality of the textiles is not here in the US • Quality and expense of eco-friendly fabrics • Dealing with foreign mills, getting goods off a boat without a loading dock, missing of deadlines from shipments • Have to find everything online, difficult with buttons and trims

What is the future of being able to design and manufacture in San Francisco?

Responses to the question generally began with a pause, sometimes followed with a comment such as: 'I take the business day by day'; 'Who knows;' or 'I think we covered that one with the challenges of doing business here'. The two themes that did emerge represented the smallest group of respondents with 25% presenting regulations or mandates from San Francisco city government and 20% commenting on the need for marketing support to continue to educate the positive benefits of local manufacturing. Table 4.3 presents the two themes, the number of interviewees that it denotes and representative responses within each theme.

Table 4.3 **Recurring themes for the future of design and manufacturing in San Francisco**

Government and city regulations (13)	• The labour department and registration is cumbersome, you are penalised for producing here • Social media, computer gaming, the next dot.com era have raised rents and pushed manufacturers and contractors out • The local registration agency is rude, unsupportive • No local support, we are too small for anyone to care about • Payroll taxes too high • The cost of doing business in SF is too high compared to other cities • San Francisco drove the industry out with the minimum wage increase • Overhead charges for labour, like healthcare and workers compensation • Duty rates for fabric and finished product exports are too high • It is more expensive to produce here than in LA or NY because of taxation
Marketing (10)	• Lack of consumer education about Made in America, quality, construction awareness, the structural integrity of products • Need local media support to build local brands • Lack of support of Made in San Francisco, what that means for the consumer, support the local garment industry • We are not LA or NY, which is OK, market Made in SF • How can a small company promote itself in a world bombarded with branding? We don't have the press here to promote us

Discussion and conclusion

To validate the responses and findings from this study, all participants were invited to a presentation given by the author in January of 2013 (see Fig. 4.1). Over 65% of the respondents attended, and it quickly became apparent that voices were accurately captured in the research. Their verbal participation also revealed how strongly they felt about the challenges and the need to continue to support each other in the continuation of the resurgence of 'locally made'.

Figure 4.1 **Invitation to research findings presentation including graphic image of cover from *San Francisco Fall Market Week—August 6–10 1934* (Manufacturers and Wholesalers Association of San Francisco 1934)**

As previously noted, the research intent was not an investigation of luxury within San Francisco designers and their brands, but rather of who was designing and manufacturing what brands in the San Francisco Bay area, and how and why they chose this method or path. Their responses validated what has been written regarding the struggles of manufacturing in San Francisco because of the shutting down of operations due to production moving offshore beginning in the 1980s for cheaper labour costs (Adachi and Lo 2008) and, more recently, with the 2002 closing of the Levi Strauss Valencia Street factory (Ioakimedes 2011). As respondents commented: 'When the big guys left [i.e. the large companies that were manufacturing locally such as Levis and others] there was not enough local business [i.e. manufacturing] to keep the cutters, sewers, print and dye houses, button, yarn, fabric and trim suppliers, here anymore'.

The value of a Made in San Francisco label

After listening to over 100 hours of responses to who was designing and manufacturing in San Francisco, it became apparent that these people were driven by the need and very strong desire to support local, because that was the 'right thing to do'. They wanted to 'know who's producing my goods … everything about how it's being made'. They were inherently aware of the higher costs required for a Made in San Francisco label, but nevertheless forged forwards due to their convictions and beliefs. As one respondent explained:

> My consumer loves us and has the loudest voice in keeping us here. Made in America is very big with the consumer, and Made in SF is very important, that is why we are not leaving here. San Francisco is a wonderful platform to emerging designers. People care about the craft of your skill, when you have it made in San Francisco it goes a long way. But our customer has really contributed the most to making us successful.

San Francisco design manufacturers are producing what this researcher has termed as the new luxury or symbol of success. The new requirement is the knowledge and prestige of being able to respond with pride and conviction to the question: 'Where was yours made?'

Consumers, both locally and globally, are seeking out this new form of luxury. The Internet has offered an affordable and easily accessible ability for consumers to have direct contact with these 'locally made' design manufacturers. This direct connection has increased the global awareness of ethical and quality-based supply chain practices in the garment industry. Consumers' direct and informed luxury purchase decisions are based on their understanding and appreciation of product supply chain practices. Where they live, be it in the same city, state or country as the production site(s) of the chosen designer label or brand rests on their perception of the ethical and socially conscious quality benefits. As eloquently defined by one respondent:

> The average consumer in Japan, lets say, is much more concerned with Made in USA, than in the US. And it's like the average consumer in Japan is like the exceptional consumer in the US, who really cares about where things are made and how they are made … It's not to say that everything that costs more is worth it, but if you do your research, which these days more people are willing to do, on everything you buy, then they find the quality and they are willing to pay a higher price.

The Internet provides a tool for the posting of diagrams, photographs or videos and the transparency of manufacturing practices that is an integral part of sourcing and communication of this 21st century luxury product definition.

Opportunities

What makes a garment or product luxurious? As the findings in this study have validated, there is a new awareness in our 21st century. Apart from qualities such as the designer name and/or brand-made product-related choices, the country, state or city of origin—a transparent supply chain—is increasingly becoming an important parameter for the definition of luxury.

This project was based in the city of San Francisco but has global relevance as the value of its findings support opportunities and challenges faced by other countries, states and cities supporting 'locally made'. In San Francisco, these designs or brands are sold at a higher retail price point, reflective of the higher manufacturing costs and other requirements of their local product design and manufacturing decisions (Tilley 2012). The relevant features of each product decision—from fibre to yarn to fabric to finishing—are complex, yet transparent and open to evaluation by the consumer, who has an implicit desire to know more about the processes of creation before they support the designer name or brand with a purchase. As well expressed by one study participant:

> If we continue to do that [be transparent in our design practice], it will be very clear to people from the onset that the product we have is inherently more valuable than any other luxury good, in any aspect.

In the 21st century, as the social and environmental meaning of how, why and where products are designed and produced continues to gain momentum, products will continue to be valuable, or luxury, only when the ideals of the company are woven within the chosen fibre, yarn, fabric, trims and manufacturing processes and locations. Worth will be contingent on what is behind the designer name or brand, inspiring confidence in the consumer for proudly wearing a garment that is luxurious because of all aspects of where it was made.

Bibliography

Adachi, R.A., and V. Lo (2008) 'Made in Chinatown', *Chinese America: History and Perspectives, The Journal of Chinese Historical Society of America*: 51-59.

Anon. (1940) 'Editorial: Fashion Week', *Time*, 19 August 1940: 67.

Anon. (1943) 'Editorial: San Francisco's Style in Ads', *San Francisco Resources*, November 1943.

Bigelow, S.B. (1979) *Fashion in History* (Minneapolis, MN: Burgess Publishing).

Binkley, C. (2010) 'How Green is My Sneaker?', *The Wall Street Journal*, 22 July 2010: D1, D6.

City and County of San Francisco (2012) *Request for Proposals for FashionSF*, 4 December 2012: 1-16.

Dubois, B., S. Czellar and G. Laurent (2005) 'Consumer Segments Based on Attitudes Toward Luxury: Empirical Evidence from Twenty Countries', *Marketing Letters* 16.2: 115-28.

Forney, J.C., D.M. Rosen and J.M. Orzechowski (1990) 'Domestic Versus Overseas Apparel Production: Dialogue with San Francisco Based Manufacturers', *Clothing and Textiles Research Journal* 8.3: 39-44.

Heine, K. (2012) 'The Concept of Luxury Brands', *Luxury Brand Management* 1.2 (Emylon Business School, France, www.conceptofluxurybrands.com).

Hethorn, J., and C. Ulasewicz (eds.) (2008) *Sustainable Fashion: Why Now?* (New York: Fairchild Books).

Ioakimedes, N. (2011) 'Made in SF', *San Francisco Magazine* (22 August 2011; www.modern luxury.com/san-francisco/story/made-sf, accessed 15 November 2012).

Kapferer, J-N., and V. Bastien (2012) *The Luxury Strategy: Break the Rules of Marketing to Build Luxury Brands* (London: Kogan Page, 2nd edn).
Krick, J. (2004) 'Charles Frederick Worth (1825–1895) and The House of Worth', *Heilbrunn Timeline of Art History* (October 2004; New York: The Metropolitan Museum of Art, www.metmuseum.org/toah/hd/wrth/hd_wrth.htm).
Lai, H.M., and R. Jeung (2008) 'Guilds, Unions and Garment Factories', *Chinese America: History and Perspectives, The Journal of Chinese Historical Society of America*: 1-10.
Ma, F., H. Shi, L. Chen and Y. Lou (2012) 'A Theory of Fashion Consumption', *Journal of Management and Strategy* 3.4: 84-92.
Manufacturers and Wholesalers Association of San Francisco (1934) *San Francisco Fall Market Week—August 6–10 1934* (San Francisco, CA: P.H. Nealey).
Masidlover, N. (2013) 'Fashion Goes Shopping', *San Francisco Chronicle*, 29 April 2013: B1, B7.
McDonough, W., and M. Braungart (2013) *The Upcycle* (New York: North Point Press).
Mistry, M. (2011) 'Is Ready to Wear the New Couture?', *The Wall Street Journal* (22 October 2011; http:/online.wsj.com/article/SB10001424052970204346104576639112470478424.html, accessed 20 January 2012).
Mulvey, K., and M. Richards (1998) *Decades of Beauty. The Changing Image of Women 1890 to 1990* (New York: Checkmark Books).
Roberts, C. (2013) 'Designs for a Fashion Mecca', *The SF Examiner*, 3 March 2013: 4-5.
Stegemeyer, A. (1996) *Who's Who in Fashion* (New York: Capital Cities Media Inc.).
Tilley, A. (2012) 'Clothing Manufacturers Enjoy a Bit of Resurgence', *San Francisco Business Times* (20 July 2012; www.bizjournals.com/sanfrancisco/print-edition/2012/07/20/clothing-manufacturers-enjoy-a-bit-of.html?page=all, accessed 20 December 2012).
Welters, L. (2008) 'The Fashion of Sustainability', in J. Hethorn and C. Ulasewicz (eds.), *Sustainable Fashion: Why Now?* (New York: Fairchild Books): 7-29.
Woolfolk, J. (2013) 'Minimum Wage: California, US, Other Cities', *Mercury News* (10 March 2013; www.mercurynews.com/politics-government/ci_22752697/san-jose-joins-other-major-cities-hiking-minimum, accessed 15 March 2013).

Dr **Connie Ulasewicz** has over 25 years of garment industry experience managing production, merchandising and sales, and is the co-author of *Made In America: The Handbook for Sewn Products Manufacturing* and *Sustainable Fashion: Why Now?* An Associate Professor of apparel design and merchandising, her research focuses on community-based sustainable practices. Email: cbu@sfsu.edu

5

Sustainable consumption

Luxury branding as a catalyst for social change

Gjoko Muratovski
Faculty of Design and Creative Technologies, Auckland University of Technology, New Zealand

Introduction

The origin of the word 'luxury' is an ancient one and comes from the Latin *luxus* meaning excess. However, according to the Oxford English Dictionary, in a contemporary context this word is associated with 'a state of great comfort or elegance, especially when involving great expense', or with 'an inessential, desirable item which is expensive or difficult to obtain'. From this perspective, it can be argued that luxury means different things to different people. Often, what some perceive as luxury others may see as a basic essential. And in a world with depleting resources the notion of luxury may take on a whole new dimension in the future.

Even though many luxury brands have a long history behind them, the term 'luxury brands' is a relatively new one—it was made popular by Wall Street analysts who tried to describe some of the world's most valuable brands when they became public (Dewey 2009). Prior to this, such companies were not known as luxury brands. These companies were mostly small family businesses operated by high-quality artisans and craftspeople that had highly specialised areas of expertise for which they have obtained a global reputation. For example, Louis Vuitton had a humble beginning as a trunk-maker, crafting innovative customised boxes and luggage that attracted the attention of affluent clients from prominent households, including that of Napoleon III (Johnston 2012). Gucci merged an idea of a refined style of living with craftsmanship by local Tuscan artisans when it came to the making of leather bags for horseman—he moved into luggage, accessories and shoes later on.[1] Haute couture fashion houses, such as Chanel and Dior, started equally small and became famed for their designs and making of fashionable clothes to their clients' specific requirements and measurements (Charleston 2004; Krick 2004). Montblanc begin its history by presenting themselves as 'manufacturers of high-class gold and fountain pens'—or writing instruments, as they call them today.[2] Hans Wilsdorf, the founder of Rolex, was a watchmaker dedicated to producing highly precise, elegant and reliable timepieces that people could wear on their wrist—which was highly innovative at the time.[3] Cartier, the French master jewellery makers, made their name by specialising in exquisite jewellery for royal houses and celebrities.[4] Hermés mastered a very narrow trade and established a harness workshop catering to European noblemen—including the Tzar of Russia, for whom he created some of the finest wrought harnesses and leather saddles (Raisbeck 2013). Burberry, the supplier of garments to kings and maharajas, began as a small local outfitter in England who invented the gabardine fabric—a waterproof, tightly woven cotton inspired by the loose linen smocks worn by English shepherds and farmers.[5] What all these producers share is that they have not defined themselves as luxurious. They focused on delivering handcrafted products of exceptional quality, and they left their reputation to do the rest. In the meantime, the concept of luxury has expanded significantly and many products once considered to be luxurious have become increasingly available to more and more people, and not only to the elites.

Problems of mass consumption

While the consumption of luxury goods can be traced back to ancient times (Al-Awaal 2013), mass consumerism is a relatively recent phenomenon. In the past, the consumption patterns of the masses—driven only by genuine needs, practicality and functionality—were vastly different from those of today. The consumption patterns of the elites, on the other hand, have not changed significantly—they are still driven by the purchase of rare, expensive and non-essential things. The introduction of mass production, advertising and globalisation significantly changed the purchasing patterns of the masses. With the industrial and cultural shift that

1 www.gucci.com/us/worldofgucci/mosaic/the_house_of_gucci/gucci_history, accessed 19 August 2013.
2 www.montblanc.com/en/flash/default.aspx/#/meet-montblanc/history, accessed 19 August 2013.
3 www.rolex.com/about-rolex/rolex-history/1905-1919.html, accessed 19 August 2013.
4 www.cartier.com/maison/history-and-stories, accessed 19 August 2013.
5 www.burberryplc.com/about_burberry/company_history, accessed 19 August 2013.

followed, new lifestyles, higher expectations and different kind of beliefs were introduced (Campbell 2004: 27; Crocker and Lehmann 2012: 385). As a result, we now have a mass culture of individuals striving to have the same or more than others around them. People's needs and wants have become relative to the circumstances of others, and this behaviour now acts as a 'social push' for ongoing growth. As some increase consumption, the rest face a higher reference point and this initiates even more consumption. The main problem here is that consumers have come to believe (or, rather, have been convinced to believe) that buying more things will make their lives better (Zukin 2004: 255; Crocker 2012: 17; Muratovski 2013a: 178).

There has never been more money, thought, effort, creativity, time or attention to detail invested in any propaganda campaign aimed at changing public behaviour as in the campaigns for creating mass consumerism (Marchand 1997: 85; Jhally 2000). In a process that can be described as 'democratisation of luxury', many things shifted from luxury to essentials. Things that were seen as luxuries in the past, such as heating, plumbing, refrigerators, washing machines, TVs and cars are now everyday essentials, and the range of 'affordable luxuries' constantly expands (Dewey 2009). By creating an impression that a better life can be achieved by buying new products, designers and advertisers help corporations to sell things that people would love to buy (Jodard 1992: 59). People were persuaded that they could satisfy their needs and desires, or overcome their fears, by purchasing more goods. Corporations started selling dreams, fantasies and relationships by connecting everyday commodities with powerful images of deeply desired social life (see Stø *et al.* 2008: 244). And, in return, this gave birth to the idea that the 'good life' is within reach and available to everyone (Schudson 2004: 566; De Grazia 2005; Holmes *et al.* 2012: 20-21).

In this pursuit of a better life, people constantly replace things that do not need replacing with things that they do not really need. As a result, the world is facing an unsustainable future and social change is necessary. This problem has given rise to the idea of 'sustainable consumption': '[C]onsumption which meets the needs of the present without compromising the ability of future generations to meet their own needs' (DEST 1996: 2; see also Jackson 2011). However, achieving this requires solutions that go beyond the development of new products or product substitutions. While reusing or recycling products can be highly beneficial, sustainable consumer behaviour can deliver far greater environmental benefits (Gardner and Stern 2002; Steg and Vlek 2009; Muratovski 2013a). This social change calls for a promotion and acceptance of concepts such as responsible consumption, consumption reduction, voluntary simplicity and sustainable lifestyles on a global scale (Jackson 2005; Peattie and Peattie 2009). One way of achieving this is by using luxury brands as catalysts for social change. As luxury brands are often seen as aspirational brands and are, therefore, admired, copied, imitated or mimicked, they are best positioned to set an example and to influence change in the society. This becomes even more evident if we take into account the notion that sustainability is, in fact, much closer to the concept of luxury than it is to mass consumption.

Mass consumption and subjective happiness

Mass consumption is based around a central idea that people can achieve happiness by accumulating goods. However, a series of surveys that examined the link between material wealth and subjective happiness concluded that intrinsic values significantly outweigh extrinsic values in terms of importance (Jhally 1998; Putnam 2000: 332-33; Kasser 2002; Thorpe 2010). According to this research, while happiness may be temporarily achieved by engaging in consumer activities, it cannot be maintained simply by owning more things; once we achieve a certain level of comfort in life, objects cease to make us happy. According to the findings, which have been consistent over a course of many years, what really makes us happy in life is not more 'stuff', but a sense of autonomy and control, good self-esteem, warm family relationships, tension-free leisure time, close and intimate friends, romance and love. In other words, people's perception of happiness is often based around interpersonal relationships with other people (Jhally 1998; Thorpe 2010; Holmes *et al.* 2012).

The advertising industry sees an opportunity in the moments when people do not feel happy or satisfied—a state often produced by 'reminding' us of what we might lack in our lives—and tries to convince people to fill this 'gap' by buying more things. As a result, many people resort to shopping not only to purchase necessities, but also in order to satisfy certain unfulfilled desires or to compensate for unfulfilled social needs (Thorpe 2010). Unfortunately, this 'retail therapy' is short-lived and people soon crave for the next consumer 'fix' as a way to curb emotional distraction (see Ehrenfeld 2008: 36). Then again, not all advertising has these persuasion abilities. For example, we do not react in the same way to advertising of fast-moving consumer goods (FMCG) as we do to that of luxury brands (see Dewey 2009).

Contrary to the FMCG advertising, in luxury brand advertising the product is never the real offer but only a substitute for something else which is of social value to us (see Jhally 1998; Neumeier 2006). Even the most luxurious 'objects of desire'—products that clearly feed an extrinsic social aspiration such as status or prestige—often have an intrinsic brand narrative that 'justifies' the high price (Farameh 2011). Contrary to the popular belief that luxury purchases are exclusively based around the notions of reputation, image or social standing, various studies have shown that these types of purchases can also act as gestures that articulate authenticity and caring in existing relationships (Miller 2001: 229; Thorpe 2010); or as means of engaging in new relationships (Sundie *et al.* 2011).

This means that luxury brands do not operate only on 'face value'; there is also an underlying social platform on which they build their communication strategies. That is why advertising often tries to uncover 'deeper veins of sentiment' that can provoke emotional responses (Fowles 1996: 167). This type of advertising is often based on 'real', but often concealed, human motives and not on the subjective reasons that people give for what they do. This idea, which has its roots in Freudian psychology, suggests that many human thoughts and actions are compensatory substitutes for desires that people feel obliged to suppress. In many cases a product is desired not for its intrinsic worth or usefulness, but because it is unconsciously a symbol of something else—a desire a person may be ashamed to admit. For instance, a person looking to buy a specific car model may argue that he or she wants it for the purposes of transport. But unconsciously this person may want this car because it is perceived as a symbol of social standing, evidence of success in business, a means for pleasing his or her partner, or attracting a new one (Muratovski 2013a).

Luxury cars are not practical and certainly not the most affordable. If we take into consideration the Porsche Boxster model, for instance, we can see that this car has limited cargo capacity, only two seats, lacks comfort, has high fuel consumption and is expensive to repair. Yet these considerations are often irrelevant to the people purchasing this car. What matters to them is the symbolic value of the Porsche and, in this case, this is related to the sexual appeal this car projects (Sundie *et al.* 2011).

Luxury brands appeal to people's hidden desires. In doing so, the advertising of luxury brands assumes a multiplex form that absorbs and fuses a variety of symbolic practices and cultural references from the fields of design, literature, media, history and popular culture. Once the right elements are collected, they are recombined around a theme that involves consumption (see Leiss et al. 1997). The power of luxury brand advertising lies in the subtle mix of reality and fantasy. And, as is often the case, when faced with a choice consumers often prefer the fantasy (or the hyper-reality) rather than the actual reality. This is because, as human beings, we constantly strive for something that is 'better' than reality and demand things that seem more exciting, more beautiful, more inspiring, more terrifying and generally more interesting (see Baudrillard 1986; Eco 1986; Sanes 2011; Muratovski 2013b). Therefore, we are constantly in pursuit of 'happiness' that in reality can never be truly achieved (see Muratovski 2010).

Sustainable consumption and subjective happiness

A recent study conducted in China confirms that the notion of subjective happiness can be applied to the context of sustainable consumption. The study, which was conducted in 14 cities, found a new emerging trend: consumers who reported green purchase intention and sustainable behaviour started developing higher scores in life satisfaction compared to consumers of more traditional, 'unsustainable' products. The study also showed that by engaging in 'prosocial spending' (buying greener products) consumers were willing to sacrifice personal interests over collective benefits and short-term losses over long-term gains (Xiao and Li 2011). This means that people have begun to view sustainable consumption as more valuable (and not simply more costly) than non-sustainable consumption. In their conclusion, the researchers behind this study argue that people should be encouraged to think in a positive way about sustainable consumption; not only because it benefits the world or the society, but also because it leads to improved wellbeing and life satisfaction (Xiao and Li 2011). On the basis of this we can argue that sustainable consumption can be promoted as an activity that provides self-fulfilment (subjective happiness). This exchange philosophy is often removed from social marketing, which is based on the idea that self-indulgent behaviour in relation to consumption is morally wrong. The problem with this construct is that the link between a citizen and consumer has been established so strongly in the 20th century that it is nearly impossible for people to accept a non-consumerist model of public behaviour (Schudson 2004). That is why, rather than opposing consumerism, critics need to embrace a consumer-driven approach towards the introduction of a social change. The way this could be done is through aspirational advertising, such as that found in luxury branding, or through luxury brands themselves. After all, people cannot be asked to change their behaviour without offering them new dreams to dream (see Stø *et al.* 2008).

Advertising and emotional manipulation

Some researchers argue that advertising trivialises real experiences and engenders materialism, cynicism, anxiety, disrespect for age and tradition, and leads to preoccupation with sex and competition. According to them, advertising is morally unsound and it outweighs any social benefits that may be gained in return (see Ling *et al.* 1992). Along the same lines, others argue that advertising is unethical because it is manipulative by nature (see Grier and Bryant 2005) and that it cannot achieve a social change because it reflects societal values rather then affecting them (see Holbrook 1987; Alexander *et al.* 2011). On the other hand, advertising critic Jean Kilbourne (2006: 12) argues that advertising is far from being a 'passive mirror of society'; instead, and with much justification, she describes advertising as a pervasive medium of cumulative influence and subtle persuasion. According to her, the influence of advertising is so strong that, for the consumer society, it performs the same role as myth did in ancient societies (see also Alexander *et al.* 2011). The cultural critic Sut Jhally agrees: 'To not be influenced by advertising would be to live outside of culture, [and] no human being lives outside of culture' (cited in Kilbourne 2006: 10).

While many maintain the idea that advertising creates market demand by manipulating people's normal motivational impulses, Leiss et al. (1997) share a different position. According to them, people already know their needs and desires, and advertising only makes them aware of certain items that might 'satisfy' these needs and desires. As this suggests, the cruel illusion of advertising is not in the appeals it makes, which are very real, but in the answers it provides (Jhally 1998). Then again, while some oppose or criticise advertising in terms of its manipulative power, others oppose it because they believe that advertising is just not as effective as people think and that its effectiveness is overstated. In *Consumer Behaviour*, Michael R. Solomon (2002: 21) cites one advertising executive who, in a testimony before the US Federal Trade Commission, said that while people think that advertisers have an endless source of 'magical tricks' and/or scientific techniques to manipulate people, in reality, the industry is successful only when it tries to sell good products and unsuccessful when selling poor ones. Furthermore, according to Solomon, there is little evidence that advertising has the capacity to create patterns of consumption. As the failure rate for new products ranges between 40% and 80%, he argues that advertisers simply do not know enough about people to influence them. While this may be the case for many generic trademarks, things are different for luxury brands. An analysis of the motives behind the purchase of a Porsche (see Sundie *et al.* 2011), or a diamond engagement ring by De Beers or Tiffany (see CIBJO 2007), or a Louis Vuitton bag (see Nagasawa 2009; Frankel 2011), shows emotional manipulation. Then again, it can be argued that the whole business concept behind the luxury brands is based on the idea of manipulating people's emotional impulses for the purpose of engaging them with unnecessary and often irrational purchases (see Dewey 2009).

Luxury brands and sustainable behaviour

When it comes to sustainable behaviour, the general perception often fluctuates around the idea that this type of behaviour can be costly, unnecessary or disruptive to everyday life. On the other hand, many luxury brands also possess the same 'negative' attributes: they are costly, unnecessary, and often disruptive to everyday life, but purchasing them is considered to be a privilege rather than a nuisance. Similarly, sustainable products often share the same 'essential' qualities of luxury goods: they call for extraordinary creativity and design; they need to be made from exceptional materials and with good quality; and they are rare and expensive (see Dewey 2009). These two concepts are not too far apart.

Some leading brands have taken a new direction and begun to introduce the idea of 'sustainable luxury' as an integral part of their own brand image (Niemtzow 2010) and, according to the BBC, sustainability is now posed to define the future of luxury (Cronin 2011). This trend, however, is not emerging because the companies are becoming more socially conscious—but because their customers are. As new generations of customers increasingly seek to align their purchases with newly discovered social values and sustainable lifestyles, they also feel conflicted about what they really need. In increasing numbers, luxury brands begin to align their values with principles of sustainability—timelessness, durability, innovation, craftsmanship and a meaningful customer experience. These are all characteristics that underlie notions of luxury, sustainability and social responsibility (Niemtzow 2010).

Learning from the alcohol and tobacco industries

Another example of similar effectiveness of brand advertising can be found in the alcohol and tobacco industries. While these products are not luxurious *per se*, these industries often adopt the same form of advertising to promote them as products that offer indulgence and pleasure, while simultaneously appealing to people's intrinsic values. For over a century, the advertisers of alcohol and tobacco have been building support for their products in mainstream culture by using advertising, product placements, celebrity endorsements and even through endorsements by medial professionals (Vaknin 2007). In an attempt to reach out to the next generation of consumers, they were consciously targeting children and teenagers (Pechmann and Reibling 2000; Kilbourne 2003).

Since the 1930s, alcohol and tobacco industries began highlighting the social benefits of their products. They promised that smoking would make people appear distinguished, smart and attractive; while drinking the right brand of liquor can help people relax after a long day and will impress neighbours and clients (Blount 2005). In popular culture these products became symbols of hope and objects of desire. They became symbols of masculinity for men, and symbols of emancipation and independence for women (Vaknin 2007). Advertising promised that, by consuming these products, people would have instant success in life (in terms of wealth and upward social mobility) and would become more attractive, cool, romantic, slimmer (for women) or stronger (for men), as well as just having more fun. Alcohol and tobacco were selling lifestyles and fantasies—an assurance that life is good, especially if you drink and smoke (Kilbourne 1988; Peck 1993; Martin *et al.* 2002; Audrain-McGovern *et al.* 2006; Vaknin 2007). Consuming these products became not only a personal choice but also a social experience, intimately bound up with broader relationships and values shared with a peer group (Szmigin *et al.* 2011). Heavy drinking and chain-smoking became the social norm (Peck 1993; Alexander *et al.* 2011).

The success of these products is staggering, especially if we take into account that alcohol and tobacco can cause serious long-term health issues (Kilbourne 2003). Furthermore, drinking alcohol and smoking are learned behaviours as few people enjoy their first cigarette or alcoholic drink. Although these products are addictive, the addiction has to be learned. Psychological addiction is created through branding and advertising (Muratovski 2013a: 186-87). The advertisers have made these products so appealing that it has taken decades of government bans and restrictions to barely slow them down. In 2012, for example, Australia became the first country to ban the use of logos and colours for cigarette packaging in an attempt to stop the tobacco industry glamorising its products—even though TV and radio commercials for tobacco products were banned from 1976, newspaper ads from 1989, and tobacco sponsorship of cultural and sport events from 1992 (Kennedy 2012).

Conclusion

The key problem in achieving social change through typical social marketing campaigns is that this type of marketing often ignores the underlying exchange philosophy that each side has something of value to offer and exchange. Social marketing asks people to engage in individual behaviour change without offering them anything in return (Szmigin 2011). On the other hand, the potential for inspiring social change based on subjective appeals, such as those seen in luxury branding, are endless. Sustainable consumption can be achieved by implying that people will feel better and be happier if they consume sustainably, even if that costs them more in the short term. This is the exchange philosophy that is missing from most social marketing campaigns but can be found in abundance in luxury brand marketing. While sustainable luxury, as a concept, will remain to be a privilege only for the wealthy, we can redefine sustainable consumption as a form of accessible luxury. Therefore, based on the success of luxury brands, it can be argued that sustainable behaviour can be promoted as a desired lifestyle as long as it is associated with positive and intrinsic appeals.

Bibliography

Al-Awaal, R. (2013) 'Control and Recognition: A History of Luxury', *Saudi Gazette* (10 February 2013; www.saudigazette.com.sa/index.cfm?home.con&contentid=20130210152622, accessed 12 March 2013).

Alexander, J., T. Crompton and G. Shrubsole (2011) *Think of Me As Evil? Opening the Ethical Debates in Advertising* (Machynlleth, Wales and Godalming, UK: Public Interest Research Centre and WWF-UK).

Audrain-McGovern, J., D. Rodriguez, V. Patel, M.S. Faith, K. Rodgers and J. Cuevas (2006) 'How Do Psychological Factors Influence Adolescent Smoking Progression? The Evidence for Indirect Effects Through Tobacco Advertising Receptivity', *Pediatrics* 117.4: 1216-225.

Baudrillard, J. (1986) 'Simulacra and Simulations', in M. Poster (ed.), *Jean Baudrillard: Selected Writings* (Stanford, CA: Stanford University Press): 166-84.

Blount, K. (2005) *What's Your Poison?: Addictive Advertising of the '40s-'60s* (Portland, OR: Collectors Press).

Campbell, C. (2004) 'I Shop Therefore I Am: The Metaphysical Basis of Modern Consumerism', in K.M. Ekstrol and H. Brembeck (eds.), *Elusive Consumption* (Oxford, UK: Berg): 27-44.

Charleston, B.D. (2004) 'Christian Dior (1905–1957)', *The Metropolitan Museum of Art* (October 2004; www.metmuseum.org/toah/hd/dior/hd_dior.htm, accessed 19 August 2013).

CIBJO (2007) *The Retailer's Guide to Marketing Diamond Jewellery* (Bern, Switzerland: CIBJO—The World Jewellery Confederation).

Crocker, R. (2012) 'Somebody Else's Problem: Consumer Culture Waste and Behaviour Change—The Case of Walking', in S. Lehmann and R. Crocker (eds.), *Designing for Zero Waste* (London: Earthscan): 11-34.

Crocker, R., and S. Lehmann (2012) 'The Culture and Politics of Zero Waste: Looking Ahead', in S. Lehmann and R. Crocker (eds.), *Designing for Zero Waste* (London: Earthscan): 385-93.

Cronin, F. (2011) 'What Will Be a Luxury in the Future?', *BBC News* (27 June 2011; www.bbc.co.uk/news/magazine-13875014?print=true, accessed 9 March 2013).

Dewey, D.N. (2009) 'Back to the Future of Luxury', paper presented at *The Luxury Marketing Council and The French-American Chamber of Commerce*, Houston, TX, 22 January 2009.

De Grazia, V. (2005) *Irresistible Empire: America's Advance Through Twentieth-Century Europe* (Cambridge, MA: Harvard University Press).

DEST (Department of the Environment, Sport and Territories) (1996) 'More With Less: Initiatives to Promote Sustainable Consumption', Environmental Economics Research Paper No.3, Commonwealth of Australia, Canberra.

Eco, U. (1986) *Travels in Hyperreality* (New York: Harcourt Brace Jovanovitch).

Ehrenfeld, J.R. (2008) *Sustainability By Design: A Subversive Strategy for Transforming Our Consumer Culture* (New Haven, CT: Yale University Press).

Farameh, P. (ed.) (2011) *Objects of Desire* (New York: Farameh Media).

Fowles, J. (1996) *Advertising and Popular Culture* (London: Sage).

Frankel, S. (2011) 'A Flourish for Fetish: Louis Vuitton Unleashes its New Objects of Desire', *The Independent* (10 March 2011; www.independent.co.uk/life-style/fashion/news/a-flourish-for-fetish-louis-vuitton-unleashes-its-new-objects-of-desire-2237545.html?printService=print, accessed 21 March 2012).

Gardner, G.T., and P.C. Stern (2002) *Environmental Problems and Human Behavior* (Boston, MA: Pearson Custom Publishing).

Grier, S., and C.A. Bryant (2005) 'Social Marketing in Public Health', *Annual Review of Public Health* 26: 319-39.

Holbrook, M.B. (1987) 'Mirror, Mirror, on the Wall: What's Unfair in the Reflections on Advertising', *Journal of Marketing* 51: 95-103.

Holmes, T., E. Blackmore, R. Hawkins and T. Wakeford (2012) *The Common Cause Handbook* (London: Public Interest Research Centre).

Jackson, T. (2005) 'Motivating Sustainable Consumption: A Review of Evidence on Consumer Behaviour and Behavioural Change', a report to the Sustainable Development Research Network, Centre for Environmental Strategy, University of Surrey, UK.

Jackson, T. (2011) *Prosperity Without Growth: Economics for a Finite Planet* (London: Earthscan).

Jhally, S. (1998) 'Advertising and the End of the World' (Northampton, UK: Media Education Foundation, documentary/videotape).

Jhally, S. (2000) 'Advertising at the Edge of the Apocalypse', in R. Andersen and L. Strate (eds.), *Critical Studies in Media Commercialism* (New York: Oxford University Press): 27-39.

Jodard, P. (1992) *Raymond Loewy* (London: Trefol Publications).

Johnston, R. (2012) 'King Louis', *GQ* (12 July 2012; www.gq-magazine.co.uk/style/articles/2012-07/12/louis-vuitton-history-of-luxury-label-and-outlets-shops-bags-shoes, accessed 19 August 2013).

Kasser, T. (2002) *The High Price of Materialism* (Cambridge, MA: MIT Press).

Kennedy, D. (2012) 'Australia Smokers Given Plain Packs', *BBC News* (1 December 2012; www.bbc.co.uk/news/world-asia-20559585, accessed 12 October 2013).

Krick, J. (2004) 'Gabrielle "Coco" Chanel (1883–1971) and the House of Chanel', *The Metropolitan Museum of Art* (October 2004; www.metmuseum.org/toah/hd/chnl/hd_chnl.htm, accessed 19 August 2013).

Kilbourne, J. (1988) 'Cigarette Ads Target Women, Young People', *Alcohol & Addiction Magazine*, December 1988: 22.

Kilbourne, J. (2003) 'Deadly Persuasion: The Advertising of Alcohol and Tobacco' (Northampton, UK: Media Education Foundation, documentary/videotape).

Kilbourne, J. (2006) 'Jesus is a Brand of Jeans', *New Internationalist*, September 2006: 10.

Leiss, W., S. Kline and S. Jhally (1997) *Social Communication in Advertising* (New York: Routledge).

Ling, J.C., B.A.K. Franklin, J.F. Lindsteadt and S.A.N. Gearon (1992) 'Social Marketing: Its Place in Public Health', *Annual Review of Public Health* 13: 341-62.

Marchand, R. (1997) 'Where Lie the Boundaries of the Corporation? Explorations in "Corporate Responsibility" in the 1930s', *Business and Economic History* 26.1: 80-100.

Martin, S.E., L.B. Snyder, M. Hamilton, F. Fleming-Millici, M.D. Slater, A. Stacy, M. Chen and J.W. Grube (2002) 'Alcohol Advertising and Youth', *Alcoholism: Clinical and Experimental Research* 26.6: 900-906.

Miller, D. (2001) 'The Poverty of Morality', *Journal of Consumer Culture* 1.2: 225-43.

Muratovski, G. (2010) 'Corporate Communication Strategies: From Religious Propaganda to Strategic Brand Management', PhD thesis, University of South Australia at Adelaide, Australia.

Muratovski, G. (2013a) 'Advertising, Public Relations and Social Marketing: Shaping Behaviour Towards Sustainable Consumption', in R. Crocker and S. Lehmann (eds.), *Motivating Change: Sustainable Design and Behaviour in the Built Environment* (London: Routledge).

Muratovski, G. (2013b) 'Totem: The Religious Dimensions of Branding', paper presented at the *2013 Popular Culture Association/American Culture Association Annual Conference*, Washington, DC, 27–30 March 2013.

Nagasawa, S. (2009) 'Luxury Brand Strategy of Louis Vuitton: Details of Marketing Principles', *Waseda Business and Economic Studies* 45: 21-40.

Neumeier, M. (2006) *The Brand Gap: How to Bridge the Distance Between Business Strategy and Design—A Whiteboard Overview* (Berkeley, CA: Peachpit, revised edn).

Niemtzow, E. (2010) 'Sustainable Luxury: New Opportunities for Growth', *The Guardian* (16 November 2010; www.guardian.co.uk/sustainable-business/sustainable-luxury-fashion-growth-shoppers, accessed 9 March 2013).

Peattie, K., and S. Peattie (2009) 'Social Marketing: A Pathway to Consumption Reduction?', *Journal of Business Research* 62: 260-68.

Pechmann, C., and E.T. Reibling (2000) 'Anti-Smoking Advertising Campaigns Targeting Youth: Case Studies from USA and Canada', *Tobacco Control* 9.2: 18-31.

Peck, R.L. (1993) 'Alcohol Advertising and Addiction: What's the Connection?', *Addiction & Recovery*, March–April 1993: 11.

Putnam, R.D. (2000) *Bowling Alone: The Collapse and Revival of American Community* (New York: Simon and Schuster).

Raisbeck, F. (2013) 'Hermès: History of the Iconic Brand in Numbers', *Marie Claire* (20 May 2013; www.marieclaire.co.uk/blogs/542797/hermes-history-of-the-iconic-brand-in-numbers.html#ZeKyVE6Y0eM8YjIm.99, accessed 19 August 2013).

Sanes, K. (2011) 'Travelling Through Hyperreality with Umberto Eco', *Transparency* (www.transparencynow.com/eco.htm, accessed 17 February 2012).

Schudson, M. (2004) 'American Dreams', *American Literary History* 16.3: 566-73.

Solomon, M.R. (2002) *Consumer Behavior: Buying, Having, and Being* (Saddle River, NJ: Prentice Hall).

Steg, L., and C. Vlek, C. (2009) 'Encouraging Pro-Environmental Behaviour: An Integrative Review and Research Agenda', *Journal of Environmental Psychology* 29: 309-17.

Stø, E., H. Thorne-Holst, P. Strandbakken and G. Vitersø (2008) 'Review: A Multi-Dimensional Approach to the Study of Consumption in Modern Societies and the Potential for Radical Sustainable Changes', in A. Tukker, M. Charter, C. Vezzoli, E. Stø and M.M. Andersen (eds.), *System Innovation for Sustainability 1: Perspectives on Radical Changes to Sustainable Consumption and Production* (Sheffield: Greenleaf Publishing): 234-54.

Sundie, J.M. D.T. Kenrick, V. Griskevicius, J.M. Tybur, K.D. Vohs and D.J. Beal (2011) 'Peacocks, Porsches, and Thorstein Veblen: Conspicuous Consumption as a Sexual Signaling System' *Journal of Personality and Social Psychology* 100.4: 664-80.

Szmigin, I., A. Bengry-Howell, C. Griffin, C. Hackley and W. Mistral (2011) 'Social Marketing, Individual Responsibility and the "Culture of Intoxication"', *European Journal of Marketing* 45.5: 759-79.

Thorpe, A. (2010) 'Design's Role in Sustainable Consumption', *Design Issues* 26.2: 3-16.

Vaknin, J. (2007) *Smoke Signals: 100 Years of Tobacco Advertising* (London: Middlesex University Press).

Xiao, J.J., and H. Li (2011) 'Sustainable Consumption and Life Satisfaction', *Social Indicators Research* 104: 323-29.

Zukin, S. (2004) *Point of Purchase: How Shopping Changed American Culture* (New York: Routledge).

Dr **Gjoko Muratovski** has over 20 years of international, multidisciplinary design and branding experience spanning from Europe and Asia, to the USA and Australia. Over the years, Dr Muratovski has been working and collaborating with companies and organisations such as Deloitte, Toyota, UN (Association of Australia), UNESCO World Cultural Heritage, World Health Organization (WHO), Greenpeace, Department of the Premier and Cabinet of South Australia, Office of the Prime Minister of Macedonia, Dumfries and Galloway Council of Scotland, and Ehrenberg-Bass Marketing Science Institute. He also served as an Advisor on Brand Development Strategies for the European-based agency IDEA+ Communications (part of the Pristop Group) whose clients include Porsche, Audi, Volkswagen, McDonald's and the Heineken Group. Dr Muratovski is currently Head of the Communication Design Department at Auckland University of Technology, New Zealand.
Email: gjoko.muratovski@aut.ac.nz

6

Luxury versus conscious consumption: are they really paradoxical?

A study of Brazilian and Portuguese luxury consumer behaviour

Ana Carolina De Pierro Bruno and Edgard Barki
FGV-EAESP, São Paulo, Brazil

Introduction

At the beginning of the 21st century, sustainable development is no longer just a concern of environmentalists and researchers. It became a recurring theme in discussions between governments, businesses, civil society and consumers. In this context, the luxury market has become the subject of much criticism, not only by drawing attention to social differences in society, but also because it is considered an industry in which many material resources are spent for the benefit of a few who seek only to satisfy their desires as consumers (Kapferer 2010). In fact, for many people, luxury and sustainability can be considered an oxymoron (Kapferer 2010).

However, when observing closely the main features of luxury products and the business model of companies in the industry, there are many similarities between luxury, sustainability concepts and conscious consumption. Since luxury products are usually not quickly discarded, because they are expected to last, and are often produced by hand and in small quantities, they can approach the concept of sustainability (Kahn 2009; Kapferer 2010).

Some companies in the luxury industry have tried to change the image consumers have about luxury products and their relation to sustainable development. Whether adopting new environmental and labour standards, or creating more environmentally responsible products (Kahn 2009), luxury brands are trying to insert themselves in this new social context where sustainability is central. For consumers, the question that remains is whether sustainability is an important factor in their luxury purchasing decisions.

This chapter aims to describe the importance given to sustainability in purchases of luxury products for Brazilian and Portuguese consumers. To achieve this objective, exploratory research was taken. Twenty-one in-depth interviews were conducted with Brazilian and Portuguese consumers of luxury products, in which it was possible to identify some differences in buying behaviour between the two nationalities.

Literature review

Luxury products and services have specific characteristics. Luxury brands carry a symbolic meaning, and the value of luxury goods and services is defined by the perception of consumers who seek economic, emotional or social satisfaction (Strehlau 2008).

Not only does the concept of luxury vary from culture to culture, so too do the reasons for, and valued aspects of the purchase of luxury items (Kapferer and Bastien 2009; Bernstein Research 2010). For the French, for example, showing individual material success is frowned upon. On the other hand, for Americans, this exposure is valued (Lombard 1989). Buying luxury for Americans should have a technical meaning (i.e. the luxury item must have functional superiority in relation to other goods; Kapferer and Bastien 2009; Bernstein Research 2010).

Luxury for the French is an intimate pleasure, valued because of the knowledge, history and details of the product instead of the use of the product itself (Kapferer and Bastien 2009). In Italy, luxury is inspired by art (Kapferer and Bastien 2009). According to Bernstein Research (2010), the Italians are obsessed with beauty and fashion. The Japanese, in turn, consume more luxury in order to have their social status recognised (Lombard 1989) and for a product to be considered as luxury it must be close to perfection (Bernstein Research 2010).

Therefore, culture is considered a relevant factor to define the way people purchase (Rapaille 2006). One of the most used frameworks to analyse different cultures is from Hofstede (2001) who defined five dimensions that describe a set of values that differentiate one country from another. The five dimensions are: (1) 'power distance'; (2) 'individualism vs. collectivism'; (3) 'masculinity vs. femininity';

(4) 'uncertainty avoidance'; and (5) 'long-term vs. short-term orientation'. In 2010, a sixth dimension was added, 'indulgence vs. restraint' (Hofstede *et al.* 2010).

Moreover, in the postmodern era, individuals create their own identities through consumption choices and lifestyles (Giddens 1991; Firat and Venkatesh 1995; Slater 1997; Schaefer and Crane 2005). However, the central role of consumption in social life has been questioned with regard to its viability in the context of depletion of the planet's natural resources (Schaefer and Crane 2005; Assadourian 2010; Prothero *et al.* 2011).

In the dynamics of modern capitalism, the engine of development is based on a continuous process of innovation and creative destruction for the production of increasingly new, better and cheaper goods and services, and, secondly, on the expansion of demand for these products, motivated by a complex social logic. This desire for novelty is intrinsically linked to the symbolic aspect as consumer goods are treated as an extension of 'self'. Thus, individuals seek to permanently complete themselves with products and services, and this desire for novelty is the perfect complement to the continuous innovation of entrepreneurs and businesses. Creative destruction thus motivates and is driven by consumer appetite for novelty (Jackson 2009). However, this excitement with the new is ephemeral, and soon consumers seek fulfilment through new products and services (Varey 2010).

On the other hand, consumers might use their power as citizens to regulate consumption and to demand products and policies that generate less social and environmental impacts (Gabriel and Lang 1995). Conscious consumption is strongly related to the idea that, in every purchase, the individual is voting for one brand over another (Lang and Gabriel 2005). Therefore, the choice to consume (or not) a particular product or brand not only shows the true value of symbolic consumption, but also the consumer's power (Connolly and Prothero 2003). There are different ways in which consumers attempt to influence products, brands or companies. Boycotts are the best known, and highlight the deliberate use of consumer behaviour as a way to achieve ethical goals (Newholm and Shaw 2007). One of the most successful elements of consumption goods in terms of ethical marketing is the Fairtrade movement (Newholm and Shaw 2007). By choosing these products consumers practice so-called 'positive consumption' or 'buycotting' (Harrison *et al.* 2005: 3).

Methodology

A qualitative methodology was chosen because it offers richer descriptions of the social world and does not depend on the study of large numbers of randomly selected cases, being more likely to confront the constraints of everyday life (Denzin and Lincoln 2000; Barr 2004). Moreover, the research also seeks to evaluate cultural differences in which the environment and the participants' frames of reference are different and relevant (Eriksson and Kovalainen 2008).

The research focused on the consumption of luxury fashion goods by Brazilian and Portuguese females aged between 20 and 35 years. Given its importance in the global demand for luxury, and the ease by which leading fashion brands can be recognised, the luxury fashion sector was chosen in order to delimit the scope of the research. For the purposes of this study, clothes, bags, shoes and accessories were considered as luxury fashion goods, which together accounted for 51% of global demand in the luxury market in 2009 (Bernstein Research 2010). In this sector, brands such as Chanel, Hermès and Yves Saint Laurent are readily recognised as luxury (Allérès 2000).

Twenty-one interviews were conducted between October 2012 and June 2013, thirteen with Brazilian consumers and eight with Portuguese. In our analysis, the interviewed consumers were codified from BR1 to BR13 and from PT1 to PT8. This sample size is consistent with other studies (Valor 2007; Ikeda and Bacelar 2008). The interviews lasted from 25 minutes to 1 hour 20 minutes and were recorded, transcribed and read line by line.

For this research luxury consumers were those people who had already bought an article of clothing, shoes or bags of a globally recognised luxury brand such as Chanel, Hermès, Prada, Gucci, among others. No distinctions were made between habitual or occasional consumers of luxury.

Results

The concept of luxury

It was observed that the concept of luxury was compatible between Brazilian and Portuguese consumers. On both sides of the Atlantic, the interviewees considered that luxury refers to abstract characteristics such as refinement, sophistication and status, but also to more functional aspects of the product, such as quality and durability. Exclusivity, defined as having something that is not accessible to all people, was the most mentioned factor:

> When I think about luxury, I think about status, power, recognition, and sophistication (PT1).
>
> Products that have durability, in which I trust, and have beauty and elegance (BR2).
>
> Luxury for me is something that is not accessible to everyone, it is something that is unique (PT7).

Luxury was also defined in terms of high prices, but the interviewees pointed out that not every expensive item can be considered a luxury one. At the same time, luxury was related to purchases in which the individual does not have to worry about the amount of money spent. So, luxury was seen as having the freedom to carry out the wishes of consumption regardless of price. Especially in the Portuguese case, spending great amounts of money at a moment of crisis was seen as a luxury:

> For me luxury is being able to choose what you will buy, at the time you want. It is having that power to control things. For example, you see something you like and you have the power to buy at that moment, because you have the purchasing power (BR8).

> It is the power of buying, it is to do whatever you want, without thinking twice, i.e., if I want to buy something, I do not even look over and buy it (PT8).

On both sides, the participants considered that luxury is something that is not necessary. However, according to one of the Portuguese interviewees, it makes people feel special. Brazilians related it to pleasure:

> Luxury is a product that is above the ordinary. It is a product that makes us feel special. It is a product that makes us feel good (PT5).

> Luxury for me is to have no limits on how much you will spend to buy a product. It is to give yourself the pleasure of buying that, without thinking on the value that you will be spending and on the time you will spend. It is something for your pleasure, independently of the time, the effort or the money you are spending (BR5).

Attraction for luxury products

Among all the factors that define the attraction to luxury products, quality and durability were the only ones that permeated all interviews, with both Brazilian and Portuguese. According to them, the intrinsic quality of these products, measured in terms of the materials used, design and durability, makes luxury brands attractive, not so much by the image of each brand, but by their high quality. As a consequence, it was not uncommon that interviewees perceived their consumption under a rational perspective, generally as a cost-effective purchase, especially in Portugal:

> The design also attracts me. Obviously the design is the first thing that jumps out. I will not say that I am thinking firstly in quality, but of course, usually where there is the best quality, you will find the best design (PT3).

> For me, the design is attractive in most of the luxury goods I look for. So, when I look for a product of the same kind which is not from a luxury brand, and then I check the luxury one, I realise that there is no comparison among them. The luxury one is much better (BR9).

Consuming luxury was also seen as a form of investment on quality products that will be used multiple times on different occasions. It was expected that the rigorous selection of materials and the manufacturing of these products would ensure that they do not easily depreciate over time. Or, if there was any problem, the after sales service of these brands would solve it. Moreover, there was also the expectation that even with the changes of trends, models of handbags, shoes and accessories would come back to fashion regularly:

> I think that buying luxury items . . . is an investment and the product has to be something of quality that will last long, and that you'll use a lot (BR3).

Brazilians valorised the idea of luxury consumption as a way of communicating a personal image; their tastes and personality. On the other hand, Portuguese interviewees were somewhat discomforted to be identified as luxury consumers:

> So when I spend a lot of money, I like to spend on something that I imagine myself wearing on several occasions and that will differentiate me from the others (BR5).
>
> I guess I do not buy products because they are more luxurious. Deep down I know that they are segmented as luxury brands, but I'm not … It is an uncomfortable word and I do not think … But it seems that I associate luxury to something that the person buys to show off. And I buy because I like it, because I feel good (PT5).

Both Brazilian and Portuguese knew luxury brands primarily through their products, advertising and media. It is generally a one-way communication, since most of them do not seek information about the brands they consume unless they are looking for a specific product. For most respondents, the image they have of every luxury brand is inspired by the company's own communications and media, as well as by their experiences in retail outlets and with the products. As they passively receive information from the brands, consumers say they cannot have a clear perception about the values and purposes of luxury companies, or even know about initiatives undertaken by them:

> I do not know anything about those [luxury] companies. I do not do any research. I am not used to have a daily contact with those companies (PT4).
>
> I am not interested about the companies behind the brands. My contacts with the brands are inside the stores. I don't even check their websites (BR12).

Conscious consumption

The opinions of Brazilian consumers about the power of consumers were divergent. Some reported believing that through purchasing decisions they could choose brands that invest sustainably or could stop buying products produced by companies considered to be unethical. When asked: 'Do you think that through consumption you can contribute to sustainable development?' one respondent stated:

> I think so … through preferring things that are sustainable … If I buy things from companies that have a strong concern with sustainability, it helps (BR9).

On the other hand, other respondents claimed that they do not feel that they have power to change the social context through consumption. For them, there is nothing that consumers can do to change the policies of the companies or to reduce environmental degradation and injustice in the world. Relating to a case of a fashion brand who was accused of using slave labour, one interviewee commented:

> So it was a story that shocked me at first, but in the end there was nothing that I could do to change it. If I stopped buying, for example, it would not change. That would not make them stop using slave labour (BR6).

The Portuguese were explicit in stating the potential power that consumers have through their purchasing decisions. They argued that the consumer can choose between consuming certain products or not, and that these decisions can make companies change the way they act on environmental issues. Thus, by increasing the consumption of products from sustainable enterprises, or by buying products based on ethical criteria, they could influence sustainable development. However, they emphasised that in practice it is difficult to choose only companies that are sustainable for all categories of products consumed:

> If there is no consumer, there will be no producers. That happens in every industry. It doesn't need to be in the luxury market. If you don't buy, companies will not produce … or they change the technique. It is the law of nature (PT3).

Believing or not that the consumer has the power to elicit social change, it became clear in most interviews that luxury consumers in both countries are not familiar with the concept of conscious consumption. Most of the answers referred to the concept in financial terms, relating it to the judicious use of the money for purchases. It was also noted that interviewees had difficulties in expressing themselves about the sustainability issue, possibly because they have no clear concept in mind. While in the first part of the interviews, participants were able to discuss their luxury consumer behaviour easily, in the second one, when asked about their perceptions of conscious consumption and sustainability, the conversation was less articulate.

Most of the time, sustainability was related spontaneously to care for the environment with regard to the materials used in the production of consumer goods, recycling and waste reduction. The social aspect of sustainability was stimulated when we discussed the perception of consumers about company policies in relation to communities and its employees, or naturally emerged when respondents mentioned cases of scandals involving companies and exploitation of child labour or slavery.

Both Brazilian and Portuguese respondents were unanimously positive about conscious consumption. Both groups considered such behaviour important and approved individuals engaged in environmental issues through consumption. Most Brazilian consumers did not consider themselves conscious.

According to Brazilians, sustainability is not a relevant factor in their purchasing decisions, especially for luxury goods. Quality and design are more important. They would not buy a product just because it is more sustainable if its aesthetics and attributes were not attractive. Opinions differ when it comes to choosing between two products with similar design and quality, but with different sustainability approaches. Some believed that if the price was not much higher, they would choose the sustainable company. However, some still would not use the criterion of sustainability, seeking some other, such as colour or packaging:

> I do not use [sustainability purposes] as a decision factor. I even think it is cool and all, but I would not buy just because the product has a sustainable purpose or not (BR2).

> If there was a luxury product that was sustainable and was similar to other products, surely I would opt for that product (BR3).

> Maybe I would pay a little more to help a cause. I still would have a luxury brand and would be helping (BR9).

Eleven of the thirteen interviewees spontaneously mentioned the case of a large fashion company accused of alleged forced labour in Brazil. Of these eleven interviewees, only one had stopped buying products from that brand, but said she buys products of similar brands and does not question their working conditions. Another one tried to avoid buying products from that brand, but did not find a compatible option and so continued buying from that brand. As for the others, they said that the news on the subject drew their attention, but as the investigations have not been more publicised in the media and they were not sure about the veracity of the facts, the allegations did not impact their consumption of the brand:

> I do not remember if I have already stopped buying something because of a negative attitude of a company. The last case which I remember that came out in the media was that of Brand X and, to be honest, I did not stop buying there ... I think it was a bit speculative, but it somehow impacted the brand image ... If I see something on a competitor's brand, I may consider. But it will have to be products that are attractive in the same way. I will not stop buying anything from a brand unless the actions of the company are absurd (BR1).

In the case of Portuguese consumers, most of them considered themselves conscious consumers, but the practice of conscious consumption differs among them. Some show concern for sustainable development, translated in buying recycled products and reducing consumption, while others have an interest in knowing the social and environmental practices of companies or do not purchase from a brand due to ethical issues.

> I have this concern [with conscious consumption]. And it is not just a concern. I buy, for instance, many products that are recyclable or that don't pollute the environment (PT5).

The Portuguese seemed to be more active in boycotting products for social and environmental reasons than the Brazilians, even though sustainability is not a determining decision factor in shopping. Moreover, they consumed more articles related to causes and brands considered by them to be sustainable:

> I did not know the origin of the fur Astrakan. And when I heard that they killed sheep, so as to remove the skin of the fetus, I was shocked. And obviously I stopped buying Astrakan. Because one thing is to kill an adult animal, but another completely different is to kill an adult animal with a baby in there and take the unborn fetus, who is not guilty of anything and did not have the opportunity to live, that's different (PT3).

Interviewees also mentioned Kiehl's products, which are related to the cause of AIDS, the clothes from a store called Hoss, where 30% of the value of the pieces is used to help homeless people, and Lanidor's shirt to target breast cancer. One commented on finding interesting initiatives such as Timberland, Portugal, where at the time of purchase one can donate €1 to plant a tree. She believed that, as people are already spending enough money on the purchase, it would not make much difference to them to donate a little.

This more conscious behaviour revealed by the Portuguese can indicate the presence of socially desirable responses on their part, especially when they are asked about their expected behaviour in hypothetical situations. According to Hofstede's (2001) dimensions, Portuguese culture is the second most likely to avoid uncertainty among all the countries studied, and is also more collectivist than the Brazilian culture. Bernardi (2006) points out that it is expected that individuals in cultures with these characteristics have higher rates of socially desirable responses. What has been observed is that there were few answers that would entail possible biases, since the interviewees provided several examples about past behaviours considered conscious. This analysis suggests that the Portuguese consumers might be more active in relation to conscious consumption than the Brazilian.

Luxury and sustainability

The concepts of luxury and sustainability were perceived by most respondents as distant or even opposed. Brazilians and Portuguese had difficulty associating luxury to issues of sustainable development, because they believed that this market is driven by factors much more attached to tradition and the use of rare materials than to sustainability. As a consequence, interviewees had the impression that luxury brands are not benchmarks of sustainability, mainly due to the use of animal skins for most of its products, and that becoming more sustainable is not an objective for the companies. Some believed, however, that the environmental impact of luxury products is reduced because they are manufactured in small quantities:

> The luxury market is driven more strongly by other attributes. So tradition is much more important than sustainability today (BR1).
>
> Yes, for me it's super important sustainable development. I do not associate with luxury brands. I do not think luxury brands are an example of sustainability (PT5).

The fact that the participants considered these concepts as separate did not prevent consumers envisaging the possibility of rapprochement between them. The development of luxury cars with clean technology, for example, was mentioned as one of the ways to enhance sustainability in the luxury car market. Another Brazilian interviewee evaluated that sustainability in luxury should be more connected to a more conscious consumption instead of just changing the raw material of products. In terms of products, a Portuguese consumer emphasised that the concepts could be closer if brands create products that harm less the environment:

> I think luxury and sustainability ... have to be more connected to the idea of having a conscious consumption. Thus, for example, I think it is very hard for these stores that have grown as a brand that sells leather shoes to no longer use leather because it is not sustainable. I think in the short term it is very difficult (BR3).

In the viewpoint of consumers in both countries, there is not currently a movement in the luxury market to become more sustainable. They claimed to have no knowledge about social and/or environmental initiatives carried out by the luxury brands they consume, since the communication of brands, both advertising and at point-of-sale, does not address this issue. Consequently, it gave the impression that luxury companies do very little in social and environmental areas:

> Companies are more concerned with explaining to the consumer why he/she is paying €500 more for a product than any other brand in terms of image, the materials used and the designers hired. They do not care to present the policies of corporate social responsibility (PT1).
>
> I know luxury brands that do have social initiatives but do not communicate them because the company doesn't see value on it (BR13).

Some interviewees associated this lack of communication to the low importance given to sustainability in consumers' purchasing decisions. Brazilian and Portuguese believed that luxury consumers generally do not demand more sustainable positioning by luxury companies. So, even if they communicated their initiatives, consumers would not change brands on this criterion alone. However, the participants declared that they would like to receive more information about the sustainability policies of these companies to, perhaps, use this criterion in a purchase situation:

> I think nowadays consumption is very superficial, people are giving more value to luxury, status, than an initiative in which a company benefits someone (BR6).

Although they believed that luxury consumers are not concerned with sustainability, interviewees believed that the companies have a responsibility to the environment and society, and if corporations established initiatives in this area they could gain the sympathy of more engaged consumers and get more followers. With more people worrying about sustainability, offering greener and more social alternatives could be seen as an interesting strategy to differentiate themselves:

> I think there is a consumer demand for the luxury sector to become more sustainable, mainly because of the mindset of the population that is changing, but I particularly think that the luxury consumer is not very focused on that (BR4).
>
> I think worrying about sustainability is good for the brand image ... It's important, it's a nice differentiation (BR2).

Brazilians believed that luxury firms could engage in sustainable development, so as to have a different appeal and to become more attractive. However, if the companies just copied the initiatives of other businesses they would risk being considered trivial, since the luxury segment is a differentiated one.

> If they start to do something that is equal, no matter if it is a good thing, it may be seen as banal. I do not know. Because I cannot see, for instance, Louis Vuitton communicating images that they are helping children (BR9).

The Portuguese, on the one hand, perceived a luxury company becoming more sustainable as a positive development. However, on the other hand, they questioned whether changes in the characteristics of products to reduce their environmental impact would not interfere in their quality and eventually have the opposite effect of that expected by the brand image. Behind this fear is the impression that companies could use recycled materials or synthetic leather to manufacture their products instead of traditional leather:

> I think it's worse for the brand to use raw materials that are more environmentally friendly, if the product damages more quickly. It will affect more the brand image than if it had continued to use materials that are not as environmentally friendly. But I think if you can use environmentally friendly products and at the same time have a good quality, of course, it is always preferable (PT6).

One of the main barriers to seeing luxury as sustainable is the use of animal fur. Both Brazilian and Portuguese consumers were resistant to replacing authentic fur for a synthetic equivalent. They valued quality and durability of leather goods and would not stop consuming it because of its impact on the environment. Likewise, they recognised that this is perhaps the most difficult aspect to be changed in the consumption of luxury, as the quality offered by this material is one of the main attributes of these products.

> I made a choice of boots: I tried some that weren't with leather inside, and others that were with leather. I bought the ones that were with leather inside and outside, because they were better (PT2).

> I think maybe in the future leather bag will be something obsolete. In the short, mid-term, I think that is difficult to change (BR3).

Therefore, the resistance of consumers showed that there is little room for change in companies if they want to become more sustainable. Design, quality, durability and exclusivity are the most decisive factors in the purchase of luxury products. If changes interfere in one of these aspects, they can jeopardise the brand image.

Conclusions

According to our exploratory research, sustainability is not a relevant aspect in purchases of Brazilian and Portuguese luxury consumers. These consumers prioritise quality, durability, design and exclusivity. In Brazil, consumers seem to use luxury products in order to communicate a different status, while the Portuguese prefer more discreet, intimate consumption. They even feel uncomfortable with the label of luxury consumers. This difference in the observed behaviour of the two nationalities might be explained by Hofstede's dimension of power distance.

One reason why sustainability is not considered as a purchase criterion is the fact that consumers have difficulty associating the concept of sustainability to luxury, believing that this is not an issue that drives this market and due to the high dependence of luxury products using animal leather. Additionally, the low interest interviewees presented in knowing about the values and purposes, as well as social and environmental initiatives of the companies whose products they consume, contributes to the impression among them that, in luxury, little is done to make the sector more sustainable. The communication of sustainability policies of these companies, in turn, is also seen as inefficient, since the participants claimed that they do not receive any information about it through advertising or from contact with sales staff.

Even taking into account that luxury and sustainability are distant concepts, consumers evaluate that luxury brands might become more sustainable. For some of them this is not only possible but necessary. The reason is that luxury companies are not exempt from the growing concern of individuals with sustainable development. But if, on the one hand, these companies have a lot to gain in terms of brand image and attraction of followers by adhering to sustainable practices, on the other hand, the consumers, especially the Portuguese, are afraid that products would lose quality.

The research also indicates that if luxury companies want to have a more sustainable approach they would need to innovate. Moreover, they need a communication strategy which clearly presents their purpose and, most importantly, a perspective which adds value and does not harm the quality or design of the products. By adopting an innovative approach to sustainability, the brand might have the opportunity to differentiate itself in the market.

As consumption in postmodernity is related to the creation of identities and desired appearances (Slater 1997), based on the symbolic content of consumed objects (Firat and Venkatesh 1995), to combine exclusivity and differentiation to conscious consumption might be a differential strategy. One of the possible benefits of this association is to reduce the stigma that luxury consumption is a selfish act.

It was observed that luxury consumption strengthens the feelings of pleasure and satisfaction in the consumer. Likewise, consumers might feel good when they realise they are contributing to sustainable development.

Although the Brazilian luxury consumers have not presented concerns about sustainability, and the Portuguese could be considered more conscious, the research indicates that it is important that companies pay attention to the changes in the social context towards a new paradigm based on sustainable development. While it is expected that companies communicate their values and actions related to sustainability, they should be cautious in conveying how the concept of sustainability is embedded in the context of the company and its brands. As they add sustainability to their business model, companies need to maintain their brand identity and positive image to consumers (Silverstein 2010).

This research has many limitations. It just studied women between 20 and 35 years old in urban centres in Brazil and Portugal. The choice of this younger target group may have resulted in very different behaviour from that observed in individuals of older age groups who have consumed luxury products for a longer time. The importance given to sustainability could be different in other age groups. Moreover, the study does not investigate other nationalities. Finally, the fact that many of the respondents were business managers or work in areas related to management may have generated biases relating to greater knowledge about how businesses operate or, more specifically, the luxury market.

The findings of this study raise additional questions that provide opportunities for future research. Besides expanding the discussion of luxury consumption and sustainability to other consumers' profiles, it would be interesting to address sustainability policies and the importance given to this issue by luxury companies. Additionally, future research could try to understand the reasons why luxury companies still do not communicate their actions more actively.

Bibliography

Allérès, D. (2000) *Luxo ... Estratégias, Marketing* (M. Gama, trans.; Rio de Janeiro, Brazil: Editora FGV).

Assadourian, E. (2010) 'Transforming Cultures: From Consumerism to Sustainability', *Journal of Macromarketing* 30.2: 186-91.

Barr, P.S. (2004) 'Current and Potential Importance of Qualitative Methods', in D.J. Ketchen and D.D. Bergh (eds.), *Research Methodology in Strategy and Management* (Oxford, UK: Elsevier): 165-88.

Bernstein Research (2010) *Black Book: European Luxury Goods: Long-Term Attractiveness & Structural Demand Drivers* (New York: Bernstein Global Wealth Research).

Bernardi, R.A. (2006) 'Associations Between Hofstede's Cultural Constructs and Social Desirability Response Bias', *Journal of Business Ethics* 65.1: 43-53.

Connolly, J., and A. Prothero (2003) 'Sustainable Consumption: Consumption, Consumers and the Commodity Discourse', *Consumption, Markets and Culture* 6.4: 275-91.

Denzin, N.K., and Y.S. Lincoln (2000) *Handbook of Qualitative Research* (London: Sage, 2nd edn).

Eriksson, P., and A. Kovalainen (2008) *Qualitative Methods in Business Research* (Los Angeles, CA: Sage).

Firat, A.F., and A. Venkatesh (1995) 'Liberatory Postmodernism and the Reenchantment of Consumption', *Journal of Consumer Research* 22.3: 239-67.

Gabriel, Y., and T. Lang (1995) *The Unmanageable Consumer: Contemporary Consumption and its Fragmentations* (London: Sage).

Giddens, A. (1991) *Modernidad e Identidad del yo: El yo y la Sociedad en la Época Contemporánea* (J.G. Aristu, trans.; Barcelona, Spain: Ediciones Península).

Harrison, R., T. Newholm and D. Shaw (2005) *The Ethical Consumer* (London: Sage).

Hofstede, G. (2001) *Culture's Consequences: Comparing Values, Behaviours, Institutions and Organizations Across Nations* (Thousand Oaks, CA: Sage, 2nd edn).

Hofstede, G., G.J. Hofstede and M. Minkov (2010) *Cultures and Organizations: Software of the Mind* (New York: McGraw-Hill, 3rd edn).
Ikeda, A.A., and F.C.T. Bacellar (2008) 'Revelando e Compreendendo o Relacionamento Professor-aluno em Marketing', *Revista de Administração Mackenzie (RAM)* 9.5: 137-54.
Jackson, T. (2009) *Prosperity Without Growth: Economics for a Finite Planet* (London: Earthscan).
Kahn, J. (2009) 'Luxury-Goods Makers Embrace Sustainability', *The New York Times*, 27 March 2009: A11.
Kapferer, J-N. (2010) 'All That Glitters in Not Green: The Challenge of Sustainable Luxury', *European Business Review*, November-December 2010, 40-45.
Kapferer, J-N., and V. Bastien (2009) *The Luxury Strategy: Break the Rules of Marketing to Build Luxury Brands* (London: Kogan Page).
Lang, T., and Y. Gabriel (2005) 'A Brief History of Consumer Activism', in R. Harrison, T. Newholm and D. Shaw (eds.), *The Ethical Consumer* (London: Sage): 39-53.
Lombard, M. (1989) *Produits de Luxe: Les Clés du Succès* (Paris: Economica).
Newholm, T., and D. Shaw (2007) 'Studying the Ethical Consumer: A Review of Research', *Journal of Consumer Behaviour* 6.5: 253-70.
Prothero, A., S. Dobscha, J. Freund, W. Kilbourne, M. Luchs, L. Ozanne and J. Thøgersen (2011) 'Sustainable Consumption: Opportunities for Consumer Research and Public Policy', *Journal of Public Policy and Marketing* 30.1: 31-38.
Rapaille, C. (2006) *The Culture Code: An Ingenious Way to Understand Why People Around the World Buy as They Do* (New York: Broadway Books).
Schaefer, A., and A. Crane (2005) 'Addressing Sustainability and Consumption', *Journal of Macromarketing* 25.1: 76-92.
Silverstein, B. (2010) 'Can Luxury Brands Sustain Themselves By Becoming Sustainable?' *The Brand Channel* (16 November 2010; www.brandchannel.com/home/post/2010/11/16/Luxury-Brands-Get-Sustainable.aspx, accessed 2 March 2012).
Slater, D. (1997) *Consumer Culture and Modernity* (Cambridge, UK: Polity Press).
Strehlau, S. (2008) *Marketing do Luxo* (São Paulo, Brazil: Cengage Learning Edições Ltda).
Valor, C. (2007) 'The Influence of Information about Labour Abuses on Consumer Choice of Clothes: A Grounded Theory Approach', *Journal of Marketing Management* 23.7/8: 675-95.
Varey, R.J. (2010) 'Marketing Means and Ends for a Sustainable Society: A Welfare Agenda of Transformative Change', *Journal of Macromarketing* 30.2: 112-26.

Ana Carolina De Pierro Bruno has a Masters in international management from Fundação Getulio Vargas/EAESP and CEMS-MIM. She is a management consultant and her areas of interest are luxury, fashion, sustainability and marketing. Email: anacpbruno@gmail.com

Edgard Barki has a PhD and Masters in business administration from Fundação Getulio Vargas/EAESP. He is an assistant professor and co-ordinator of BoP Lab Brazil. He was co-organiser of the books *Varejo para Baixa Renda* (*Retail for Low Income*) and *Negócios com Impacto Social no Brasil* (*Business with Social Impact in Brazil*) and was co-author of the book *Varejo no Brasil* (*Retail in Brazil*). His areas of interest are the base of the pyramid, emerging markets, retail and marketing. Email: edgard.barki@fgv.br

7

Are luxury purchasers really insensitive to sustainable development?

New insights from research

Jean-Noël Kapferer
Advisor to the President of Groupe INSEEC

Anne Michaut-Denizeau
HEC Paris, France

Luxury is now in the spotlight of sustainable development

Luxury refers to a concept, an economic sector and a specific strategy. There are endless discussions on what luxury is (Berry 1994; Vigneron and Johnson 1999; Wiedmann *et al.* 2007), not to talk about ethical discussions on luxury since Aristotle or Seneca. Based on the recent review paper by De Barnier *et al.* (2012), in this chapter we shall refer to luxury as high quality products and services whose high price far exceeds their functional value, are sold through selective distribution channels and produced in rather small quantities, often by hand, with an image tied to prestigious clients.

Luxury is also a macroeconomic sector, highly visible yet relatively small. According to Bain (2013), its aggregate sales are comparable to those of Walmart—at least €212 billion for personal products and accessories. Luxury is also a specific strategy, invented over time by those brands that now lead the sector: its goal is to grow in volume without diluting the brand prestige by offering feelings of exclusivity, rarity and privilege. Not all so-called luxury brands adopt the 'luxury strategy' (Kapferer and Bastien 2012); others go down a more mass-produced route, albeit communicating a glamorous public image. A lay person would not see the difference, however, and would perceive them all as luxury items.

By its enduring long-term growth and high visibility in all capital cities of the world, despite recessions and economic crises, the luxury sector has recently captured the attention of sustainable development (SD) advocates. This started as early as 2007 when WWF published *Deeper Luxury* (Bendell and Kleanthous 2007), while another non-governmental organisation (NGO), Corporate Knights, published its Global 100 Rating in 2012.[1] Luxury companies are now scrutinised by many NGOs, each focusing on one specific facet of SD, for the concept of SD is itself multifaceted. Since 1987, when the UN released the Brundtland Report (WCED 1987), a widely used definition of SD is: 'Development that meets the needs of the present without compromising the ability of future generations to meet their own needs'. SD has three pillars: environmental, social and economic, although most people associate SD with saving the planet and maintaining biodiversity. In the present chapter, we refer to the full meaning of the concept.

As a very old human activity, luxury has always been the object of criticism from philosophers and moralists. This is why ethics was for long the major source of concern for this industry. How ethical is it to indulge in luxury? How ethical is it to sell non-essential products and services to people who cannot afford them?

Today, the angle of attack has changed, with pressure coming from SD advocates and NGO groups. Some focus on the opaque traceability of most of the gold, diamonds, rubies and other gemstones coming from under-developed countries or war zones. Others on labour conditions in under-developed countries where some luxury brands have their products made, only to finally assemble them in Italy to get the 'Made in Italy' label. Some SD advocates focus on production processes (e.g. use of hazardous chemicals, water use in cotton production or for golf resort maintenance). Finally, the distribution side of luxury is also scrutinised (e.g. storage, logistics, transportation).

Political authorities have also criticised luxury. Thus, in 2012, the mayor of Beijing criticised luxury brands for creating social disharmony through the public exhibition of the wide wealth differences between Chinese citizens. Financial analysts themselves are now examining how much effort luxury brand manufacturers make in terms of SD. These analysts consider that the high reputation of the luxury brand must remain intact to be able to sustain their high pricing power and subsequent high margins. SD could become a problem from a shareholder perspective if stains start appearing on a brand's reputation, as this could affect the share price. Luxury brands are very averse to bad publicity.

1 http://global100.org/, accessed 22 June 2014.

Research on luxury and sustainable development

Research on consumers' sensitivity to sustainability issues has mostly focused on fast-moving consumer goods (FMCG), exploring who buys sustainable products, such as organic food, and their motivations and behaviours (Boulstridge and Carrigan 2000; Carrigan and Attala 2001; Newholm and Shaw 2007; Gupta and Ogden 2009). Low value commodity products, such as those advertised on TV and distributed globally via supermarkets and hypermarkets, are those that symbolise our consumer society.

Overall, the main finding from this research is the attitude–behaviour gap. Despite favourably expressed attitudes towards SD, purchasers of goods and services do not always act on their expressed opinions and the market share of ethical, environmentally conscious products remains small, at least in Europe and the USA. Sustainable products are seen as desirable but are not necessarily purchased. Furthermore, a social desirability bias may be being demonstrated by those who report that they take SD into account when purchasing goods and services (Chung and Monroe 2003).

Closer to our concerns, academic research has also analysed the fashion sector (Shaw *et al.* 2006; Morgan and Birtwistle 2009), looking at how environmental and ethical concerns did (or did not) influence the choices of fashionistas and young purchasers. Critics of the fast fashion industry, exemplified by brands such as C&A, H&M, Target, Mango and Zara, have pointed out devastating stories behind their daily casual clothing (Black 2011; Siegle 2011; Cline 2012).

Until recently, the specific case of sustainable luxury purchasing behaviour had not been much researched. One reason is size. In comparison with the FMCG industry, luxury is a tiny microeconomic sector. Bain (2013), a luxury consultancy, estimates the personal luxury market at €212 billion, which is less than Walmart's total revenue in 2012. Also, compared with the 'fast fashion' industry, which thrives by enticing people to buy products they already have in their closet, luxury promotes totally different values. Luxury sells products that are meant to last, are often handmade under the best conditions, mostly by talented artisans with passion and time. The slogan of a famous luxury watch brand says that their watches are bought to be transferred to the next generation. This is why the issue of sustainable luxury looked for so long to be a truism—isn't such artisanal work by definition sustainable? Isn't a Hermès leather belt, made to last decades, the symbol of sustainability too?

Research on luxury consumers' sensitivity to SD is only just beginning. Are luxury consumers ready to adopt SD as one of their main purchasing criteria? A pioneering work, on which we base our hypotheses, is Davies *et al.* (2012). This indicates that UK consumers' propensity to consider ethics is indeed significantly lower when contemplating luxury purchases compared to commoditised purchases. This research does not explicitly discuss SD, but its concern with 'ethical production' is similar to our concern with SD. Ethical production conditions came last among the luxury purchasing criteria list (and joint fifth out of eight in the commodity purchasing criteria list).

In Davies *et al.*'s study, three factors explain the difference in purchasers' attitudes towards luxury and commodity products. First, luxury purchases are an exceptional act for most of the population. As a result, consumers may not consider the possible negative impacts of their purchase compared, for instance, with the repeat purchasing of detergents or textiles for everyday use. Second, luxury purchases are, for most people, exceptional and special acts. Consumers may wish to protect these moments by ignoring external problems. Third, most consumers are not aware of what brands do in terms of SD. With the exception of Stella McCartney or Edun, luxury brands do not talk about their SD credentials. As a result, there is a lack of knowledge among the general public and there are no identified luxury brands that could be considered 'sustainable'. Since luxury brands insist on their creativity, their craftsmanship and their passion for excellence, luxury as a whole seems sustainable by definition. At least in the food and wine industry one can identify a clear organic segment in-store. So, among the luxury brands, which are focusing on SD?

To those factors we could add a further one—are the sustainable luxury brands' appeal, quality and creativity exceptional enough to qualify them as 'luxury brands'? Are they known enough to sustain desirability? Is there enough 'glamour in the green' (Kapferer 2010)? Or are they more a premium brand, positioned high on SD performance. It has been shown (Kapferer and Bastien 2012) that 'luxury' and 'premium' are very different business models and types of brands. Luxury sells dreams, premium sells the notion 'best of class' on some criteria that can be measured.

Our research is an extension of Davies *et al.*'s in two ways. First, if luxury consumers are not particularly sensitive to ethical or SD questions when they purchase a luxury object, what could make them sensitive? When questions about ethics and/or SD are asked in a survey, respondents may not perceive immediately what the interviewer is referring to. These concepts are quite abstract or wide. This is why, in any questionnaire about SD, one should first explain the full meaning of SD with its three facets (environmental, economic, social). Our first hypothesis is that data which reveal luxury consumers' insensitivity to SD may be due either to the vagueness of the concept, but also to its lack of clarity: mentioning a sweatshop or inhumane working conditions in fast fashion factories talks more than the concept of SD itself. To avoid this problem we undertook a first study, in 2012, with two improvements. We made the three pillars of SD explicit at the start of the questionnaire and we asked for reactions to actual SD misbehaviours. The goal was to investigate the capacity of actual negative information about luxury brands to emotionally move luxury consumers. It might well be that, under an apparent lack of interest, there is latent capacity to mobilise consumers against some brands, even the most prestigious, precisely because they should behave as models. Second, we wished to test further hypotheses related to the drivers of luxury consumers' sensitivity (or lack of) to SD when purchasing high ticket items. Some hypotheses are suggested in

Davies *et al.*'s research, others stem from the arguments advanced by the luxury industry itself to promote its inherent sustainability. Some companies' SD reports also appeared to support these hypotheses. Industry arguments can be found on the websites of Comité Colbert (the organisation that collectively defends the French luxury brands) and Fondazione Altagamma (the equivalent in Italy). The critical arguments are found in Bendell and Kleanthous (2007).

We now present the 13 propositions that could influence luxury consumers when considering SD in their purchasing decisions:

- The 'parenthesis of pleasure' hypothesis (Davies *et al.* 2012): consumers do not want to be annoyed by negative thoughts during their luxury purchase experience
- The 'exemplarity assumption': as luxury brands are held up as the paragon of all qualities they are surely also exemplar in terms of SD (Davies *et al.* 2012)
- The lack of information hypothesis: not being aware of any brand that stands out strongly on SD issues, consumers cannot take this criterion into account when making purchasing decisions
- The luxury industry insisting on the fact that it is non mass-produced, consumers' lack of sensitivity may be based on their perception that luxury brands produce so little quantities that neither the probability of a negative effect nor the magnitude of eventual negative consequences could ever be significant
- The luxury industry promotes the perception that luxury is so respectful of product quality, with its small production facilities (ateliers), that it cannot be detrimental in terms of SD
- The assumption that, since it is so highly priced, luxury must have taken care of everything, including SD and ethics
- The perception that luxury purchases are too infrequent to have any form of negative impact on SD
- The perception that luxury brands talk little about SD because they actually have nothing to say about it. So a SD purchase criterion would not help differentiate one from another
- The perception that luxury and SD are fundamentally contradictory. For instance one might criticise the fact that luxury stimulates envy, and pushes a lot of ordinary people to spend large amounts of money on unnecessary and expensive products. This is especially true today when luxury is aimed at the masses (Nueno and Quelch 1998)
- The perception that luxury satisfies a minority (happy few) while the majority is still trying to survive or satisfy their elementary needs (health, housing, education, jobs)

- The perception that, in periods of economic crisis, it is bad for social harmony for some people to conspicuously exhibit luxury purchases
- The perception that a few luxury brands are priced very high and yet have their products made in low-wage countries
- The current perception that it is 'classy' to purchase SD oriented products. This notion of 'green class' was suggested by interesting research from Griskevicius *et al.* (2010) who found that early buyers of hybrid powered cars did not want to save the planet per se, but did want to be seen as innovators and leaders

Each of these 13 hypotheses was operationalised in the questionnaire.

Methodology

To answer the two main research questions presented above, we undertook two surveys, one in 2012 with 966 luxury buyers, the other in June 2013 with 192 luxury buyers. Today, thanks to Internet surveys, it is possible to reach large samples of actual luxury buyers. Surveys can also contribute to the measurement of the state of public opinion about luxury and sustainable development. Since this programme of research was funded by the Pernod-Ricard Chair, beyond academic interests, this information is useful to the actors of the luxury market. Also, to help the luxury industry make proper decisions about SD, large samples are necessary as they add credibility to the conclusions.

In each of these surveys we focus on actual luxury customers to understand the motivations underlying either their total disinterest or, on the contrary, their high sensitivity to SD as it relates to luxury. By 'actual luxury customers' we mean people who buy luxury products. Luxury products may be seen by everybody, but their ownership remains selective among the population. There is luxury because not everybody can afford it. Luxury prices are intentionally discriminatory. It is also likely that, beyond obvious economic reasons, one motivation to refuse to buy luxury products is that they signal wealth inequality and so damage the social pillar of SD. Here, it is not our aim to analyse why people do not buy luxury products. We wish instead to focus on those who are the actual clients of luxury brands today. Our two surveys are based on people who declared a recent purchase of any of the following products: a bottle of wine above €40; a lipstick above €35; a pair of shoes above €350; eyewear above €350; and a jacket above €400. With the exception of lipstick all products could be relevant to either male or female respondents. The price level of the products (wine, shoes, dresses, jacket) is drawn from quantitative research on the threshold price of luxury in 20 product categories (Kapferer and Laurent 2011): the selected prices are actually the median of the answers. Last, but not least, in each questionnaire we reminded respondents of the full meaning of SD with its three pillars (environmental, social and economic).

Results

Are luxury and sustainable development perceived as contradictory?

One goal of the first survey (2012) was to evaluate the degree of sensitivity to SD issues among actual luxury buyers. In all, 966 French luxury buyers were selected from a larger national panel while respecting quotas to ensure representativeness. BVA, a leading polls institute, was in charge of the fieldwork. Certainly, the results cannot be generalised to the whole world—they reflect the attitudes of buyers living in a mature, economically developed country, and one that produces a range of top-end luxury goods.

Table 7.1 **Actual luxury buyers' perceptions about luxury and SD (*n* = 966)**

	Total agree	Total disagree
Considering its price, it would be a scandal if luxury did not respect SD	69%	11%
Luxury is late vis-à-vis of SD norms and standards	52%	13%
Luxury induces people with little money to buy expensive goods	60%	15%
Luxury is somehow a waste	44%	24%
Luxury is a symbol of inequality, source of social disharmony	41%	27%
Luxury is not very ethical	41%	23%
Luxury and SD are contradictory	33%	34%
Luxury promotes long lasting high quality products, this is SD	44%	18%
Luxury maintains local and traditional know-how, this is SD	58%	12%

As shown in Table 7.1, the results demonstrate that luxury buyers have a critical view of this sector. Sixty-nine per cent say that, considering their high price, it would be a scandal if luxury brands did not respect SD standards. Price is an argument that allows people not to worry about SD when they purchase luxury goods: how could excellence be based on misbehaviours? The least one can assume is that they are free from any criticism as to sourcing, production processes, etc. Surprisingly, for 52% of respondents, the luxury sector 'looks late on these matters'; this could be due to the fact that the most visible luxury brands (clothing, leather, watches, jewellery, cosmetics) do not communicate on SD (unlike the automotive ones, for example, which talk about CO_2 emissions, hybrid engines, electrical cars). The next items demonstrate how high the ambivalence vis-à-vis luxury is, even among the buyers themselves. Interestingly, they are mostly sensitive to the negative impacts on social harmony, not so much on the ecological facets of SD: the luxury sector is clearly seen by 60% of respondents as expanding its clientele among people who may not have enough money to justify such purchases, with luxury considered a waste by 44% (just looking at gas consumption of supercars, or the multiple layers of packaging). As a whole, 41% of respondents say luxury is not very ethical. Luxury buyers' opinion is balanced with regard to the contradiction between luxury and SD: 33% say it is contradictory while 34% say it is not. Finally, the level of agreement with two classic arguments from the luxury industry is high: 'luxury promotes long lasting quality products' (44% agree vs. 18% who disagree) and 'luxury defends a tradition of excellence and local know-how' (58% vs. 12%). These arguments stress the contrast with FMCG products, which are often made in poor working conditions. Since 33% of the sample declares that luxury is in direct contradiction with SD, this perception seems based more on the disruption of social harmony than on poor labour conditions or destruction of rare resources.

What information would make consumers react strongly?

Former research has shown that consumers were less concerned about SD when they purchased luxury goods than when they bought commodities (Davies *et al.* 2012), so what kind of information about concrete misbehaviours would make them react strongly? As analysed above, one main reason why consumers may not use SD as a criterion when buying a luxury good is that they make the wrong assumption: held as a symbol of excellence, luxury is 100% clean, almost by definition. This is called the fallacy of 'clean' luxury. But if some concrete misbehaviours were revealed, how shocking would it be?

Table 7.2 **What news about luxury brands would be shocking? (*n* = 966, scale 1 to 10, % answering 9 or 10)**

1) To kill animals for their fur	54%
2) To kill many crocodiles to make one luxury bag	53%
3) Made in China to benefit from low production costs	54%
4) Destroying inventory instead of selling it at a discount	52%
5) 5* golf resorts and hotels in countries that lack water	48%
6) 100,000 litres, the fuel consumption of a mega yacht	48%
7) Excessive packaging	36%
8) Out of season fruits	33%
9) Teenagers buying luxury items	27%

In the survey of 966 actual luxury buyers, we presented a list of such alleged misbehaviors to test their emotional sensitivity. Table 7.2 presents the items ranked by decreasing order of sensitivity: respondents could answer from 1 (I do not care at all) to 10 (very shocking). We report here the percentage declaring either 9 or 10. It is in all cases very high. Animal defence is clearly the most sensitive issue (54% say they would be very shocked): this does not mean that the leather industry is threatened. The literature review on sustainable purchasing behaviour highlights the gap between expressed attitudes and behaviour. As a matter of fact, Stella McCartney, a designer who refuses to sell leather and uses only substitutes, remains isolated in the sector. Leather is still held worldwide as a luxury material. But the recent ban in California on *foie gras* shows that this sensitivity may now impact public policy. In the UK, Amazon has just announced it would not sell *foie gras* any more. Items 3 and 4 relate to hidden practices of the luxury industry. This sector is made up of companies with very different business models. Some, such as Louis Vuitton, refuse to relocalise production: they sell only Made in France products. Some others do not hesitate to reduce production costs by manufacturing in China. This is seen as extremely shocking by 54% of the sample. Another typical practice is that luxury fashion houses do not hesitate to discount their unsold collections through specialised websites or stores. But the most prestigious luxury brands refuse to slash their prices. To protect the idea of luxury timeless value they prefer to destroy their inventory, a fact that strongly shocks 52% of the sample. Differences in the lives of tourists and inhabitants in so-called paradise spots where water is often rare is also very shocking for 48% of the sample. Golf resorts need enormous quantities of water. Among the least sensitive items (36%) is the luxury habit of over-packaging. Nice packaging seems a part of the luxury retail experience. Finally, the fact that today's youth indulges in buying luxury accessories is not shocking, at least for the sample of 966 actual luxury buyers.

Exploring sensitivity and insensitivity to sustainable development

The first survey showed that luxury buyers had ambivalent attitudes vis-à-vis taking SD into account when purchasing. This ambivalence does not prevent these people from buying. It also showed how negative interviewees' reactions could be to some specific information on brands' misbehaviors. What Davies *et al.* (2012) called consumers' 'lesser sensitivity' could actually transform into anger and ill will. A second survey was undertaken to explore the beliefs of those people who did (or did not) care about SD when purchasing luxury. We have already presented 13 such beliefs, which are potential motivators. To avoid rationalisations we do not use direct questions such as: 'Why are you concerned (or not) by sustainable development when you buy a luxury product?'. We infer the weight of a belief on consumers' sensitivity to SD from statistical analysis of the correlations between this particular belief and the dependent variable (sensitivity or non sensitivity). In all, 192 luxury buyers answered the second questionnaire .

Are insensitivity and sensitivity two faces of the same coin?

A first unexpected result of this second survey is that 'insensitivity to SD concerns when purchasing a luxury product' is not the opposite of 'I tend to choose luxury brands that are known to be ethical and concerned by SD' nor of 'I am ready to pay more for a luxury product respectful of SD' or 'I would immediately boycott a luxury brand if I learned it is not engaged in SD and pro-environmental actions'. Originally, these four questions were supposed to tap the same uni-dimensional underlying factor (luxury sensitivity to SD), three questions being positively worded and one negatively (no concern for SD). Table 7.3 presents the matrix of Pearson correlations between these four items. These correlation coefficients measure the strength and direction of the linear relationship between two variables. Unexpectedly, the insensitivity item has a zero correlation with the three others, indicating that they load on two distinct factors. Had this item loaded on the same factor as the three other items, its correlation coefficients with these items should have been significant and negative. Being close to zero means these are two independent factors.

Table 7.3 **Insensitivity and sensitivity are not correlated (matrix of correlations between items)**

	When I buy a luxury product I never ask myself what the brand does for SD	**I tend to choose luxury brands that are engaged in SD**	**I would stop buying a luxury brand if I learned it did not respect SD**	**I am ready to pay more for a luxury product that respects SD**
When I buy a luxury product I never ask myself what the brand does for SD	1	–.073	–.072	–.052
I tend to choose luxury brands that are engaged in SD	–.073	1	.470	.587
I would stop buying a luxury brand if I learned it did not respect SD	–.072	.470	1	.459
I am ready to pay more for a luxury product that respects SD	–.052	.587	.459	1

How can one explain this lack of correlation? The frequency distribution of these items reveals no skewedness: respondents answered using the full 1 to 10 scale. The social psychological literature on the relationships between attitudes versus behaviours (Fishbein and Ajzen 1975) or between verbal intentions and behaviours (Boulstridge and Carrigan 2000) has shown that both variables were less correlated than expected. But we have here a zero correlation between the item measuring what people do while purchasing (they never think of SD) and three attitudinal items (I tend to, I would stop buying, I would pay more).

One must then admit that 'being totally insensitive' is not the contrary of being engaged in SD. Insensitivity seems to be a kind of 'non involvement' rather than direct opposition to being engaged in SD. The opposite of SD engagement would, for instance, be SD deniers who claim that concern for SD is artificially made up by the media or by anti-economic growth activist groups.

The drivers of sensitivity and insensitivity are not the same

Looking at the determinants of each factor (insensitivity and sensitivity to SD) provides further insights on consumers' psychology. In fact the drivers of each of these two factors are totally different (see Table 7.4).

Table 7.4 **Levers of insensitivity and sensitivity to luxury and SD (n = 192, correlations between each perception and the dependent variable)**

	DV: I would stop buying a luxury brand if I learned it did not respect SD standards	DV: When I buy a luxury product I never ask myself what the brand does for SD
1	Today the real class is to buy luxury products respectful of SD (r = .625)	When I buy a luxury product I think only of my own pleasure (r = .499)
2	Considering their price, respecting SD is the least you can expect from luxury brands (r = .617)	I am totally unable to tell what brands are engaged on SD or ethical issues (r = .415)
3	Luxury does not promote social harmony, it makes inequality visible (r = .513)	Luxury purchase is too rare to have any negative impact on SD (r = .380)
4	Luxury brands do not talk about SD because they are not totally clean (r = .498)	Luxury is about the egoistic pleasure of a minority (r = .343)
5	I am shocked by luxury brands that relocalise in low-cost countries to reduce their costs (r = .486)	For me, fundamentally, luxury and SD are contradictory (r = .317)
6	In an economic crisis it is indecent to buy luxury (r = .477)	I do not see how to reconcile luxury and social demands of SD (r = .288)
7	Luxury is a superficial lifestyle (r = .453)	

What drives insensitivity? What are the salient motives or beliefs justifying it at the time of purchase? The first driver is the wish to think only about pleasure at this very moment, as indicated by the size and significance of the Pearson correlation coefficient (r = .499). This result corresponds to the 'parenthesis of pleasure' hypothesis, examined above. It is well known that luxury purchasing also fulfils an escape function (Kapferer and Bastien 2012). Buyers of luxury goods want to forget the real world with its many problems, leaving it outside the store and, while purchasing, experience a few moments of intimate privilege and exception. The second reason underlying their lack of concern is they have no idea of any luxury brand positioned on SD (r = .415). Third, they perceive luxury as too rare a purchase to have any impact on the major problems of SD (r = .380). In fourth position, for them, luxury is for the pleasure of only a minority (r = .343). Finally, they really believe that luxury and SD are deeply contradictory and that nothing can be done about this (r = .288).

What, then, are the beliefs and opinions most correlated with SD sensitivity, measured by an intention to immediately stop buying a luxury brand if it was proven it did not behave correctly? The first driver of this sensitivity to SD in luxury purchases is that such purchases are the only ones to give 'class' (r = .625). This remarkably echoes what Griskevicius *et al.* (2010) call 'green conspicuousness'. Smith (2010) also had noticed that the early buyers of the Toyota Prius, the first car with a hybrid engine, had not bought it to protect the planet or reduce their fuel consumption, but to show they were really in advance, forerunners. Today, for these people engaged in sustainable luxury, buying green luxury creates more 'class' than traditional luxury. The second driver of SD sensitivity (r = .617) is the assumption that, at such high prices, luxury brands must have checked that their sourcing, production and logistical processes are fully in line with SD requirements. If this assumption was shown to be false then luxury consumers would immediately retaliate by stopping buying the brand that had betrayed their trust.

Interestingly, the third motivator, which is highly correlated with SD sensitivity and its consequence (willingness to stop buying), reveals that these buyers do acknowledge an inherent weakness of luxury: it is not good for social harmony (it shows off the inequality of revenues; r = .513). Fourth, these buyers believe that the absence of communication on SD by luxury brands is due to the fact that they may not be so innocent (it could then backlash; r = .498). The fifth driver of sensitivity to SD in luxury (r = .486) is related to the belief that some luxury brands, although very expensive, try to save costs by delocalising production to any other low-wage country (e.g. Prada, Zegna). Remember that in the first survey such information was judged shocking by 54% of the sample of luxury buyers. The sixth driver of sensitivity to SD for luxury is a shame factor related to the economic crisis (r = .477). These buyers feel that it is indecent to exhibit luxury purchases during crises, yet they nevertheless bought some luxury items. As a result, luxury brands must not increase this guilt. Engaging in SD is a way to alleviate it.

Finally, the luxury buyers engaged in SD admit that luxury is indeed a superficial lifestyle. This is why they could abandon a brand if it was seen to be not doing enough in terms of SD.

Implications for management

Luxury brands are conscious that the time to procrastinate is over. François-Henri Pinault, CEO of Kering, a world leader in luxury apparel and accessories, recently said: 'If we wait for consumers to insist upon sustainability as a condition for purchasing, nothing will happen. It is up to us to see to it that environmental products become the new norm'. Since luxury companies belong to financial groups, or are themselves listed, they have so far hesitated to act more quickly, begging the eternal question: 'What about the return on SD? What if luxury buyers are not ready to pay more for the extra costs of SD?' For buyers of a €10,000 watch, a 5% increase in price is not a problem. But a lot of the growth in the luxury sector has been achieved by selling lower priced items. People buying a €3,000 watch are far more price sensitive.

This research shows that SD is certainly a desirable concept, but there is, as yet, no overwhelming demand for it. However, among luxury buyers, differentiation and class will now come from SD oriented purchases. It is luxurious to drive without petrol and, in California, to drive a Tesla car instead of a Ferrari. Even if luxury consumers do not think about SD when buying a luxury product, they may react emotionally if they discover that the brand damages SD standards, with social media quickly spreading such information. This is too big a risk.

One main source of the potential negative reactions of luxury consumers is their false assumption that, because of their high prices, luxury brands must have taken care of SD already. If consumers learn this is not the case, it would backfire. Finally, SD will be the only way for new luxury brands to emerge. New brands and companies will create a new segment—that of sustainable luxury brands—which bears modern 21st century values, thus endangering the whole species of traditional luxury brands if they do not react proactively.

To conclude, the luxury future starts today. Luxury brands should lead the way, be exemplary on all accounts, and not wait till explicit demands are made by the public.

Bibliography

Bain (2013) *The Luxury Report* (Paris and Milan: Bain Monographs).

Bendell, J., and A. Kleanthous (2007) *Deeper Luxury* (London: WWF-UK).

Berry, C.J. (1994) *The Idea of Luxury: A Conceptual and Historical Investigation* (Cambridge, UK: Cambridge University Press).

Black, S. (2011) *Eco-Chic: The Fashion Paradox* (London: Black Dog Publishing).

Boulstridge, E., and M. Carrigan (2000) 'Do Consumers Really Care About Corporate Responsibility? Highlighting the Attitude–Behavior Gap', *Journal of Communication Management* 4.4: 355-68.

Carrigan, M., and A. Attalla (2001) 'The Myth of the Ethical Consumer: Do Ethics Matter in Purchase Behaviour?', *Journal of Consumer Marketing* 18.7: 560-77.

Chung, J., and G.S. Monroe (2003) 'Exploring Social Desirability Bias', *Journal of Business Ethics* 44.4: 291-302.
Cline, E. (2012) *Overdressed: Responsible Shopping in the Age of Cheap Fashion* (New York: Penguin Books).
Davies, I.A., Z. Lee and L. Ahonkhai (2012) 'Do Consumers Care About Ethical Luxury?' *Journal of Business Ethics* 106: 37-51.
De Barnier, V., S. Falcy and P. Valette-Florence (2012) 'Do Consumers Perceive Three Levels of Luxury? A Comparison of Accessible, Intermediate and Inaccessible Luxury Brands', *Journal of Brand Management* 19: 623-36.
Fishbein, M., and I. Ajzen (1975) *Belief, Attitude, Intention, and Behaviour: An Introduction to Theory and Research* (Reading, UK: Addison-Wesley).
Griskevicius, V., J. Tybut and B. Van den Bergh (2010) 'Going Green to Be Seen: Status, Reputation and Conspicuous Conservation', *Journal of Personality and Social Psychology* 98.3: 392-404.
Gupta, S., and D.T. Ogden (2009) 'To Buy or Not to Buy? A Social Dilemma Perspective on Green Buying', *Journal of Consumer Marketing* 26.6: 376-91.
Kapferer, J-N. (2010) 'All That Glitters is Not Green: The Challenge of Sustainable Luxury', *The European Business Review*, November–December 2010: 40-45.
Kapferer, J-N., and V. Bastien (2012) *The Luxury Strategy: Break the Rules of Marketing to Build Luxury Brands* (London: Kogan Page, 2nd edn).
Kapferer, J-N., and G. Laurent (2011) *Luxury Price Thresholds: An International Comparison* (Paris: HEC Research Reports).
Morgan, L.R., and G. Birtwistle (2009) 'An Investigation of Young Fashion Consumers' Disposal Habits', *International Journal of Consumer Studies* 33: 190-98.
Newholm, T., and D. Shaw (2007) 'Studying the Ethical Consumer: A Review of Research', *Journal of Consumer Behaviour* 6: 253-70.
Nueno, J.L., and J.A. Quelch (1998) 'The Mass Marketing of Luxury', *Business Horizons* 41.6: 61.
Siegle, L. (2011) *To Die For: Is Fashion Wearing Out the World?* (London: Fourth Estate).
Shaw, D., G. Hogg, E. Wilson, E. Shui and L. Hassan (2006) 'Fashion Victim: The Impact of Fair Trade Concerns on Clothing Choice', *Journal of Strategic Marketing* 14: 427-40.
Smith, J. (2010) 'Premium Customers Hold Key to Success in Electric Cars', *The Times*, 5 May 2010.
Vigneron, F., and L.W. Johnson (1999) 'A Review and Conceptual Framework of Prestige-Seeking Consumer Behaviour', *Academy of Marketing Science Review* 1: 1-17.
WCED (World Commission on Environment and Development) (1987) *Our Common Future* (Oxford, UK: Oxford University Press).
Wiedmann, K.P., N. Hennings and A. Siebels (2007) 'Measuring Consumers' Luxury Value Perception: A Cross-Cultural Framework', *Academy of Marketing Science Review* 7: 1-21.

Jean-Noël Kapferer is a world renowned expert on branding, author of *Reinventing the brand, The New Strategic Brand Management* and co-author of *The Luxury Strategy: break the rules of marketing to build luxury brands*. Ph.D Kellogg Business School, he taught at Northwestern University before joining HEC Paris and is now Advisor to the President of Groupe INSEEC. He directs executive seminars on luxury all around the world.

Anne Michaut-Denizeau is an affiliate professor at HEC Paris. Her research expertise is on new product management and, more recently, on sustainable development. She manages luxury programmes at HEC Paris. Email: michaut@hec.fr

Part III

8

Luxury Lodges New Zealand and prospects for elegant disruption

Martin Perry
School of Management, Massey University, Wellington, New Zealand

Introduction

Luxury brands are identified partly by prices that make consumption of them something to which most people can only aspire, giving those with the required purchasing power an elite experience and sense of prestige that sets them apart from people at large. This can be associated with conspicuous consumption and the urge to impress others through a public display of wealth; but not all luxury goods and services are necessarily associated with such motivations (Moscardo 2013: 278). As in the case of New Zealand's luxury lodges, luxury can be associated with comparatively remote and private settings with access to undeveloped natural environments a large part of the luxury offering. The motivations driving luxury consumption are potentially diverse and, in some circumstances, may emphasise attributes that are consistent with sustainable forms of economic activity (Bendell and Kelanthous 2007; Mastrelli 2007). In many respects this should not be surprising. It has long been recognised that growing affluence gives capacity to devote resources to minimising the environmental impacts of economic activity and that increased income brings shifts in the distribution of expenditure in favour of environmental goods (Jänicke 2008). This process explains the success of eco-efficiency initiatives such as the uptake of renewable energy, waste reduction and resource conservation (Dryzek 1997). The possibility has been raised that something more than this can occur with the purchase of luxury goods and services. Bendell (2012) has coined the term 'elegant disruption' to show how consumer aspirations for luxury brands can be associated with changes in patterns of consumption, production or exchange that go beyond incremental improvements in economic efficiency.

The concept of elegant disruption links luxury, entrepreneurship and sustainability, but there is a larger literature that examines the opportunity for sustainability to support new entrepreneurship. This chapter distinguishes two alternative models: co-evolution and social bricoleurs. The chapter first explains these alternative perspectives and then examines them further through a case study of New Zealand's luxury lodges. Of the three perspectives examined in the chapter, elegant disruption is most consistent with luxury having potential to make a significant contribution to the advancement of sustainable forms of economic activity. Other perspectives indicate that a contribution to sustainability will depend on the extent to which luxury lodges bring a competitive reaction incorporating sustainability from incumbent enterprises in the accommodation market or suggest that the contribution will be modest.

This chapter uses the case of luxury lodges in New Zealand to examine the barriers and opportunities for some form of elegant disruption to occur. The central research questions in the case study are:

- Do luxury lodges in New Zealand confirm the potential for luxury consumption to promote sustainability in accordance with the concept of elegant disruption?
- How does the experience of New Zealand's luxury lodges fit with the concepts of co-evolution and social bricoleurs as applied to sustainability-based entrepreneurship? Do either of these concepts better capture the position of luxury lodges than elegant disruption?
- What are the implications of the case of New Zealand's luxury lodges for the larger application of the conceptualisation of elegant disruption?

Scope of the study and research method

The main purpose of this chapter is to evaluate whether the concept of elegant disruption appears to have application beyond the limited cases that have so far informed its development. The chapter focuses on elegant disruption because it is a comparatively novel concept developed by a researcher who has led much of the debate around sustainability and luxury consumption. The evaluation takes two main forms. First, it draws on the wider green entrepreneurship literature to identify two opposing conceptions of the capacity for new enterprise to push forward a transition to a more sustainable economy. This discussion immediately highlights a weakness in the way that the idea of elegant disruption has been developed without reference to the larger entrepreneurship literature. Second, the chapter presents a case study of luxury lodges in New Zealand to comment further on elegant disruption by examining how far it appears to fit efforts to integrate sustainability with luxury lodge accommodation.

The case study focuses on lodges affiliated to Luxury Lodges of New Zealand[1] for two reasons. First, luxury lodges provide one of the few examples of a locally produced luxury item supporting new entrepreneurship in New Zealand with the country not having a strong presence of affluent consumers. For example, New Zealand immigration laws give special access for potential residents with wealth of at least NZ$10 million (US$8.5 million), but this scheme has attracted only around 25 new residents a year since 2009 (Heather 2013). Lodges rely on international visitors, with overseas buyers also explaining New Zealand's other main luxury industry, the manufacture of racing and super yachts. Second, as an activity linked to tourism, luxury lodges present a significant test of the potential for elegant disruption. As discussed by Yin (1989: 47), examining an extreme or unique case provides a rationale for conducting a case study as it gives opportunity to observe patterns that may not be recognised when standard cases are examined. Bendell's (2012) conceptualisation of elegant disruption drew on cases involving fashionable consumer accessories where the challenges to being sustainable are less complex than in the case of tourism.

While leisure tourism has long since ceased to be the exclusive domain of an affluent, educated, elite social class, a distinct luxury segment remains in the form of exclusive locations, forms of accommodation and modes of travel (Towner and Wall 1991; Ryan and Stewart 2009). Within this sector a 'new luxury' can be observed in the way luxurious travel destinations are being promoted on the basis of experience, authenticity and rarity rather than the traditional luxury attributes of exclusivity, superiority and elite group membership (Moscardo and Benckendorff 2010). This may encompass serious efforts to offer a luxury service based on sustainable design and management, but the relationship between tourism and luxury remains problematic (Moscardo 2013: 278). Luxury consumer expectations for facilities such as spas and pools, infrastructure such as landing strips and helicopter pads, as well as the long haul travel frequently associated with luxury tourism, create large ecological footprints (Gössling *et al.* 2002; Ryan and Stewart 2009). So-called eco-experiences based on small-scale, exclusive access to natural environments may not change behaviour or beliefs once the experience ends and may act as a beach head for other forms of tourism to enter once isolated locations (Moscardo and Benckendorff 2010). More immediately, it has been shown that some luxury

1 www.lodgesofnz.co.nz, accessed 6 May 2014.

hotels have been slow to address environmental or social responsibility issues (Bohdanowicz 2005; Maresco and Lyons 2005; Bohdanowicz and Zientara 2009).

The case study draws on information collected from interviews of the owners or managers of four lodges, an executive of the lodge association and publicly available information of all lodges that form part of Luxury Lodges of New Zealand. The interviews were loosely structured around four main topics: (1) the origins of the lodge and owner motivations and business objectives; (2) guest profile and any changes in the market served by the lodge; (3) the owner/manager's understanding of guest motivations; (4) the owner/manager's perceived importance of sustainability to luxury lodges and their own sustainability actions. It is important to stress that the case study is not attempting to provide an evaluation of the sector as whole. The purpose of the case study is to capture experiences and motivations of lodges that have engaged with sustainability and to gather their evaluation of the role that lodges might play in leading a transformation towards more sustainable forms of visitor accommodation. Insight from among those actively engaging with sustainability provides a preliminary assessment of the disruptive potential of this form of luxury. While the case study is based on a small number of interviews, it can be noted that lodges belong to an association that establishes common performance standards for member lodges and requires that entry to the group is through the recommendation of at least two existing members. Individual lodge owners do, therefore, have insight into how their own motivations and objectives compare with those of other lodge owners.

The chapter commences by outlining the idea of elegant disruption before considering alternative conceptions of green entrepreneurship. Some description of New Zealand's luxury lodges and their contributions to sustainability is then given before discussing which of the three perspectives on sustainability and entrepreneurship best fit this case.

Pathways for and alternatives to elegant disruption

Disruptive innovation as defined by Christensen (1997) shakes up the organisation of markets and fundamentally challenges the continuance of established business models and the incumbent enterprises that perfected such models. Disruptive innovation is open to small-scale entrepreneurialism. Being guided by their understanding of what best satisfies existing customers, and being constrained by what their network of suppliers and support services are configured to provide, incumbents can be slow to spot emerging technologies. New enterprise, in contrast, can pursue innovations that are typically introduced in the context of marginal, niche applications that appear inferior and unthreatening to mainstream offerings but ultimately may be disruptive. Sustainability is viewed as one source of creative disruption (Hart and Milstein 1999: 23), with some even seeing improved environmental outcomes as being the inspiration for a new industrial revolution (Braungart and McDonough 1998; Lovins *et al.* 1999; Rainey 2006; Porter and Kramer 2006, 2011). Whether the opportunities presented by the undoubted growth of interest in sustainability will be taken by small or large enterprises, or some combination of both, is not yet clear (Hockerts and Wüstenhagen 2010). There is discussion, for example, that the sustainability revolution is not following the path of other late 20th century industrial revolutions in which venture capital-funded new enterprise played a big part (Kenney 2009).

Among those seeing the prospect of a sustainability-informed industrial revolution, Bendell (2012) speculates that the luxury sector is on the cusp of being overtaken by new business models that make sustainability integral to luxury consumption in a process he refers to as elegant disruption. According to this claim, five trends are being capitalised upon by a new generation of luxury brands that are making sustainability attributes an integral aspect of luxury (Bendell 2012: 12):

- Evolving tastes: consumers are turning away from long established luxury brands that are perceived to have lost mystique compared with new providers
- Critical transparency: consumers are showing more awareness of the conditions under which luxury goods and services are provided and favouring those demonstrating social responsibility
- Hyper-connectivity: as part of the growth of social media, consumers are seeking direct engagement with the entrepreneurs supplying luxury, to feel part of a community
- Cultural shifts: the shift of economic wealth towards East Asia has potential to loosen the dominance of Western brands as affluent Asians take an increasing share of the expenditure on luxury goods and services
- 'Transmodernism': changing perceptions of luxury producing greater diversity in the places and attributes associated with luxury

Elvis and Kresse is one of Bendell's (2012) exemplars informing optimism for the possibility of elegant disruption. This company makes luxury goods from waste and combines this with opportunities for buyers to engage with the enterprise in ways consistent with the drivers of elegant disruption. The business has built its brand on an initial success, converting disused fire hoses into handbags, belts and other luxury fashion accessories sold through some of the world's most luxurious department stores such as Harrods in London. The business model includes donating 50% of all profit from sales to charities associated with the wastes used (in the case of the fire hose accessories, the Fire Fighters Charity is the beneficiary). Designer shopping bags from used coffee bean sacks, with profits shared with coffee grower programmes, has been another Elvis and Kresse enterprise. The business model relies on learning how to make use of discarded material and identifying 'story-laden wastes' that enable the final product to be the basis for a deep association between the consumer and the company.[2] Company founder Kresse Wesling has ambition to disrupt the established luxury brand companies by directly communicating with potential consumers on the same wavelength rather than utilising traditional advertising and marketing channels.

Doubts about elegant disruption

Bendell (2012) acknowledges two sources of doubt over the possibility of the luxury sector being disrupted through sustainable innovation. First, novel business models based around their sustainability attributes need to be scaled up sufficiently if they are to become a significant challenge to incumbent luxury brands. Clearly, for Kresse Wesling's enterprise, the volume of waste going to landfill still far outstrips understanding of how value can be built into waste, but this leaves many uncertainties about the ability to identify viable waste streams to support a coherent product range. Second, such sustainability driven enterprises may simply concentrate a consumer's interest and help to justify continuing patronage of 'normal' goods and services. This is possible where conversion to sustainable business models is associated with fringe enterprises, which to some degree lessen the pressure on mainstream enterprises to reconfigure their business operations.

These concerns link to questions in the wider literature on sustainable or green entrepreneurship which have highlighted a number of limitations to the disruptive potential of new enterprise. First, the scope for new enterprise to capitalise on sustainability provides start-up opportunities, but the challenge remains in having to dislodge large, incumbent enterprises (Hockerts 2006). Second, experience indicates that many sustainability-based start-ups either become absorbed into larger enterprises that do not share the same commitment to sustainability or they remain as small-scale niche activities (Hockerts and Wüstenhagen 2010; Holt 2011). Third, the extent to which disruptive innovation ultimately favours new rather than incumbent enterprise depends on the speed with which the innovation is taken up (Perry 2010). When innovation unfolds over time, incumbents have the capacity to take control of emerging technologies should they start to show promise, as in the way that new biotechnology start-ups are frequently acquired by 'big pharma' companies once it appears that a discovery has commercial potential (Gray 2002). Sustainable business practice relies partly on supportive regulation to create the markets for environmental goods and, as in the case of biotechnology, dependence on regulation tends to slow the rate of change and affords big business opportunity to shift regulation in its favour (Hockerts and Wüstenhagen 2010). Two conceptions that respond to these constraints on new enterprise are co-evolution and social bricoleurs.

2 See www.elvisandkesse.com, accessed 6 May 2014.

Co-evolution

Hockerts and Wüstenhagen (2010) characterise sustainable entrepreneurship as progressing through a dynamic interaction between 'Emerging Davids' and 'Greening Goliaths' and argue that the co-evolution of both types of business is more likely to result in sustainability than either of the two forms of enterprise acting alone. According to this interpretation, each scale of enterprise has aspects that cause reaction and facilitate opportunity for the other, so it is the sequential steps of each that drives progress. This is demonstrated in the way, for example, that once sustainability attributes are demonstrated to be of some market interest, providers of leading premium brands move to imitate the offering through extensions of their existing offerings. Demonstration of market demand can then induce a second wave of new entrepreneurship that has more growth ambition, better information and more resources than the first wave of new start-ups. Through both the greater threat to their market share and the further development of the market, incumbents may then react with further commitments to their sustainability-based business lines. With their greater capacity to combine cost and sustainability advantages than new entrants, the second wave of entrepreneurship tends to be squeezed as sustainability becomes part of the mainstream. This process of co-evolution has been observed in the food sector where dominant supermarket chains have successfully adapted to the new markets for local, organic and Fairtrade foods that were pioneered by green entrepreneurs who originally envisaged building alternative food networks (see Hockerts and Wüstenhagen 2010; Perry 2010).

Entrepreneurs as social bricoleurs

Where green entrepreneurship remains within the realm of small-scale values rather than profit-driven enterprise it has been characterised as belonging to 'social bricoleurs' (Zahra *et al.* 2009) or 'bioneers' (Schaltegger 2002). These entrepreneurs exist on the margin between the social and private sectors and are distinguished by a motivation to achieve environmental and social change more than an aspiration to build a profit-maximising business. While not driven by business ambition they can have certain advantages that enable them to survive alongside commercial enterprise. They can present their enterprise as radically different to established offerings and build a market from those who share their ideals. Seeding a market with social bricoleurs is a starting point for co-evolution; but not all instances of such seeding necessarily bring reaction from incumbents or produce a second wave of more substantial entrepreneurship. A tendency for single-issue campaigning can be one reason for failing to engender a larger transformation (Hockerts and Wüstenhagen 2010: 487). For example, within the food sector, green enterprises have variously aligned themselves to a Fairtrade or local produce agenda obtaining support from one faction but without offering a balanced sustainability agenda (Morgan 2010). Furthermore, Hockerts and Wüstenhagen (2010: 487) suggest that idealistic over-attachment to their particular sustainability mission can keep bricoleurs in small and exclusive market niches.

Luxury lodges and elegant disruption

Lodges are predominantly owner-managed independent undertakings driven by the values and lifestyle aspirations of the owner rather than by corporate commercial objectives. Of the 27 lodges that comprised Luxury Lodges of New Zealand in 2013, most have existed only since the 1990s and continue to be governed by their owner-founders. As explained by one interviewee:

> A feature of the New Zealand luxury lodge industry has been the role played by migrant entrepreneurs who have been inspired by the New Zealand environment and have been motivated to provide accommodation that complements their feelings for the environment. They have invested substantial resources in developing high quality facilities in excess of what is economically sensible in terms of delivering a reasonable return on the investment (lodge manager).

Lodge owners are motivated as well by the ability to exercise their personal interest in the services associated with providing lodge accommodation, such as fine cuisine and the blending of art and consumption (as in the interior design and furnishings). The vision also variously encompasses a goal of providing access to the landscape and natural environment in ways that retain qualities that attracted the investor to New Zealand, of which an aspect is the absence of intrusive commercial development.

The motivations among local lodge owners are similarly affected by lifestyle considerations and a personal conception of what constitutes an appropriate form of tourism for New Zealand. The ownership considerations have created space for sustainability concerns to be reflected in the design and management of the lodges. Of course, where the lodge is purpose-designed the opportunity to incorporate energy efficiency and other sustainability features, such as some use of renewable energy generation and locally-sourced recycled building materials, is greater than where a lodge is retro-fitted into an existing building. As well, the ability to claim a good sustainability performance is assisted by the scale of operation:

> There are some inherent features of luxury lodges that build on the environmental benefits of small-scale tourism. The physical operation generates less waste as . . . all food is prepared just-in-time to client orders: there are no set menus and no buffet bars to stock. There is no space required for reception areas and building space is used efficiently with no need to heat or light large communal areas (lodge owner).

Lodge operations and management further demonstrate owner affiliation to minimising the environmental footprint of the lodges. The luxury aspect common to lodges is the emphasis on a personalised, hosted experience that provides an informed introduction to the locality around the lodge. As expressed by three interviewees:

> A luxury lodge provides an experiential service based around an intimate, personal experience that introduces guests to the very best on offer in the surrounding environment (lodge manager).
>
> Nothing supplied by the lodge is pre-packaged. Guests are hosted with a set of activities including menus agreed in discussion between the designated host and the guest. This tends to steer guests to places and activities that most visitors would not participate in or be less likely to encounter (lodge manager).
>
> Our approach to luxury is to give people a sense that they are more like family friends visiting part of the family than paying guests (lodge owner).

This limits lodges to comparatively small-scale operations that range from three guest rooms to maximum capacities that rarely exceed the ability to accommodate more than 30 overnight guests. A few lodges have leisure amenities such indoor sports facilities, extensive private settings including a golf course and heliport, but the majority do not. Luxury lodges in New Zealand are thus a different type of product to lodges in low income countries that are located within game reserves or in areas of natural beauty without a history of international visitors (see Ryan and Stewart 2009). At the extreme, the Kaimata Retreat, located on the Otago Peninsula, comprises three guestrooms and a single shared lounge, dining and kitchen area. The luxury component is primarily in the dramatic siting of the lodge and the hosting provided by the on-site owners. Like other parts of New Zealand, the environment around the lodge is under stress particularly in terms of the loss of natural ecosystems and the gravely endangered indigenous wildlife (de Freitas and Perry 2012). The lodge could be simply a well-appointed overnight stay, enjoying access to landscape views. To varying degrees, through engagement with the hosts, guests are exposed to the lodge owners' passion and concerns for the surrounding environment. Other lodges may not confront their guests with the urgency of New Zealand's environmental challenges to the same degree, but most are primarily offering access to protected, natural environments.

Lodges directly engage with sustainability in a variety of ways (Table 8.1). Twelve of the 27 member lodges have sought Qualmark Enviro accreditation (New Zealand's main accreditation scheme judging the environmental performance of accommodation services), with seven achieving the highest level of accreditation (Enviro Gold). Of the four lodge owners/managers interviewed all were accredited and this was explained as a reflection of the interviewees' personal belief in the importance of showing environmental concern rather than as a way of influencing visitor choices. An aspect of the accreditation is involvement in community-based environment programmes, which in the case of the lodges includes support for wildlife protection initiatives and the regeneration of degraded ecosystems. Enviro accreditation also encourages demonstration of energy and water conservation and the use of 'best for the environment' cleaning products. Stressing 'genuine New Zealand hospitality', and being reliant on off-site service providers to augment their guest experience, gives the lodges reasons to integrate into their communities and to be viewed as 'good neighbours'. The use of local, seasonal produce and local labour are frequently emphasised. This integration helps to support services that rely on the protection of wilderness and indigenous culture. Luxury means high standards of cleanliness but two of the four lodges visited do offer an 'environmental choice' to minimise the extent of daily linen and towel changing. Others consider such an offering inconsistent with their product but have other ways to reduce resource use, such as providing a refillable bottle in place of bottled water and stressing the quality of their own water supply.

Table 8.1 **Luxury lodge examples of sustainability actions**

Source: Lodge websites accessed July 2013.

Lodge	Examples of sustainability actions
Blanket Bay www.blanketbay.com	• Qualmark Enviro Gold accreditation • Lodge owner is a director of WWF (America) • Negotiated access to a shared recycling collection service for themselves and other businesses in the nearby community • Lodges constructed using local building materials and local craftsman helped to revive local building skills • Support Department of Conservation pest eradication in areas around the lodge • Carbon emissions calculated • Waste composting on site and jointly with a neighbouring Wellness Centre • Minimise bottled water by providing self-fill bottles and encouraging use of the lodge's own bore water
Tiritiri Lodge www.tiritirilodge.com	• Qualmark Enviro Gold accreditation • Support of a programme to reintroduce the endangered South Island robin • Support a community-based action group promoting the uptake of environmental initiatives • More building includes extensive energy efficiency features beyond those justified by savings in energy costs • Environmental policy statement emphasises ecological responsibility and integration within the local community • Environmental choice offered to guests to reduce linen/towel usage
Pen-y-bryn Lodge www.penybryn.co.nz	• Qualmark Enviro Silver Gold accreditation • Heritage building adapted to include energy efficiency features • On-site composting
Kaimata Retreat www.kaimata.com	• Qualmark Enviro Silver Gold accreditation • Lodge constructed from locally-sourced materials • Bio diesel heating system installed • Regeneration of land with native vegetation • Remote, small lodge emphasising interaction with nature around the lodge

At the same time, some limitations need to be acknowledged with respect to the sustainability contributions. As expressed by one lodge owner interviewed:

> The mission and vision statement of the lodge stresses environmental responsibility and emphasis on fitting in with the locality and offering a specific experience ... the level of client interaction and our emphasis on introducing ... the local environment results in guests having a better chance of gaining appreciation of the environment than they would if visiting a luxury hotel; but we have some guests whose only interest is to go hunting and shooting.

Lodges with extensive landholdings can be controversial where this limits public access to areas of cultural and scenic importance or introduces new development (for example, see Remmerswaal 2003). Given the preponderance of new, purpose-designed lodges, some of the environmental gains are facilitated by their modern construction which gives more attention to energy efficiency than was done in the past. Indeed, Qualmark Enviro accreditation criteria were questioned by one interviewee who doubted that they were a reliable assessment of sustainability performance:

> The Qualmark system uses crude indicators to judge environmental performance. It is a tick box exercise that takes little notice of how changes in performance are achieved. It gives credit if annual utility expenditure is reducing, assuming this reflects energy conservation efforts whereas it may reflect changes in occupancy and temperatures (lodge owner).

Furthermore, lodges rely primarily on international visitors to New Zealand, but the environmental impact of long haul air travel is not part of the Qualmark assessment. As noted by one interviewee:

> I want to be sustainable and we have done a lot of things to support being sustainable, but I don't know if we can be with our guests travelling from far away (lodge owner).

Nonetheless, the various efforts taken in support of minimising the direct environmental impacts, and focus on service rather than physical amenity, do suggest unusual levels of responsibility compared with other forms of holiday accommodation.

The next part of this chapter turns to the second research question: 'How does the experience of New Zealand's luxury lodges fit with the concepts of co-evolution and social bricoleurs as applied to sustainability-based entrepreneurship? Do either of these concepts better capture the position of luxury lodges than elegant disruption?'

Luxury lodges and disruptive entrepreneurship

Some application of the disruptive trends Bendell (2012) identifies as supportive of elegant disruption is evident in the case of New Zealand's luxury lodges (Table 8.2). The lodges are part of a worldwide phenomenon in which various forms of boutique scale luxury accommodation have started to compete with international hotel chains. Lodges base their luxury on the provision of a service tailored to the individual customer and seek to genuinely treat visitors as house guests rather than as paying customers. New Zealand's proximity to Asia is helping to maintain the country's growth as a visitor destination, including both Asian nationals and expatriates on work assignments in the fast growing Asian economies. Originally best known as an adventure tourism location, the development of a luxury traveller market is partly dependent on attracting people away from places more widely recognised as providers of luxury accommodation. This builds on New Zealand's recent emergence as a high quality wine producing country and through the heightened priority to natural landscape as a motivation for travel (Molloy 1993; Pawson 1997).

Table 8.2 **Drivers of elegant disruption and application to luxury lodges**

Bendell's trends supporting elegant disruption	Mechanism of change	Application to luxury lodges in New Zealand
Evolving tastes	Luxury has lost mystique with consumers favouring new forms of luxury open to small enterprise innovation	Lodges are part of a growth in small-scale, hosted accommodation as an alternative to international luxury hotels
Critical transparency	Luxury consumers seek deeper engagement with their purchasing and exercise sensitivity to the conditions of production	Lodges provide authentic experiences based on personalised service
Hyper-connectivity	Consumers seek to engage with the suppliers of their favoured luxury purchases	Direct interaction between owner/manager and guest
Cultural shifts	Expansion of luxury consumption in East Asia weakens dominance of established Western luxury brands	New Zealand is comparatively proximate to East Asia
Transmodernism	Diverse understanding of what constitutes progress allows style leadership to originate outside established fashion centres	New Zealand is a new luxury travel destination building on a growth in appreciation of natural, undeveloped landscape

By offering a personalised service tailored to individual guests, without necessarily providing high levels of private amenity, lodges offer a particular form of luxury. Luxury hotels differ in their higher levels of physical amenity in the context of a venue where consumption is comparatively conspicuous and guests can publicly display their affiliation to a brand that is well known and widely aspired too.

The distinction is captured partly by the identification of two levels of luxury (Low cited in Moscardo 2013: 278). Lodges may be viewed as an aspect of the search for a 'new luxury' in which luxuries aim to 'evoke and engage consumers' emotions while feeding their aspirations for a better life' (Silverstein and Fiske 2003: 48). Unlike established luxury hotels, lodges do not aspire to combine high volume with exclusive pricing.

Affirming one of Bendell's (2012) drivers of elegant disruption, the lodge owners and managers use social media hoping to build a community around their lodge, but the significance of this is limited. As expressed by one interviewee:

> The visitor profile is predominantly people in their 50s and older and they are often not the most active with things like Facebook (lodge owner).

A practical problem, too, as identified by one lodge manager, is that with most guests staying no more than three nights, even during the summer peak, and most guests not planning a return trip to New Zealand, the interest in staying in touch with the lodge is frequently low.

While luxury lodges reflect some aspects of Bendell's drivers for elegant disruption they also illustrate his two sources of doubt (Table 8.3). As discussed above, these doubts are uncertainty that sustainable luxuries can be scaled up and that they generate an overall shift in consumer purchasing in favour of sustainable options.

Table 8.3 **Constraints on elegant disruption**

Constraint	Impediment to overcome	Prospect for luxury lodges
Ability to scale-up sustainable luxury	The business model must be capable of expanding without damaging the rarity value of the luxury and while building broader aspiration for the sustainable attributes	Essence of the lodge product is small-scale, personal service. Business expansion can be less important than maintaining lifestyle
Rebound and displacement	Availability of the sustainable luxury should act to discourage patronage of other goods and services rather than be viewed as a justification for discounting environmental attributes of other purchases	New Zealand lodges exist within the context of New Zealand as an international travel destination. Travellers tend to maintain an interest in visiting other destinations without New Zealand becoming a generally preferred destination

First, to be a disruptive phenomenon of significance to a larger transition to sustainability there must be strong, unsatisfied aspiration that drives a change in the preferences of mainstream consumers. Bendell's (2012) illustration is Tesla and its development of a luxury, high performance, electric vehicle that aims to change the image of electric vehicles and increase the prospects for a wider acceptance of the technology (see Waters 2013). This relies on the Tesla luxury electric car first establishing itself akin to the Ferrari sports car whose annual production remains well below the potential demand (Kapferer and Bastien 2009: 70). Such an aspirational brand influences how the larger population of people who aspire to, but cannot own, a Ferrari conceive of the attributes of a vehicle that they would like to own. In a similar way Tesla aims to change the perception of electric cars by first developing an aspirational brand. Applied to luxury lodges, this implies a two-step process if there is to be an incidence of elegant disruption: first, encourage aspiration for the luxury; second, diffuse the sustainability aspects of the aspirational product to mainstream offerings. There are reasons to doubt that New Zealand's luxury lodges can take the first of these steps.

According to the 'anti laws of marketing', to retain its luxury credentials a luxury brand must have far more people who know it and dream of it than people who buy it (Kapferer and Bastien 2009: 70) as 'true' luxury should excel in the practice of distributing rarity (Kapferer and Bastien 2009: 71). New Zealand's luxury lodges are linked to international marketing initiatives such as Small Luxury Hotels of the World[3] that are partly attempting to build an aspirational brand. They may also seek inclusion in international rankings of exclusive destinations. Equally, many of the lodges belong to national marketing initiatives too in addition to the Luxury Lodge of New Zealand membership, which reflects a reality that many of the lodges are not sufficiently secure to be able to emphasise their rarity value or to forsake efforts to increase demand for their product. This economic insecurity has tended to increase in recent years with one interviewee stating:

> The GFC [global financial crisis] unleashed a perfect storm for the luxury lodge segment that they have not fully recovered from. It encouraged people to hang on to their wealth given their uncertainty as to the security of their wealth ... wealthy individuals turn to high end hotels at the expense of lodges (lodge manager).

The same lodge manager also noted how lodge visitors have changed in behaviour:

> In the past, there would have been little or no interest in sharing a helicopter: today it is more likely that people will wish to share than book out the helicopter for their own use.

Even assuming that confidence returns to the luxury market, it is also evident that New Zealand's luxury lodges are challenged to sell their particular brand of luxury with its emphasis on offering a personal experience rather than high physical amenity:

> Isolation and the lack of facilities are an issue with some guests, including the small size of rooms ... sometimes not large enough for the amounts of luggage our guests have. Complaints are few but it is evident that some guests are under-whelmed (lodge owner).

3 www.slh.com/, accessed 28 May 2014.

A form of exclusivity is supported by some lodge owners but without the purpose required to promote elegant disruption. A desire to scale-up the venture or encourage a larger shift in visitor behaviour is not part of the ambition of the lodge owners interviewed. Rather than seeking to expand their operations, lodge owners may see their importance as demonstrating the viability of small-scale ventures geared to high value visitors in place of the mass market tourism on which the larger industry depends. This view was put by one interviewee in the following way:

> Luxury lodges are merely the top end of a national industry that should emphasise small-scale, customised travel experiences. The possibility exists for New Zealand to go further in developing a more selective industry based on fewer travellers that individually stay longer and spend more ... In this regard the focus of Air New Zealand and government promotion of tourism on expanding visitor numbers is wrong (lodge owner).

Such a transition would result in New Zealand's tourism becoming an exclusive product whereas elegant disruption occurs only when sustainability attributes become part of mainstream products.

Second, Bendell (2012) identifies rebound and displacement effects as potential constraints on elegant disruption and this is certainly evident in the case of luxury lodges. Lodges rely mainly on international travellers who are visiting New Zealand rather than being attracted specifically by the attributes of the lodge at which they stay. As stated by one lodge manager interviewed: 'High net worth individuals typically wish to experience different places and the lodge is simply part of that larger motivation'. Another lodge owner wished to believe that a stay at the lodge changed their guests' appreciation of the environment but was uncertain this occurred:

> Many [guests] go away with a deeper appreciation of the environment and having reflected on the importance of protecting nature but for long distance travellers [around 95% of the lodge's guests] New Zealand may be a once only trip given they have the world to choose from and we probably don't change their future travel decisions (lodge owner).

This makes a lodge different to other luxury goods and services that are consumed in their own right. Lodges are mainly consumed as an ancillary to the 'main attraction', with the lodge tending to encourage this with the emphasis on hosting a visit to their locality as part of a larger visit to New Zealand. The ability of a lodge to change perceptions of desirable travel experiences is constrained by the product being centred on the environment to which travellers are introduced, rather than the lodge itself. Some guests may view the environment as primarily a playground for hunting wildlife or as a scenic backdrop for golf played on an exclusive course. As expressed by one interviewee:

> Some guests, perhaps many, are likely to stay in other six star destinations in Thailand, Bali and Sumatra as well as Africa. They rationalise the impact of their travel wherever they go ... We even get right wing Texans staying who would argue that they do great things when they go hunting

> in Africa by putting a price on endangered wildlife that protects them from poachers. The first thing they may do [here] is go hunting for thar [by helicopter] (lodge owner).

Similarly, while lodge owners may see it as positive that the lodge employs local staff, one interviewee commented:

> Some guests from Asia may live in homes with housekeepers and servants and have no problems with staying in lodges where there are low paid staff. They are capable of treating [our] lodge staff as minions (lodge owner).

Hosts would need to articulate a clear environmental message to provide guests with a consistent outcome. This, in theory, might be possible since one of the signifiers of a luxury can be the way that it dominates the client and acts as an adviser, educator and sociological guide to those not yet sharing the culture and values on which the luxury is built (Kapferer and Bastien 2009). Preserving the status of a luxury brand is partly about maintaining a distance from the client based on promoting attributes that can be recognised as denoting luxury but that may not yet be shared by the consumer of the luxury. This works within limits of maintaining the image of the luxury as a reward; it is not an opportunity for overt advocacy of preferred behaviours, as would be required to ensure all lodge guests took a consistent message from their experience. As observed by one lodge manager interviewed: 'Visitors to luxury lodges tend to see their expenditure and impact as helpful regardless of the activity they engage in while staying at the lodge'.

Co-evolution or social bricoleurs?

Given reasons to doubt that luxury lodges have attributes capable of contributing to an elegant disruption, it is appropriate to consider whether other models of green entrepreneurship fit luxury lodges. Within the scope of the present study, it is possible to offer some preliminary observations on the potential of lodges to engender a co-evolution towards sustainability, or whether they are better viewed as examples of social bricoleurs.

The possibility that luxury lodges will bring a reaction from mainstream luxury accommodation providers is doubtful for broadly similar reasons as question the likelihood of lodges contributing to an elegant disruption. In a co-evolutionary process, mainstream luxury accommodation providers (mainly comprising luxury hotel chains) might respond by developing small-scale establishments outside their existing locations close to areas of natural beauty. To date there has been no such reaction in New Zealand. Without insight into the strategic planning of the large hotel groups, the prospects that a reaction may arise can only be speculated upon. The growth of international groupings of luxury lodge and luxury boutique hotels such as Small Luxury Hotels of the World has potential to raise the market significance of the sector. For the present, the scale of lodges means that, even if operating at high levels of occupancy, they are not building a market that challenges the viability of large hotels. Instead there is a degree to which the lodges are helpful to mainstream hotels as their customer base is principally international visitors to New Zealand who combine their lodge stay with time in other places and forms of accommodation. A comment from two of the lodge managers interviewed is that, as part of their focus on introducing guests to New Zealand, they encourage visitors to sample other locations and make use of other forms of accommodation. It can also be noted that major hotel chains are able, and have responded, to sustainability concerns without adjusting their scale of operation. The pressure to do so has less to do with the emergence of alternative accommodation providers than with the financial benefits of better energy and waste management, and the need to respond to concerns raised about the environmental impacts of international travel (Bohdanowicz 2005; Bohdanowicz and Zientara 2009).

The mix of commercial and lifestyle objectives among lodge owners is consistent with an aspect of being a social bricoleur who are envisaged as being motivated to address social needs rather than to build growth-orientated enterprises. In Zahra *et al.*'s (2008) classification, social bricoleurs are a form of social enterprise different to social constructionists and engineers by a focus on small-scale local needs and their lack of ambition to covert an entire sector of economic activity. Lodges may be viewed as a form of social enterprise through their dependence on the motivations of owners to provide a standard of service that is personally satisfying rather than being a product of profit maximising objectives. As noted above, some broader social benefit may also be claimed in their support of low volume, high value tourism which imposes less pressure on the environment than mass market tourism. The emphasis on local knowledge is inconsistent with Zahra *et al.*'s (2008) description of social bricoleurs. According to their typology, bricoleurs build their enterprise on 'intimate knowledge of both local environmental conditions and locally available resources' with the attention to previously indiscernible or unrecognised social needs being a principal contribution of this form of entrepreneurship (Zahra *et al.* 2008: 524). The preponderance of international or immigrant entrepreneurs among lodge owners, and the extent to which lodges are reliant on overseas visitors, are at odds with the emphasis on local knowledge and needs. A form of local attachment occurs in the extent to which lodges seek to integrate within their local economies, partly through their interest in providing lodge guests with destination experiences and in offering an authentic experience of which one aspect is the use of local resources. Rather than being uniquely positioned to discover local social needs, as in Zahra *et al.*'s (2008: 524) account of social bricoleurs, luxury lodge entrepreneurs may be more distinguished by their willingness to draw on local resources rather than the making of purely commercial operating decisions. A consistency is that lodge entrepreneurs, sometimes being wealthy individuals, are not reliant on numerous external resources to achieve their objectives and they do not see themselves as developing a business model that replaces other forms of luxury accommodation.

Conclusion

Where luxury accommodation: is located within or near to areas of natural beauty; emphasises low impact visitor experiences; and promotes awareness of environmental issues, then tourism is an area where sustainability and luxury have the potential to be mutually supportive. Luxury Lodges of New Zealand is a collective marketing group representing 27 independently owned and operated lodges that is making this connection. Judged against other forms of premium accommodation, the investment in sustainability features is high. With a focus on providing luxury through an experience customised to the individual guest rather than through high levels of physical amenity, and with exclusive access to destination attractions, luxury lodges are able to claim a commitment to sustainability. Nonetheless, judged against the benchmark of elegant disruption, this case study reveals reasons to doubt that luxury lodges have wider significance as a model that shows how luxury consumption can be at the forefront of a transition to sustainability. Of two contrasting interpretations developed in the larger context of green entrepreneurship, preliminary observations suggest social bricoleurs is the concept closest to luxury lodges. This places lodges as a form of social enterprise and recognises how they are motivated by a vision of a preferred form of visitor accommodation in which commercial considerations are not paramount. An alternative proposition—that lodges may participate in a co-evolutionary shift towards sustainable business practice—is considered unlikely given that mainstream accommodation providers serving the luxury segment are not threatened by a significant loss of their market. Neither are mainstream providers being directed to new business practices or being challenged to respond to sustainability concerns in ways that cannot be incorporated within their existing business models.

As accommodation providers in their own right, lodges can be credited with helping to achieve the aspirations of New Zealand's destination marketing agencies to have the country viewed as a 'pure' location distinguished by high commitment to wilderness and ecosystem protection. A truly disruptive luxury changes the attributes of a product or service that consumers as a whole aspire to gain access to. Luxury lodges in New Zealand incorporate sustainable business aspects into their offering and, while this chapter has offered no direct comparison with other types of luxury accommodation, it does suggest that the commitment to sustainability is high among luxury lodges. This occurs partly because of the scale of lodge operations whereby a comparative lack of physical luxury is offset by the focus on delivering a personalised service customised to individual guests. Nonetheless, the difficulty of identifying a pathway through which the luxury lodge product will scale-up, and the fact that the perception of lodge guests about the value of sustainability does not seem to be influenced by their stay at a luxury lodge, are reasons to doubt the disruptive potential of luxury lodges. Luxury lodges in New Zealand are a niche product that compromise on some aspects of luxury, but which are generally experienced as part of a one-off visit to New Zealand that does not cause any reconsideration of either the appropriate places to visit or forms of travel in which to participate.

Bibliography

Bendell, J. (2012) *Elegant Disruption: How Luxury and Society Can Change Each Other for Good*, Asia Pacific Work in Progress Research Paper Series 9 (Brisbane: Asia Pacific Centre for Sustainable Enterprise, Griffith University).

Bendell, J., and A. Kelanthous (2007) *Deeper Luxury* (Godalming, UK: WWF).

Bohdanowicz, P. (2005) 'European Hoteliers' Environmental Attitudes: Greening the Business', *Cornell Hotel and Restaurant Administration Quarterly* 46: 188-204.

Bohdanowicz, P., and P. Zientara (2009) 'Hotel Companies' Contribution to Improving the Quality of Life of Local Communities and the Wellbeing of Their Employees', *Tourism and Hospitality Research* 9.2: 147-58.

Braungart, M., and W. McDonough (1998) 'The Next Industrial Revolution', *The Atlantic Monthly*, October 1998: 82-92.

Christensen, C. (1997) *The Innovator's Dilemma: When New Technologies Cause Great Firms to Fail* (Boston, MA: Harvard University Business School Press).

de Freitas, C., and M. Perry (2012) *New Environmentalism: Managing New Zealand's Environmental Diversity* (Dordrecht, The Netherlands: Springer).

Dryzek, J. (1997) *The Politics of the Earth: Environmental Discourses* (Oxford, UK: Oxford University Press).

Gray, M. (2002) 'The Micro Level Matters: Evidence from the Bio-Pharmaceutical Industry', *Zeitschrift für Wirtschaftsgeographie* 46: 124-36.

Gössling, S., C. Hansson, O. Horstmeier and S. Saggel (2002) 'Ecological Footprint Analysis as a Tool to Assess Tourism Sustainability', *Ecological Economics* 43: 199-211.

Hart, S., and M. Milstein (1999) 'Global Sustainability and the Creative Destruction of Industries', *Sloan Management Review* 41.1: 23-33.

Heather, B. (2013) 'Surge in Rich Gaining NZ Residency', *New Zealand Herald* (30 September 2013; www.stuff.co.nz/business/industries/9223975/Surge-in-rich-gaining-NZ-residency, accessed 24 October 2013).

Hockerts, K. (2006) 'CaféDirect: A Social Entrepreneurial Fair Trade Success', in F. Perrini (ed.), *The New Social Entrepreneurship: What Awaits Social Entrepreneurial Ventures* (Cheltenham, UK: Edward Elgar).

Hockerts, K., and R. Wüstenhagen (2010) 'Greening Goliaths Versus Emerging Davids: Theorizing About the Role of Incumbents and New Entrants in Sustainable Entrepreneurship', *Journal of Business Venturing* 25: 481-92.

Holt, D. (2011) 'The Longitudinal Evolution of Environmental "Ecopreneurs" from the 1990s: Mergers and Acquisitions and the Waste Management Industry"', G. Eweje and M. Perry (eds.), *Business and Sustainability: Concepts, Strategies and Changes* (Bradford, UK: Emerald).

Jänicke, M. (2008) 'Ecological Modernization: New Perspectives', *Journal of Cleaner Production* 16: 557-65.

Kapferer, J., and V. Bastien (2009) *The Luxury Strategy* (London: Kogan Page, 2nd edn).

Kenney, M. (2009) *Venture Capital Investment in the Greentech Industries: A Provocative Essay*, Berkeley Roundtable on the International Economy Working Paper 185.

Lovins, A., L. Lovins and P. Hawken (1999) *Natural Capitalism: Creating the Next Industrial Revolution* (New York: Little Brown).

Maresco, P., and B. Lyons (2005) 'Achieving Growth in the Luxury Market', *Strategic Finance*, May 2005: 47.
Mastrelli, T. (2007) 'Luxury With a Conscience', *Hospitality Design* 29.6: 87-92.
Molloy, L. (1993) 'The Interpretation of New Zealand's Natural Heritage', in M. Hall and S. McArthur (eds.), *Heritage Management in New Zealand and Australia* (Auckland: Oxford University Press).
Morgan, K. (2010) 'Local and Green, Global and Fair: The Ethical Foodscape and the Politics of Care', *Environment and Planning A* 42: 1852-67.
Moscardo, G. (2013) 'Marketing and Sustainability', in G. Mascardo, G. Lamberton, G. Wells, W. Fallon, P. Lawn, A. Rowe, J. Humphrey, R. Wiesner, B. Pettitt, D. Clifton, M. Renouf and W. Kershaw (eds.), *Sustainability in Australian Business: Principles and Practice* (Milton, Queensland: John Wiley & Sons Australia).
Moscardo, G., and P. Benckendorff (2010) 'Sustainable Luxury: Oxymoron or Comfortable Bedfellows?' paper presented at the *Global Sustainable Tourism Conference*, Nelspruit, South Africa, 15–19 November 2010.
Pawson, E. (1997) 'Branding Strategies and Language of Consumption', *New Zealand Geographer* 53.2: 16-21.
Perry, M. (2010) *Controversies in Local Economic Development* (Abingdon, UK: Routledge).
Porter, M., and M. Kramer (2006) 'Strategy and Society: The Link Between Competitive Advantage and Corporate Responsibility', *Harvard Business Review*, December 2006: 1-17.
Porter, M., and M. Kramer (2011) 'Creating Shared Value', *Harvard Business Review*, January–February 2011: 1-17.
Rainey, D. (2006) *Sustainable Business Development* (Cambridge, UK: Cambridge University Press).
Remmerswaal, L. (2003) *Cape Kidnappers: David Versus Goliath Plus the Council* (www.converge.org.nz/watchdog/05/08.htm, accessed 29 May 2013).
Ryan, C., and M. Stewart (2009) 'Eco-Tourism and Luxury: The Case of Al Maha, Dubai', *Journal of Sustainable Tourism* 17.3: 287-301.
Schaltegger, S. (2002) 'A Framework for Ecopreneurship: Leading Bioneers and Environmental Managers to Ecopreneurship', *Greener Management International* 38: 45-58.
Silverstein, M., and N. Fiske (2003) 'Luxury for the Masses', *Harvard Business Review*, April 2003: 48-57.
Towner, J., and G. Wall (1991) 'History and Tourism', *Annals of Tourism Research* 18: 71-84.
Waters, R. (2013) 'Inside Business: Real Tests Still Lie Ahead for Tesla', *Financial Times* (3 July 2013; www.ft.com/intl/cms/s/0/b81abf26-e3fc-11e2-b35b-00144feabdc0.html?siteedition=intl#axzz2hv8RzGU2, accessed 17 October 2013).
Yin, R. (1989) *Case Study Research Design and Methods* (Newbury Park, CA: Sage).
Zahra, S.A., E. Gedajlovic, D.O. Neubaum and J.M. Shulman (2009) 'A Typology of Social Entrepreneurs: Motives, Search Processes and Ethical Challenges', *Journal of Business Venturing* 24: 519-32.

Martin Perry teaches business and sustainability in the School of Management, Massey University (Wellington). With an academic background prior to his current appointment in geography and urban planning, his research interests are mainly in the area of local economic development and small enterprise. His most recent books include *New Environmentalism: Managing New Zealand's Environmental Diversity* (published by Springer and co-authored with Chris de Freitas) and *Controversies in Local Economic Development* (Routledge) which was voted best book 2011 by the UK-based Regional Studies Association. Email: m.perry@massey.ac.nz

9

Diversity of human capital as a driver for corporate responsibility engagement

The case of the luxury industry

Catarina Pessanha Gomes and Masaru Yarime
University of Tokyo, Japan

The emergence and evolution of corporate responsibility: from philanthropy to innovation

Corporate responsibility (CR)[1] emerged these last decades as a response to civil society's pressure for increased consideration of sustainable development objectives into business practices. As the negative impacts of globalisation become more visible (Korten 1995, Stiglitz 2006), corporations started to deal with growing expectations from civil society to address sustainable development challenges, among them environmental problems, including forest degradations, mining destruction, climate change and social issues such as workers' and communities' rights (Auld *et al.* 2008). The increased organisational capacity of non-governmental

1 This article does not use the term 'corporate social responsibility' as some authors argue that it may exclude the environmental responsibilities of the private sector (DesJardins 1998).

organisations (NGOs) gave rise to protest movements that could lead to reputational damage, loss of fidelity and negative financial performances. This contributed to the emergence of CR as a voluntary initiative of the business sector to go further than mere compliance and to tackle its economic, environmental and social responsibilities (Halme and Laurila 2009) in an equal and balanced way.

However, CR initiatives used to be largely focused on ethical actions with little significant strategic impact to business firms, presenting no real change for the environment or society. Indeed, early critics of CR pointed out that CR actions were mainly concentrated on areas with no link with the company's core business activities, such as charity and philanthropy, rather than addressing the environmental or social challenges of the industry, and therefore creating only marginal societal impact (Porter and Kramer 2006). Furthermore, CR could be a source of competitive disadvantage for firms, as they were giving financial resources without positive repercussion (Aupperle *et al.* 1985).

Nevertheless, recent development in the CR concept indicates that it has the potential to transform markets trends, provide firms with competitive advantage and create meaningful societal impact. Previous discussions on the impacts of CR both in financial performances and society were not distinguishing between different types of CR, ignoring the fundamental dissimilarities between various initiatives with different purposes and impacts. In order to remedy this gap, Halme and Laurila (2009) developed a typology based on the relationship between different types of CR and the core business, target and expected benefits. This action-oriented typology distinguishes between 'philanthropic', 'integrative' and 'innovative' CR (Table 9.1).

Table 9.1 **Comparison of CR types**

Source: Adapted from Halme, M., and J. Laurila (2009) 'Philanthropy, Integration or Innovation? Exploring the Financial and Societal Outcomes of Different Types of Corporate Responsibility', *Journal of Business Ethics* 84.3: 325-15. With kind permission from Springer Science and Business Media.

	Philanthropic CR	**Integrative CR**	**Innovative CR**
Relationship to core business	Outside of firm's core business	Close to existing core business	Enlarging core business or developing new business
Target of responsibility	Extra activities	Environmental and social performance of existing business operations	New product or service development
Expected benefit	Image improvement and other reputation impacts	Improvements to environmental and social aspects of core business	Alleviation of social and environmental problems

Firms engaging in philanthropic CR are pursuing reputation preservation, therefore engaging in activities outside the business firm and receiving no direct business benefit from them. By contrast, firms who concentrate their CR activities in integrative CR are internalising the negative externalities in their core business, by implementing policies to improve environmental and social operational impacts in their core business. The expected benefits of this approach include cost and risk reduction and reputational improvement. The last type of CR sees environmental or social problems not as constraints but as a source of business innovation and creativity, and seeks to develop new products to solve these issues. This approach has strong potential benefits both for business and society because it is built on a win-win approach. By creating new products, services or business models beneficial for the environment and society, the company is also strategically investing in its future, and in a source of competitive advantage. While it is often argued that both integrative and innovative CR could bring more benefits to the firm and to society than philanthropy (Hillman and Keim 2001; Porter and Kramer 2006), innovative CR could potentially be the more profitable approach (Halme and Laurila 2009). Yet there is still lack of empirical research on the potential benefits and implementation barriers to this innovative form of CR.

Organisational challenges to innovation: the business case for diversity

Previous research considered the potential of innovation for sustainability, either in creating new products or, from an environmental or social perspective, superior production processes such as ecodesign or sustainable design (Carrano and Thorn 2006), or investing into organisational innovation such as changes in the organisational structure, corporate strategy and management techniques to create a favourable ground for the implementation of sustainability strategies (Preuss 2010).

However, innovation requires the promotion of human capital leading to imaginative mindsets and increased learning capabilities (Griffiths 2004), characteristics that tend to emerge in a diverse environment. Indeed, empirical research connected highly diverse teams to different thinking processes, increased creativity, and unconventional knowledge (Cox 1994; Higgs *et al.* 2005; Leung *et al.* 2008). In particular, diversity in educational backgrounds and gender were associated with greater innovative performances (Østergaard *et al.* 2011).

Yet in order to benefit from diversity, companies need an appropriate organisational culture and management strategy so that innovative performance will be actually achieved. In this sense, the organisational culture appears as a moderator of the relationship between diversity and organisational performance

(Dwyer *et al.* 2001). According to these authors, diversity benefits from an informal organisational culture characterised by flexibility and spontaneity. Therefore, internal conditions, such as organisational culture and diversity management, are essential to create favourable conditions for innovation and organisational performance.

The luxury sector: late adopter of corporate responsibility

The luxury sector was reticent to adopt and communicate their CR practices. According to Lochard and Murat (2011), the longevity of its products, often transmitted from generation to generation, constitute an opposition to the often-criticised mass consumption and mass production system principally responsible for resource depletion. Furthermore, the nature of luxury sector businesses does not have an obvious impact on the environment, unlike heavy impact industries such as energy or chemical industries.

The criticism expressed by civil society regarding CR practices of luxury companies (Bendell and Kleanthous 2007), especially regarding the sourcing and use of materials, was a wake-up call for the major actors in this industry. NGOs such as Global Witness, PETA and Greenpeace took robust action concerning the sourcing of diamonds, the use of animal skin or the toxicity of the cosmetics industry, by alerting consumers to the hidden practices of major luxury companies. In response, CR started to appear as fundamental in order to preserve brand image and corporate reputation—key strategic issues for the luxury sector. Even though CR was only considered under its philanthropy and integration forms, and few companies saw its potential to leverage competitive advantage.

However, considering CR as a competitive advantage could open new markets and business opportunities to the industry. Indeed, wealthy consumers have increased their expectations for the CR of luxury brands, a tendency that is not limited to developed countries. About 57% of wealthy Americans are willing to pay more for socially and environmentally responsible products (Le Monde 2010 (Lochard and Murat 2011) and this trend is shared by two-thirds of Chinese luxury clients (Lau 2010). In order to maintain and conquer these new markets, which are strategically important for the future of luxury brands, firms should reconsider CR as a business advantage. Moreover, the trend of ecodesign and eco-products is penetrating the luxury market and a number of new luxury eco-brands are emerging, conciliating luxury products and services with sustainable development objectives and responding to the aspiration of the wealthy responsible consumer (Lochard and Murat 2011). For the time being, these brands remain marginal but constitute an important phenomenon, and historical luxury brands should consider that seriously in order to preserve their central position. It all points to the fact that sustainable development will increasingly be an additional element of distinction and prestige for luxury brands. Indeed, as sustainable development becomes of greater value in our society, it will be increasingly desired by all but only available to a few: a perfect match with the essence of luxury (Bastien and Kapferer 2012). As we have seen, market opportunities for more strategic CR do exist, but in order to engage in meaningful strategies, the sector has to reflect on its strengths and transformative potential in order to create a meaningful impact in the society. In this regard, luxury firms have a major impact on consumer behaviour (Bendell and Kleanthous 2007) and therefore could propagate environmentally and socially responsible consumption behaviour patterns both to elite and mass consumers. Moreover, luxury firms have a considerable transformative potential in other industries (Bendell and Kleanthous 2007), which could be used to stimulate the offer of eco-products if those are desirable and unique in the mass market. Innovative CR of luxury firms should therefore concentrate on engaging with consumers on sustainability by diffusing new values and consumption behaviour, as well as increasing their offer on eco-products and environmentally friendly design and conception.

Objective and methodology

As previously discussed, diversity can be a source of innovation and creativity for companies with an inclusive organisational culture, even though there is a lack of empirical research on how organisational structures, strategies and management techniques addressing the issue of diversity relate to the firm's CR, particularly in the luxury sector.

Therefore, our research objective is to answer the following questions:

- Which luxury companies are pursuing innovative CR strategies?
- What is their organisational culture regarding diversity?
- Are they considering diversity as a potential driver for innovation and creativity?

The research methodology encompassed a research design that entailed a qualitative analysis of the company's CR and diversity strategy. A case study approach was selected in order to allow in-depth studies of individual companies and comparisons between cases. The sample size included companies selected on the basis of highest annual revenue in the financial year 2009 (Lochard and Murat 2011). The sample group includes: Louis Vuitton Moët Hennessy (LVMH); Estée Lauder (ELC); Richemont; Luxottica; Shiseido; L'Oréal; Ralph Lauren; PPR; Swatch; Coach; Tiffany & Co.; Hermès; Armani; Hugo Boss; Prada; Burberry; and Safilo.

The data were collected mainly from publicly available secondary data sources, such as information contained in annual reports, sustainability and environmental reports and organisational profiles. Such sources have been used in previous assessments of CR strategies (Arnold 2010). Data were collected and analysed on the economic, environmental and social dimensions of CR (see Table 9.2).

Table 9.2 **Indicators for CR strategy**

Economic indicators	Environmental indicators	Social indicators
• Code of ethics • Supply chain management • Stakeholder engagement • Contribution to society • Sustainability reporting • Sustainability communication to consumers • Executive commitment to sustainability • Employee engagement	• Water management • Energy management • Waste management • Environmental management system • Transport • Material sourcing • Biodiversity protection and conservation • Renewable energies • Product design	• Employee training • Employee empowerment • Health • Safety • Product safety • Human rights • Customer feed-back

In order to evaluate the firm's strategies regarding these issues, an index of corporate commitment to CR was constructed, evaluating policies in the three areas of environmental, economic and social sustainability. Each indicator is scaled on three levels: high; medium; and low sustainability (Kinderyte 2010). The detailed performances of the 17 companies can be found in Appendix 9.1. These findings were analysed using a cluster matrix analysis (Miles and Huberman 1994) for the purpose of identifying common strategic orientation regarding CR as philanthropic, integrative or innovative.

As for the analysis of the diversity management and organisational culture, data were collected on policies for the promotion and inclusion of diversity (gender, age, ethnicity, nationalities, disabilities and sexual orientation), as well as data on the company's vision and discourse around diversity.

Results and discussion

Characterising CR strategies is challenging because, as with other business strategies, they are multidimensional and often encompass several objectives and elements. The cluster analysis revealed three main common patterns of behaviour and discourse around sustainability, namely integrative CR, innovative CR and philanthropic CR (see Table 9.3).

Table 9.3 **Cluster analysis of CR strategies**

Companies	CR score	CR strategy	Objective	Characteristics
ELC LVMH L'Oréal Shiseido PPR	High	Innovative CR	Sustainability-driven innovation seen as a competitive business advantage	• Ecodesign and green innovation • Communication with consumers on sustainability issues • Integrated environmental management
Tiffany Richemont Burberry Luxottica Hermes Boss Swatch	Moderate	Integrative CR	Preserve reputation and brand integrity by acting as an ethical and responsible company	• Manage negative environmental operational impacts • Control risks in the supply chain
Coach Safilo Ralph Lauren Armani Prada	Low	Philanthropic CR	Compliance with national law and regulation	• Charity and sponsorship • Traditional employee volunteering

Cluster 1: Innovative CR

This cluster includes ELC, LVMH, L'Oréal, Shiseido and PPR. All of these firms have high scores regarding economic, social and environmental performances.

Companies in this cluster approach CR from a strategic perspective, in order to obtain a competitive advantage in the industry, by conciliating innovation and traditional skills. This group of companies believes that sustainability pursued with innovation and creativity can be a part of their business model and they emphasise the role of sustainability innovation in their corporate sustainability strategy. By doing so, they concentrate their CR efforts on their core business, in order to create value both for the company and for society.

Therefore, companies in this cluster are concentrating their sustainability efforts on key aspects for luxury brands. Common characteristics of this cluster include integrating environmental performance when designing luxury products, improving their offer of eco-products and communicating their sustainability initiatives to consumers. This emphasis on innovation is supplemented by a risk management approach aimed at managing their operational environmental and social impacts, as well as various forms of corporate philanthropy. Some representative examples of this cluster's initiatives are the development of environmentally friendly products considering their life-cycle, including material sourcing, biodiversity protection, and end-of-life impact management, such as green chemistry or eco-bags, as well as direct communication to consumers about sustainability, for example in the form of smartphone applications to orient clients towards sustainable consumption.

Cluster 2: Integrative CR

Tiffany, Richemont, Burberry, Hugo Boss, Luxottica, Swatch and Hermes have a moderate score on their CR performances.

They consider CR as a means to maintain an ethical image and avoid brand criticism in order to preserve their reputation of excellence and prestige. As reputation is the main competitive advantage of luxury companies, their CR strategy is oriented towards the preservation and diffusion of the image of a responsible business.

Therefore, they concentrate their CR efforts on managing operational risks, managing negative environmental impacts, controlling risks in the supply chain on issues such as human and labour rights through codes of conduct and audit programmes, and via strategic philanthropy in the communities in which they operate. We could quote the adhesion to mechanisms to diffuse and regulate practices in the industry, such as the Responsible Jewellery Council,[2] which is committed to the regulation of human rights, and social and environmental practices in the gold and diamond supply chain. Other examples include environmental management systems to regulate CO_2 emissions, water and waste. Strategic philanthropic activities include supporting NGOs' work with local communities or the transmission of traditional skills to apprentices.

Cluster 3: Philanthropic CR

Coach, Ralph Lauren, Prada, Safilo and Armani have low scores regarding their involvement with CR.

This group of companies consider CR mostly under its traditional compliance and moral philanthropy form, such as setting up charitable foundations or sponsorships, employee volunteering in non-strategic areas, and risk management and CR to cope with risk associated with supply chains. There is no inclusion of environmental sustainability or policies to reduce negative environmental impacts. Four out of the five companies have a general opacity concerning working conditions in terms of training, health and safety; most of the companies appear as a CR blank screen to the public. Common characteristics include sponsorship of the arts and charities through corporate foundations and employee volunteering programmes.

2 www.responsiblejewellery.com/, accessed 29 May 2014.

Results analysis

An analysis of the organisational culture and diversity management programmes of these companies revealed different patterns among the clusters, regarding the perception and organisational culture of CR and diversity management (Table 9.4).

Table 9.4 **Research findings regarding CR and diversity management**

Cluster	CR strategy	Number of companies	Vision of diversity	Organisational culture regarding diversity
1	Innovative CR	5	Diversity perceived as a business advantage, fostering innovation and a better understanding of consumers	Inclusive culture: strong promotion of various types of diversity through diversity management programmes, bodies and recruitment policies
2	Integrative CR	6	Respect for diversity is seen as a component of responsible business	Equal opportunity culture: promotion of individual talent without discrimination through monitoring
		1	Strategic importance of understanding and promoting diversity as it contributes to the business strategy	Inclusive culture: strong promotion of various types of diversity through diversity management programmes, bodies and recruitment policies
3	Philanthropic CR	5	No consideration of diversity beyond compliance	Several cases of discrimination and harassment despite official policy of non-discrimination and harassment in codes of conduct

Companies in the innovative CR cluster perceive diversity as a business advantage to foster innovation, sustainability and a better understanding of the variety of consumers and stakeholders. Indeed, they refer to diversity as part of their corporate culture, a competitive success factor as diversity is a source of creativity and innovation. Companies affirm that diversity contributes to emerging new values and the ability to adapt business strategy to a changing environment. In order to enable diversity to play its expected role, this group of companies encourages an inclusive culture regarding various types of diversity and implements several actions to promote the heterogeneity of its workforce. The consideration of diversity is large; all companies promote at least two types of diversity, with L'Oréal emphasising on six types of diversity (age, gender, nationalities, ethnic and cultural background, social promotion, disability). In order to promote the heterogeneity of the workforce, several actions are implemented such as:

- Creation of dedicated management bodies such as a diversity committee
- Training on diversity in order to raise employee awareness
- Career management, recruitment programmes and communication actions
- Work and life balance measures to promote gender diversity and support for employee parents (nurseries, reducing overtime, flexibility in working time)

Companies in the integrative CR cluster approach diversity from an ethical perspective, where behaving as a responsible employer is seen as a component of doing business in an ethical manner. Emphasis is placed on respect for individual employee's capacities without discrimination, not on the promotion of diversity per se or on heterogeneity in the workforce. Creating a respectful and fair work environment and equality of opportunity are the objectives of this corporate culture.

The consideration of different types of diversity is narrower than for innovative CR firms, putting emphasis on the promotion of gender diversity, while only monitoring other types of diversity. Common actions regarding diversity include:

- Monitoring of diversity
- Fair treatment and recruitment processes

Nevertheless, one of the companies in the integrative CR cluster, Luxottica, presents a dissident example due to its vision of diversity as a competitive advantage. This company targets specifically the promotion of diversity with a diversity and inclusion advisory board, culture team, student mentoring programme, associate opinion survey, diversity training and supplier diversity programmes.

In the philanthropy CR cluster, the consideration of diversity is limited to strict compliance actions, affirmations of non-discriminations and prohibition of harassment, but no specific measures are implemented to promote diversity. Moreover, three out of the five companies have been involved in lawsuits for discrimination and violation of labour rights. For example, Prada Japan was sued for discrimination and harassment (Alexander 2013). Moreover, a former Giorgio Armani Corp. employee is suing the couture fashion house for sexual harassment (McCormack 2013). Armani also received negative reviews for racism and xenophobia when, in 2005, a former Armani manager was awarded compensation after a tribunal ruled he was forced out of his job for being HIV positive.[3] Finally, in 2006, four former employees of the company's Ralph Lauren stores filed a lawsuit alleging violations of wage and working time laws.[4] The plaintiffs purported to represent a class of employees who allegedly had been injured by not properly being paid commission earnings, not being paid overtime, not receiving rest breaks, being forced to work

3 'HIV-positive Armani Exchange Mexico Employee Claims Discrimination', The Friends of Aids Foundation Community Journal, http://friendsofaids2.blogspot.dk/2011/11/hiv-positive-armani-exchange-mexico.html, accessed 4 April 2013.

4 'US: Polo Ralph Lauren Accused of Labor Violations', Corpwatch, www.corpwatch.org/article.php?id=13642, accessed 27 March 2013.

off the clock while waiting to enter or leave stores and being falsely imprisoned while waiting to leave stores.

Conclusion

Based on our analysis of the companies' CR strategy and corporate culture regarding diversity, we draw the following conclusions.

Companies in the luxury sector aiming at integrating CR into their business strategy and investing in sustainability innovation perceive diversity as strength and support it with an inclusive organisational culture. Companies that aim to be a responsible company are integrating environmental and social concerns into their business operations, and conceive respect for diversity as part of being an ethical employer; their diversity management can be characterised as an equal opportunity culture. In contrast, luxury firms that have not considered CR in their core business do not support diversity beyond legal compliance, and their diversity management has been the object of criticism and even lawsuits.

On the other hand, we identified one dissident case that does not confirm our hypothesis: the case of Luxottica shows there are several factors that can moderate the relationship between CR strategy and diversity promotion. It is important to consider other factors such as the business environment, national culture and legislation, and the influence of civil society, as well as the firm's strategic position and industrial structure.

In conclusion, diversity remains an important success factor for companies aiming at innovation and a better understanding of a changing world. In the luxury sector, a diversified management is critical as companies reach new geographical markets and a variety of consumer profiles. However, diversity needs to be managed appropriately in order to get its benefits. Diversity management that encompasses training programmes, management programmes and support of work–life balance, coupled with an organisational culture that promotes employee initiative and consideration of employee opinion, is critical to receive the benefits of diverse teams. In this sense, companies should invest in organisational innovation if they aspire to promote innovation in products and processes regarding CR.

Bibliography

Alexander, E. (2013) 'Prada Vs the UN', *Vogue* (28 May 2013; www.vogue.co.uk/news/2013/05/28/prada-rina-bovrisse-lawsuit---un-statement-released, accessed 12 June 2013.

Arnold, M.F. (2010)'Competitive Advantage from Corporate Responsibility Programmes', in C. Louche, S.O. Idowu and W.L. Filho (eds.), *Innovative CSR: From Risk Management to Value Creation* (Sheffield: Greenleaf): 102-19.

Auld, G., S. Bernstein and B. Cashore (2008) 'The New Corporate Social Responsibility', *Annual Review of Environment and Resources* 33: 413-23.

Aupperle, K.E., A.B. Carroll and J.D. Hatfield (1985) 'An Empirical Examination of the Relationship Between Corporate Social Responsibility and Profitability', *Academy of Management Journal* 28.2: 446-63.

Bendell, J., and A. Kleanthous (2007) *Deeper Luxury: Quality and Style When the World Matters* (London: WWF UK).

Bastien, V., and J-N. Kapferer (2012) *Luxe Oblige* (Paris: Eyrolles).

Carrano, A.L., and B.K. Thorn (2006) 'A Multidisciplinary Approach to Sustainable Product and Process Design', *Journal of Manufacturing Systems* 24.3: 209-15.

Cox, T. (1994) *Cultural Diversity in Organizations: Theory, Research and Practice* (San Francisco, CA: Berrett-Koehler).

DesJardins, J. (1998) 'Corporate Environmental Responsibility', *Journal of Business Ethics* 17.8: 825-14.

Dwyer, S., O.C. Richard and K. Chadwick (2003) 'Gender Diversity in Management and Firm Performance: The Influence of Growth Orientation and Organizational Culture', *Journal of Business Research* 56.12: 1009-11.

Griffiths, A. (2004) 'Corporate Sustainability and Innovation', *Innovation: Management, Policy & Practice* 6.2: 6-9.

Halme, M., and J. Laurila (2009) 'Philanthropy, Integration or Innovation? Exploring the Financial and Societal Outcomes of Different Types of Corporate Responsibility', *Journal of Business Ethics* 84.3: 325-15.

Higgs, M., U. Plewnia and J. Ploch (2005) 'Influence of Team Composition and Task Complexity on Team Performance', *Team Performance Management* 11.7/8: 227-14.

Hillman, A., and G. Keim (2001) 'Shareholder Value, Stakeholder Management, and Social Issues. What's the Bottom Line?', *Strategic Management Journal* 22.2: 125-15.

Kinderyte, L. (2010) 'Methodology of Sustainability Indicators Determination for Enterprise Assessment', *Environmental Research, Engineering and Management* 52.2: 25-27.

Korten, D. (1995) *When Corporations Rule the World* (San Francisco, CA: Berrett-Koehler Publishers).

Lau, J. (2010) 'Foreign Luxury Companies Take Note: Chinese Consumers Favour CSR' (http://blogs.ft.com/beyond-brics/2010/07/21/67251/, accessed 21 July 2010).

Leung, A.K., W.W. Maddux, A.D. Galinsky and C.Y. Chiu (2008) 'Multicultural Experience Enhances Creativity: The When and How', *American Psychologist* 63.3: 169-81.

Lochard, C., and A. Murat (2011) *Luxe et Développement Durable: La Nouvelle Alliance* (Paris: Eyrolles).

McCormack, D. (2013) 'Female Armani Fashion Boss Accused of Sexually Harassing Female Assistant and Dropping Her Pants in New York City Office', *Daily Mail* (16 January 2013; www.dailymail.co.uk/news/article-2263161/Armani-boss-Laura-Giulini-accused-sexually-harassing-female-assistant-New-York-office.html, accessed 10 March 2013).

Miles, M., and A. Huberman (1994) *Qualitative Data Analysis* (London: Sage).

Østergaard, C.R., B. Timmermans and K. Kristinsson (2011) 'Does a Different View Create Something New? The Effect of Employee Diversity on Innovation', *Research Policy* 40.3: 500-509.

Porter, M.E., and M. Kramer (2006), 'Strategy and Society: The Link Between Competitive Advantage and Corporate Social Responsibility', *Harvard Business Review* 84.12: 78-15.

Preuss, L. (2010) 'Barriers to Innovative CSR: The Impacts of Organisational Learning, Organisational Structure and the Social Embeddedness of the Firm', in C. Louche, S.O. Idowu and W.L. Filho (eds.), *Innovative CSR: From Risk Management to Value Creation* (Sheffield, UK: Greenleaf): 331-21.

Stiglitz, J.E (2006) *Making Globalization Work* (London: Penguin Books).

Catarina Pessanha Gomes is a PhD candidate at the Copenhagen Business School in the Department of Intercultural Communication and Management. She has a Master's degree in Sustainability Science from the University of Tokyo and worked in the sustainability team of the Sustainable Procurement Practice Group for the United Nations Office for Project Services. Her research interests include corporate sustainability and responsibility, specifically in the fashion and cosmetic industry, and social entrepreneurship. Email: catarinagomes2411@gmail.com

Masaru Yarime is Project Associate Professor of Science, Technology and Innovation Governance (STIG) at the Graduate School of Public Policy (GraSPP) of the University of Tokyo. He has an appointment as Honorary Reader of University College London (UCL) in the Department of Science, Technology, Engineering and Public Policy (STEaPP). His research interests focus on corporate strategy, public policy and institutional design for promoting science, technology and innovation for sustainability. He contributes to many international initiatives, including the United Nations Environment Programme (UNEP) Finance Initiative on Environmental Risk Integration in Sovereign Credit Analysis, Greenhouse Gas (GHG) Protocol Technical Working Group on GHG Risk Management Protocol, Intergovernmental Panel on Climate Change (IPCC) Working Group III (Mitigation of Climate Change) Fifth Assessment Report, and the Expert Group to develop a guide on and a catalogue of policy support tools and methodologies of the Intergovernmental Platform on Biodiversity and Ecosystem Services (IPBES). Currently he is serving on the editorial boards of international journals, including *Sustainability Science, Environmental Innovation and Societal Transitions, Journal of Corporate Citizenship* and *Frontiers in Energy Research—Energy Systems and Policy*. Email: yarimemasa@gmail.com

Appendix 9.1 **Corporate responsibility evaluation indicators and company ratings**

CR evaluation Indicator	Companies																
	A	**B**	**C**	**D**	**E**	**F**	**G**	**H**	**I**	**J**	**K**	**L**	**M**	**N**	**O**	**P**	**Q**
Code of ethics	1	2	2	2	2	2	1	2	1	1	1	0	1	1	1	1	1
Supply chain management	2	2	2	2	2	2	2	2	0	0	2	1	2	0	2	0	0
Risk management	2	2	2	2	2	1	2	2	2	2	1	1	1	1	1	0	0
Stakeholder engagement	2	2	2	2	2	2	2	2	2	0	0	0	2	0	0	0	0
Contribution to society	2	2	2	2	2	2	2	2	2	2	2	0	2	1	2	1	1
Sustainability reporting	2	2	2	1	0	2	2	0	0	0	0	0	0	0	0	0	0
Sustainability communication to consumers	2	2	2	2	2	2	0	0	0	0	0	0	0	0	0	0	0
Executive commitment to sustainability	2	2	2	2	2	2	2	0	0	0	0	0	0	0	0	0	0
Employee engagement	2	2	2	1	0	2	2	2	2	1	1	0	2	0	2	0	0
Governance	1	2	2	1	2	2	2	2	2	0	0	0	0	0	0	0	0
Water management	2	2	2	2	2	0	2	0	1	2	0	2	0	0	0	0	0
Energy management	2	2	2	2	2	2	2	1	0	2	1	2	0	0	0	0	0
Waste management	2	2	2	2	2	1	0	1	1	1	0	2	0	0	0	0	0
Environmental management system	2	1	1	1	1	0	0	0	1	0	0	0	0	0	0	0	0
Transport	2	2	2	2	2	0	2	1	0	0	1	0	0	0	0	0	0
Material sourcing	1	2	1	2	2	2	2	1	0	0	1	2	0	0	0	0	0
Biodiversity conservation	2	0	2	2	2	2	0	0	0	2	0	0	0	0	0	0	0
Renewable energies	1	1	1	1	1	1	1	0	0	1	0	1	0	0	0	0	0
Product design	2	2	2	2	2	1	1	0	1	2	0	0	0	0	0	0	0
Employee training	2	1	1	2	2	1	2	2	1	2	2	2	1	1	0	0	0

CR evaluation Indicator	Companies																
	A	**B**	**C**	**D**	**E**	**F**	**G**	**H**	**I**	**J**	**K**	**L**	**M**	**N**	**O**	**P**	**Q**
Employee empowerment	2	2	2	2	2	2	1	1	2	0	0	0	0	0	0	0	0
Health	2	2	2	2	2	2	0	2	0	1	2	1	1	1	0	0	0
Safety	2	2	1	2	2	1	1	1	2	2	1	1	0	1	0	0	0
Product safety	1	2	1	2	2	0	0	0	1	0	1	1	0	1	0	0	0
Human rights	2	2	2	2	2	2	2	2	2	2	2	0	1	1	0	0	0
Customer feed-back	2	2	2	0	0	0	0	0	0	0	0	0	0	0	0	0	0
TOTAL	47	47	46	45	44	36	33	26	23	23	18	16	13	8	8	2	2

Notes: A: ELC; B: L'Oréal; C: Shiseido; D: LVMH; E: PPR; F: Tiffany; G: Richemont; H: Burberry; I: Luxottica; J: Hermes; K: Boss; L: Swatch; M: Coach; N: Safilo; O: Ralph Lauren; P: Armani; Q: Prada.

Appendix 9.2 **Diversity initiatives and perceptions**

Company	Promoting diversity	Monitoring diversity	Promoting work-life balance	Prohibiting harassment and discrimination
ELC	2	1	0	1
L'Oréal	2	1	1	1
Shiseido	2	1	1	1
LVMH	2	1	1	1
PPR	2	1	1	1
Tiffany	0	1	0	1
Richemont	0	1	1	1
Burberry	0	1	0	1
Luxottica	2	1	0	1
Hermes	1	1	0	1
Boss	0	1	1	1
Swatch	0	1	0	0
Coach	0	0	0	1
Safilo	0	0	0	1
Ralph Lauren	0	0	0	1
Armani	0	0	0	0
Prada	0	0	0	1

Note: Evaluation scale: 0: low; 1: medium; 2: strong.

10

The wild side of luxury

Can nature continue to sustain the luxury industry?

Xenya Cherny-Scanlon
International Union for Conservation of Nature (IUCN), Gland, Switzerland

Introduction

Wild and fashionable

From wool and leather to perfumes and fine foods, wildlife is a major source of raw materials for the luxury industry.[1] Natural materials, such as fine silks and wools, rare leathers and pearls, are sought after by affluent consumers and are closely associated with luxury brands. Exotic and unique animal and plant species lend themselves to the concept of luxury, which is based on rarity and beauty (Kapferer 2010). Indeed, the inherent scarcity of wildlife resources aligns well with the luxury management strategy of maintaining the exclusivity of products through limited supply (Heine 2013). Furthermore, numerous luxury brands capitalise on the enduring appeal of the wild by using charismatic animals in their marketing and branding strategies, and sometimes turning them into corporate logos—Jaguar and its famous 'leaper' and Lacoste with its signature crocodile are just two obvious examples (Chevalier and Mazzalovo 2012). This has led to calls for the luxury industry to assume its moral responsibility by 'giving back' to wildlife species that

1 While many definitions of luxury and luxury goods exist, for the purposes of this article these are defined as non-essential products which are sold at a premium price, whose supply is naturally limited, and that require a high level of skills and/or craftsmanship along the value chain.

are often the source of its inspiration and profits. Some luxury companies have taken steps in this direction, for example by joining the Save Your Logo campaign.[2] However, a more meaningful engagement which goes beyond mere philanthropy is urgently called for (Archer 2011; Bendell 2012).

In recent decades, the use of wildlife in the fashion and luxury industry, particularly fur, has been a major bone of contention. While the non-lethal uses of wildlife are varied and many, such as the shearing of wool or the harvesting of nuts, the area of the highest controversy is understandably the lethal use of animals for their hides, especially if they are killed specifically for this purpose rather than as a by-product of the food industry. Some leading designers, notably Stella McCartney, are well known for their anti-fur and anti-leather stance, alongside numerous celebrities who eschew animal-derived products on ethical grounds.[3] Nonetheless, global trends show an unwavering demand for wildlife products.[4] Wildlife is, as ever, en vogue. If anything, wildlife products are today increasingly viewed as luxury items—an extravagance rather than a necessity (TRAFFIC 2008).

CITES: 40 years of regulating wildlife trade

The Convention on International Trade in Endangered Species of Wild Fauna and Flora (CITES) was established in 1973 as a response to growing concerns that over-exploitation of wildlife through international trade was contributing to the rapid decline of many species of plants and animals around the world. Today, CITES has been ratified by 180 countries. The Convention's primary aim is to ensure that trade is not detrimental to the survival of species in the wild.

To achieve this, CITES regulates international wildlife trade through a system of permits and certificates. The level of regulation that trade in any individual species undergoes is dependent on whether the species is listed in the CITES' appendices.

Appendix I lists species that are endangered, allowing international trade only in exceptional circumstances. Appendix II species are those that may become endangered if their trade is not regulated, and thus require controls in the form of trade quotas and other measures. Appendix III species are those subject to domestic regulation.

There are approximately 5,500 fauna species and 29,500 flora species protected under the three CITES' appendices, with the overwhelming majority of these (97%) still traded.

2 www.saveyourlogo.org/, accessed 29 May 2014.

3 The killing of animals for food, fashion and other human needs is a deep philosophical debate that goes well beyond the scope of this article, which focuses on the existing international legal framework for wildlife trade.

4 '20 Trends for Fall/Winter 2013–2014', http://en.vogue.fr/fashion/fashion-inspiration/diaporama/20-trends-for-fall-winter-2013-2014/12208, accessed 13 September 2013.

Wildlife trade: big business

Wildlife trade is a growing, and lucrative, business. Today, close to 35,000 animal and plant species are traded internationally under conditions set by CITES (see Box). There are over 13 million recorded trade transactions in the CITES' database, offering a statistical perspective on the global volume of legal international trade in wildlife (CITES 2013).

While the CITES Secretariat does not put a concrete figure on legal wildlife trade, it is estimated to be worth over US$300 billion a year, according to the wildlife trade monitoring network TRAFFIC.[5] By its very nature, it is almost impossible to obtain reliable figures for the value of illegal wildlife trade; however, estimates range between US$5 billion and US$20 billion annually, excluding timber and marine wildlife (CITES 2013: 7). It has been suggested that the illicit trafficking of wildlife products is the fourth largest illegal trade after narcotics, human trafficking and counterfeit goods (Mostov and El Hadad 2013).

Some of the highly traded species are destined for the luxury markets. Trade in just three species of python is worth at least US$1 billion per year at the end of the value chain (Kasterine *et al.* 2012: 26). The price of a vicuña wool scarf starts at around US$1,000 (CITES 2013: 7). Delicacies such as caviar and truffles are prised by gourmets around the world, while essential oils are widely used in the beauty industry. Agarwood, the world's most precious aromatic substance, is far more valuable by weight than gold (Persoon 2007: 24). Despite the current economic crisis, nature-based luxury products continue to fetch record prices.

Growing consumer demand

There are clear signs that our growing appetite for nature-based luxury products is putting serious strain on some animal and plant populations, and in some cases the danger of these species going extinct in the wild is becoming very real. According to the International Union for Conservation of Nature (IUCN), one in four mammals and nearly one in five reptiles are today threatened with extinction (IUCN 2014).

Trade and growth in global consumption are major factors pushing many of these species to the brink. For example, growing numbers of newly wealthy people in emerging economies are becoming consumers of luxury products previously reserved only for the elite. China has emerged as the fastest-growing luxury consumer force in the world (Bain 2012).

However, unlike the growing awareness of dwindling supplies of precious metals and gemstones (Hardyment 2013), limited availability of wildlife as a resource for the luxury industry is a largely overlooked issue. For instance, the *Fashioning Sustainability 2013* report, while acknowledging that 'in the long term the natural

5 www.traffic.org/trade/, accessed 3 May 2013.

resources will run out if we continue business as usual' (Deloitte 2013: 8), does not explicitly mention wildlife among resources that will face increasing scarcity in the 21st century. Yet when wildlife populations collapse, the impacts can be far-reaching, not only on the environment and livelihoods, but also on the luxury industry. The unprecedented CITES ban on all international trade in wild sturgeon fish and caviar in 2006 sent ripples through the entire fine food industry from which, by mid-2014, it has not recovered, despite the relaxation of some of the sanctions.[6]

The very sustainability[7] of the luxury value chain ultimately depends on the survival, and sustainable use, of wildlife species in their countries of origin. Can our natural world continue to supply the raw materials for food, clothing, medicine, furniture and perfumes on a planet of seven billion, rising to nine billion consumers, by 2050?

The luxury imperative: taking control of the value chain

The luxury industry can be rather opaque when it comes to disclosing information along the chain of custody. As a leading luxury industry sustainability report by the Swiss-based private Bank Sarasin pointed out in 2012 (Ashida 2012):[8]

> The challenge facing luxury brands is to develop sustainable supply chain management systems, especially so that they are able to trace the origin of the raw materials and products they use. Far more transparency is therefore required.

This call for transparency and sustainability in the luxury industry supply chain echoes another one, made five years earlier, by WWF's seminal *Deeper Luxury* report (Bendell and Kleanthous 2007: 29), which argued that:

> Luxury brands will continue to be criticised until they provide independent guarantees of the sustainability and ethical credentials of their animal-derived products.

Raw materials represent a major part of the luxury industry's value chain and account for a significant share of its environmental impact. For instance, over half

6 See Princesse d'Isenbourg et Cie website: www.caviar.co.uk/caviar-cites.html, accessed 8 June 2014.

7 The term 'sustainability' has many definitions. The one used in this article is that contained in the 1987 *Our Common Future* report, which defines sustainability as meeting the current generation's needs without compromising those of future generations (WCED 1987).

8 www.sarasin-alpen.com/internet/ieae/media_relations_news_ieae.htm?reference=138745&checkSum=A1569DE32FD404813E193E37AB4D7E70, accessed 9 June 2014.

(57% or €83 million) of all environmental impacts of luxury sport and lifestyle brand PUMA are associated with the production of raw materials (including leather, cotton and rubber), according to the company's first ever environmental profit and loss account.[9]

Continued supply of raw materials for the luxury industry depends on well-managed populations of animal and plant species, both in the wild and elsewhere, such as farming operations. This requirement under CITES is known as 'non-detriment findings', which are intended to guarantee that trade does not threaten the survival of these species in the wild. Indeed, it could be argued that this kind of findings should be made for all wildlife species in trade, not just those controlled by CITES.

In the corporate world, there have been attempts to set minimum standards for the sourcing of raw materials, for example Kering's code of business practice at the group level which includes guidelines for leather, exotic skins and fur,[10] or industry-wide animal sourcing principles developed by members of the Sustainable Luxury Working Group, which includes Burberry Ltd., Cartier, Gucci and LVMH (BSR 2011). Another notable initiative being taken in this regard is the launch of the first fully traceable luxury eco-bag by Gucci in 2013, which is accompanied by a passport certifying the leather's provenance from ranches in Brazil that do not cause deforestation, the origins of the handle made from fast-growing bamboo, as well as the work of craftsmen in Gucci's factory in Florence (Armstrong 2013).

At the same time, the luxury sector still has significant ground to make up in the area of sustainability. According to a recent sustainability report from the ASEAN region, which accounts for a large share of wildlife-sourced products used in the luxury industry, 80% of companies still do not measure sustainability in their supply chain (PWC 2013: 5).

Luxury companies looking to implement sustainable strategies throughout their supply chain must ensure that raw materials are of high quality, that negative environmental and social impacts are minimised, and that the supply chain metrics are continuously improved (Kumar *et al.* 2012). Ensuring the sustainability and traceability of wildlife products will help advance all of these objectives.

Case studies

The case studies below examine several CITES-regulated species used in the luxury industry for wool (vicuña and the Tibetan antelope), leather (crocodiles and pythons) and delicacies (sturgeons and truffles[11]), selected on the basis of sourcing

9 http://about.puma.com/puma-completes-first-environmental-profit-and-loss-account-which-values-impacts-at-e-145-million/, accessed 13 September 2013.

10 www.kering.com/en/sustainability/targets, accessed 16 September 2013.

11 Truffles are not currently regulated by CITES but, as the author argues, could benefit from such regulation.

methods and species' management strategies. These case studies are largely based on secondary, publicly available sources, supplemented by the author's primary research and first-hand interviews with luxury executives as well as legal, trade and conservation experts. They are intended to provide insights into how the luxury industry can contribute towards ensuring the sustainability of wildlife trade by taking control of its supply chain.

Wool: in search of the golden fleece

Vicuña

Vicuña is the smallest member of the Camelidae family, a cousin of llamas and alpacas. Considered as 'the fibre of gods' by the Incas, vicuña's unique and precious fleece was used exclusively to produce emperors' clothes. The ritual shearing of the animals, known as 'chaccu', took place every three to five years, after which the animals were released back into the wild.

Following the European conquest, vicuña were nearly driven to extinction due to indiscriminate slaughter. By 1960, some 6,000 individuals remained out of an estimated two million 500 years earlier. In response to the perilous state of vicuña populations, the Andean countries signed the Convention for the Conservation of Vicuña in 1969. Following the entry into force of CITES, international trade in vicuña was prohibited in 1975.

By 1987, some populations had recovered so significantly that trade in cloth made from wool sheared from live animals was partially reopened. A further breakthrough for vicuña was achieved when the government of Peru, assisted by CITES, gave local communities the legal rights to manage vicuña populations and benefit from trade, as long as they protected the animals from poaching.

In 1994, the International Vicuña Consortium, comprised of three companies, including Agnona (which was later acquired by the Ermenegildo Zegna Group) and Loro Piana, received the first authorisation of legal vicuña trade from Peru (Zegna 2011). In the words of Paolo Zegna, chair of the Zegna Group: 'The reappearance of the vicuña on the international market, free of any moral concern, was greeted with enthusiasm by our customers'.

Today, the Peruvian vicuña population, estimated at a healthy 190,000, is farmed sustainably to the benefit of local communities, the environment and the luxury industry. While certain benefit-sharing issues have not been fully resolved, vicuña is a hallmark example of sustainable sourcing of a luxury product entirely from the wild.

Photo credit: David Torres Costales

Shahtoosh

The story of the Tibetan antelope, also prised for its gossamer wool, called 'shahtoosh', is very similar to that of vicuña—bar the happy ending. Like vicuña, shahtoosh, a Persian word meaning 'king of wools', was historically obtained non-violently; however, waiting for the antelope to shed its precious coat naturally was too much to ask for in the era of modern consumerism. According to People for the Ethical Treatment of Animals (PETA) India, it now takes five dead antelopes to make one shahtoosh shawl (India Today 2012).

Despite CITES trade bans, there are signs that poaching and significant illegal trade continues (Benson *et al.* 2013). A shahtoosh shawl would fetch between US$2,000 to US$15,000 or more depending on size and quality on the illegal market (AME Info 2003). Meanwhile, Kashmiri artisans are at risk of losing the age-old shahtoosh weaving tradition, which requires exceptional craftsmanship. Many are increasingly turning to pashmina as a substitute (India Today 2012).

To achieve a reversal in the fate of the Tibetan antelope, urgent leadership from range countries and the industry is required. By learning from the vicuña example, they can work with local communities to provide economic incentives for the antelope's conservation and thereby ensure the sustainable supply of its precious wool for the luxury market under strict conditions.

Leather: a slippery tale

Crocodilians

Hunted for their skins, crocodiles and alligators were, like many other reptiles, endangered in the 1960s and 1970s. After World War II, between 11 and 12 million crocodiles skins were sold every year (Boisteaux *et al.* 2013). The commercial success of leather from the Nile crocodile, the American alligator and others led to their near extinction.

With declining wild populations, the concept of crocodile farming began to gather momentum. Following the entry into force of CITES, trade in wild skins from unmanaged populations was banned. These measures both put a stop to unregulated and illegal hunting for skins and gave a much needed impetus to the crocodile ranching industry, which was seen as a way to reduce pressure on wild populations and create commercial incentives for the conservation of crocodilians. By the late 1970s and 1980s many programmes were being developed in Australia, Indonesia, Papua New Guinea, USA, Venezuela and Zimbabwe.[12] Ranching proved to be a successful way to restore wildlife populations back to health; American alligator farming alone has generated US$600 million since it was introduced (Boisteaux *et al.* 2013). A high-end crocodile handbag can fetch up to US$90,000 (Rex 2010).

Today, crocodiles are traded under internationally agreed and controlled conditions to ensure the survival of the species in the wild. A universal tagging system for all crocodilian skins entering international trade, which identifies their country of origin and distinguishes between ranched and wild specimens, has been put into place. Between 2000 and 2010, over one million skins were sold annually from some 30 countries (Caldwell 2010). The market has since decreased due to lower demand, in part linked to the emergence of other fashionable reptile skins such as pythons.

12 See IUCN Species Survival Commission Crocodile Specialist Group website: www.iucncsg.org/pages/Farming-and-the-Crocodile-Industry.html, accessed 22 April 2013.

Photo credit: Herry Lawford

Pythons

In recent years, exotic skins, in particular python skins, have become a major fashion trend. The EU is the world's biggest importer of reptile skins (Kasterine *et al.* 2012). Today, nearly half a million python skins are exported from South-East Asia annually and the trade is estimated to be a billion dollar a year industry. Most recently, however, python trade has been in the spotlight for all the wrong reasons.

'It would appear a substantial proportion of the skins in trade are sourced illegally from wild animals, beyond agreed quotas, and using false permits to launder the skins', says Tomas Waller, chair of IUCN Species Survival Commission's Boa and Python Specialist Group.[13] Moreover, investigative journalists have uncovered some gruesome slaughter methods carried out in Asian python slaughterhouses, such as skinning live animals.

In the wake of controversy surrounding python trade, several luxury companies, including the Swatch Group, put in place a voluntary moratorium on the leather imported from South-East Asia.[14] In addition to CITES having listed pythons on its

13 www.iucn.org/media/news_releases/?11551/Study-raises-concern-over-international-trade-in-python-skins, accessed 9 June 2014.

14 www.swatchgroup.com/en/services/archive/2010/watch_bracelets_made_from_exotic_leathers, accessed 25 April 2013.

Appendix II, the EU currently has a ban in place on skins sourced from Malaysia. The Swiss parliament voted in early 2012 to ban imports of python skins from Indonesia on the grounds of perceived cruelty during slaughter.

Does this herald the end of legal, or at least, sustainable python trade? Not necessarily. The 2012 report *The Trade in South-East Asian Python Skins* by the International Trade Centre, TRAFFIC and IUCN (Kasterine *et al.* 2012; Natusch 2013) identified several positive aspects of trade and recommended that the fashion industry implements a traceability system along the length of the supply chain to allow identification of skins and to complement the existing CITES permitting system.

The first steps towards such a system were made in 2013 when UN agencies, key exporting countries, the luxury industry and reptile experts came together to discuss conservation concerns, technological options, law enforcement and other essential measures to achieve sustainable python trade.[15] It will likely build upon existing successful initiatives, such as the Marsh to Market programme developed in Louisiana, USA, which provides economic, community and conservation benefits from sustainable alligator trade. Furthermore, in late 2013, Kering, the International Trade Centre and IUCN formed a partnership focusing on improving sustainability, transparency, animal welfare and local livelihoods for the python skin trade.[16] These recent developments give hope that pythons may one day become a success story of a CITES-listed species used in the luxury industry.

Photo credit: Mark Auliya

15 http://unctad.org/en/Pages/MeetingDetails.aspx?meetingid=266, accessed 9 June 2014.
16 www.iucn.org/?14068/Kering-IUCN-and-ITC-form-partnership-to-improve-python-trade, accessed 9 June 2014.

Delicacies: taste of the wild

Numerous fine foods and delicacies—be it caviar from Beluga sturgeon and Alba's white truffles sought after by European gourmets, or sea cucumbers and shark fin soup considered a high point of Asian cuisine—come directly from the wild. Our insatiable appetite for rare palate-pleasing tastes has already driven several of these species to the brink of extinction and continues to bring a growing number of species under CITES controls.

Caviar: from opulence to oblivion?

Caspian sturgeon, whose salt-cured roe is used to produce the prised Beluga, Ossetra and Sevruga caviar, may be one species for which CITES controls came too late. Once a delicacy of choice for royalty and aristocracy alike, caviar from wild sturgeons has today all but vanished from the world's finest dining tables.

Following decades of uncontrolled exploitation across its range, Beluga sturgeon populations, whose unfertilised eggs are considered the finest in the world, have been decimated. This resulted in CITES taking the unprecedented step in January 2006 of suspending trading in all wild sturgeon fish and caviar. The suspension was in response to rampant corruption and illegal trade in one of the world's most expensive foods, which fetches up to US$10,000 per kilo.[17] In 2006, Russian authorities estimated that for every registered 1,000 tonnes of caviar, there are between 12,000–14,000 tonnes placed on the black market (Fletcher 2006). One guess puts the value of illegal caviar trade at many times that of legal commerce, itself worth €244 million (Ahlenius 2008).

Several years after the ban, wild sturgeon populations in the Caspian Sea, which used to account for 90% of world caviar trade, and elsewhere, have yet to recover. In 2010, IUCN ranked sturgeon as one of the most threatened groups of animals. According to the fine foods company Princesse d'Isenbourg et Cie, CITES suspension 'forged profound implications to connoisseurs and vendors' perspective on the ethics of wild caviar and its sustainability',[18] prompting many to turn to caviar coming from farmed sturgeons.

Today, despite the relaxation of some trade sanctions and management and enforcement measures put in place by range countries, the prospects for caviar ever coming from the wild again in the future are rather uncertain. According to CITES expert Mathias Lörtscher, in the case of sturgeons, CITES failed to get the results it had hoped for (Jorio 2013):

> To protect the sturgeon we tried labelling all the containers of caviar sold. This did not have the desired effect: today the wild sturgeon cannot be marketed because there are so few specimens left.

17 www.iucn.org/?4928/Sturgeon-more-critically-endangered-than-any-other-group-of-species, accessed 9 June 2014.

18 www.caviar.co.uk/caviar-cites.html, accessed 9 June 2014.

Photo credit: THOR

Truffles in trouble?

Northern Italy is home to one of the most sought-after objects of gastronomical desire—white truffles—for which connoisseurs are willing to pay upwards of $5,000 per kilo. For example, a 750 g white truffle sold for US$210,000 in 2007 (Weird News Asia 2007). These underground treasures are unearthed by the 'trifulaus' (truffle hunters) and their specially trained dogs. In recent years, harvested volumes in France and Italy have been declining quite significantly due to pollution and forest degradation, and some say climate change (Büntgen *et al.* 2012). After peaking at €27 million in 1997, Italian white truffle exports have stabilised at around €5 million per year over the past decade (Galluzzo 2013).

The trend is clear—more cultivated truffles, less wild ones. According to truffle producer Domenico Trivelli (Warner 2012):

> It used to be that 20 years ago 90% of what we sold came directly from the hunters. Before long, 90% of what we sell will be from planted reserves.

While there have been attempts to cultivate both white and black truffles, including in Australia, China, New Zealand, USA and elsewhere in Italy, the best truffles are still believed to come from the wild. 'The wilder, the better', says trifulau Romina Casette in an interview to *The Atlantic* (Dart 2011).

At the moment, however, truffle connoisseurs do not have reliable information as to where their precious fungi come from. Trifulaus are notoriously unwilling to share information on their harvests. Some truffle producers admit to selling cultivated truffles in guise of wild ones (Warner 2012) and a New York chef recently acknowledged having smuggled white truffles from Italy (Duckor 2012). In the absence of a transparent, well-regulated truffle trade, the market is rife with speculation and fraud. 'The whole thing always feels like a drug deal, first of all', New York restaurateur Frank Prisinzano told *Bon Appetit* magazine (Duckor 2012).

Faced with an uncertain future in the wild, it would appear that truffles could benefit from better regulation under CITES. At the moment, they are not listed on any of the Convention's appendices, and there seems to be some confusion as to whether they can be listed at all as, being fungi, they are neither animal nor plant, which are the two types of wildlife mentioned in the Convention's text. Nevertheless, CITES does provide for the protection of fungi following a decision taken back in 2002 (Alvarenga *et al.* 2002). So if there is a will by truffle producing countries to propose their listing, then there is a way. The question is whether these countries will choose this option before wild truffles become as elusive as, say, wild sturgeons.

Conclusions

As CITES' 40 years of experience shows, it is possible to manage wildlife trade sustainably and thereby secure the future for many unique and precious animals and plants that are essential for the luxury industry. For this to happen, the industry has to work collaboratively with governments, local communities, conservation organisations and consumers to ensure legal, sustainable and traceable international wildlife trade for which CITES provides a solid set of ground rules. One positive development in this respect is the growing engagement of the luxury industry in CITES.

The inherently limited availability of wildlife resources must compel the industry and consumers to recognise that some luxury products cannot be 'democratised' or mass produced, and that some may not even be available to sample or to savour in one's lifetime. This would in fact reinforce the true meaning of luxury as something rare, unique and exclusive. Trade bans remain the most powerful and contentious tool in the CITES' arsenal, used only as the last resort. However, as some anti-trade advocates point out, as long as wildlife products are legally traded in international commerce, the economic incentives for killing such animals are overwhelming (Hoyt 1994).

At the same time, a most worrisome trend has emerged whereby some shady market players are 'banking on extinction', stockpiling illegally trafficked wildlife products in the hope of supplies dwindling even further and prices going up. In other words, species extinction may be an incentive-driven process via the price mechanism (Mason *et al.* 2012). Placing monetary value on conserving species in the wild, generating alternative sources of income (e.g. from wildlife tourism), and finding ways to lift people out of poverty in countries where much of our natural wealth is found, are just some options being explored to break the downward spiral of scarcity–value–exploitation–more scarcity.

Furthermore, establishing a well-controlled legal market for wildlife products is of paramount importance. In the case of wild sturgeons, rampant corruption and criminal activity in some range countries have dwarfed attempts by CITES to provide economic incentives for their conservation and sustainable trade. Some observers point out that, all too often, CITES is relegated to being 'an ambulance at the bottom of the cliff', a last-resort mechanism after management systems collapse (Aguilar *et al.* 2007: 22). Upstream, early engagement between the international community, the luxury industry, governments and conservationists is therefore all the more important. For example, faced with a growing threat to wildlife from organised crime, CITES has joined forces with Interpol, the UN Office on Drugs and Crime, the World Bank and the World Customs Organisation by establishing the International Consortium on Combating Wildlife Crime. The luxury industry has an obvious interest in supporting these law enforcement efforts.

The main strategies currently employed by the luxury industry to secure a sustainable supply of wildlife resources are strictly managed sourcing from the wild and captive breeding/farming/ranching operations. However, another key strategy that is currently under-utilised by the industry is pre-emptive action—actively engaging in conservation programmes aimed at ensuring the survival of wildlife species early on, whether or not they are subject to CITES regulation. Voluntary certification schemes, such as the FairWild[19] standard for plants or the Wildlife Friendly® label given to products that deliver concrete conservation benefits to endangered species, are already being used for some luxury products (e.g. Patagonian 'green' cashmere[20]) and will no doubt gain prominence in the years ahead.

Sustainable management of wild animal and plant species will ultimately mean a greater 'taming' of the wild. At the moment, we are seeing a notable shift from wild-sourced to farmed wildlife resources (e.g. crocodiles, caviar, truffles). As a result, truly 'wild' products will continue to demand a premium price to retain the luxury cachet, whereas sourcing from farming/ranching operations will be more acceptable alternatives for 'masstige' products. For this, clear identification of wild versus farmed products that enables tracing the product to its origin, for example one based on the universal tagging system used for crocodiles, is a must-have. At the same time, animal welfare aspects must be fully addressed to comply with the ethical standards set by conservation organisations and the luxury industry itself.

In most cases where CITES' controls for wildlife trade were met with success, this was achieved thanks to the full involvement of local communities by ensuring that

19 www.fairwild.org.

20 See Wildlife Conservation Society website: www.wcs.org/press/press-releases/green-cashmere-wildlife-friendly.aspx, accessed 9 June 2014.

they directly benefit from such trade and therefore have a stake in securing the species' survival in the wild. Likewise, industry leadership in taking threatened species 'under its wing' and investing in their survival and sustainable use as the source of luxury products would be a much welcome development. Today, the future of the Tibetan antelope may well hinge on whether there will emerge an industry champion prepared to do for the Tibetan antelope what Agnona, Loro Piana and the Zegna Group did for vicuñas 30 years ago. A legal requirement for sourcing wildlife products non-lethally wherever possible would also go a long way towards ensuring sustainability of trade and reinforcing its ethical credentials.

Finally, the face of the luxury consumer is changing. The 'Facebook generation', who rely primarily on social media for information about the ethical and environmental performance of the luxury industry, wants to be associated with brands that are thoughtful and responsible (Four Seasons 2012). Could these new luxury consumers disrupt the industry, often criticised for its apathy and indifference, and propel it into action? Or will they simply conform to existing norms and maintain the status quo? A recent good news story in this regard comes from China where the younger generation has been instrumental in changing attitudes towards the consumption of shark fin soup, once a delicacy served at weddings and banquets, and which has grown increasingly popular with China's newly rich, pushing several shark species towards extinction as a result. Fronted by celebrities such as the Chinese basketball star Yao Ming, and spread virally via the country's largest social media network Sina Weibo, a public awareness campaign has mobilised many young people who succeeded in putting shark fin soup 'out of fashion' (Denyer 2013). This example illustrates perhaps the greatest ingredient of success in managing wildlife resources sustainably—a shift in mindset.

In conclusion, transparency and traceability can be a competitive leverage for luxury brands by adding value to local producers, upholding the positive brand image, and giving luxury consumers peace of mind in line with their expectations. In addition to improving its environmental performance, taking control of the value chain would enable luxury companies to better manage risks, tighten quality controls and achieve greater vertical integration, thereby reinforcing their brand value and attractiveness to investors. It is no mere coincidence that the luxury companies singled out as sustainability leaders by Bank Sarasin (Ashida 2012) are the ones who have made the greatest investment in both transparency and sustainability of their supply chains. According to a leading industry publication, *The Business of Fashion* (Young 2013):

> Being benevolent now means better business because, in the end, transparency and traceability are concepts anchored in building consumer trust.

Today, the luxury industry has a unique opportunity to lead the way in achieving a step change in how we use the gifts of nature—and, in doing so, secure its own sustainable future.

Bibliography

Aguilar, S., A. Brooke, X. Cherny-Scanlon, L. Gordon and S. Jinnah (2007) 'Summary of the 14th Conference of the Parties to the Convention on International Trade in Endangered Species of Wild Fauna and Flora', *Earth Negotiations Bulletin*, 18 June 2007: 21-61.

Ahlenius, H. (2008) 'The Economy of Legal Wildlife Trade', *Environment and Poverty Times* 5: 10-11.

Alvarenga, K., P. Nuengsigkapian, M. Schulman, S. Speier and E. Tsioumani (2002) 'Summary of the 12th Conference of the Parties to the Convention on International Trade in Endangered Species of Wild Fauna and Flora', *Earth Negotiations Bulletin*, 18 November 2002: 21-30.

AME Info (2003) 'Shahtoosh: The Lethal Cost of Luxury' *AME Info* (www.ameinfo.com/29009.html, accessed 21 May 2013).

Archer, P. (ed.) (2011) 'Raconteur on Sustainable Luxury', *The Times*, 6 July 2011.

Armstrong, L. (2013) 'Eco-Fashion: Why Green is the New Black for Gucci', *The Telegraph*, 2 March 2013.

Ashida, M. (2012) *The Quest for Authenticity: Can Luxury Brands Justify a Premium Price?* (Basel, Switzerland: Bank Sarasin).

Bain (2012) *Luxury Goods Worldwide Market Study, China Edition* (Shanghai, China: Bain).

Bendell, J. (2012) *Elegant Disruption: How Luxury and Society Can Change Each Other For Good* (Brisbane, Australia: Asia Pacific Centre for Sustainable Enterprise, Griffith University).

Bendell, J., and A. Kleanthous (2007) *Deeper Luxury: Quality and Style When the World Matters* (London: WWF-UK).

Benson, C., K. Harris, R. Kantai, K. Neville and T. Rosen (2013) 'Summary of the 16th Conference of the Parties to the Convention on International Trade in Endangered Species of Wild Fauna and Flora', *Earth Negotiations Bulletin*, 3 March 2013: 21-73.

Boisteaux E., R. Crossley, J. Leprovost and C. Valissant-Binkley (2013) *Wild and Precious* (Paris: Editions de la Martinière).

BSR (2011) *Sustainable Luxury Working Group: Animal Sourcing Principles* (8 February 2011; www.bsr.org/files/SLWG_Animal_Sourcing_Principles.pdf, accessed 9 June 2014).

Büntgen, U., S. Egli, J. Camarero, E. Fischer, U. Stobbe, H. Kauserud, W. Tegel, L. Sproll and N. Stenseth (2012) 'Drought-Induced Decline in Mediterranean Truffle Harvest', *Nature Climate Change* 2: 827-29.

Caldwell, J. (2010) *World Trade in Crocodilian Skins, 2006–2008* (Cambridge, UK: UNEP-WCMC).

Chevalier, M., and G. Mazzalovo (2012) *Luxury Brand Management: A World of Privilege* (Singapore: John Wiley & Sons).

CITES (2013) *CITES at 40: Regulating the World's Wildlife Trade* (Geneva: CITES Secretariat).

Dart, J. (2011) 'The Sustainable White Truffle', *The Atlantic* (28 November 2011; www.theatlantic.com/health/archive/2011/11/the-sustainable-white-truffle/248697/, accessed 8 June 2014).

Deloitte (2013) *Fashioning Sustainability 2013* (Copenhagen, Denmark: Deloitte).

Denyer, S. (2013) 'In China, Shark Fin Soup is Losing its Fashion', *The Independent* (21 October 2013; www.independent.co.uk/voices/comment/in-china-shark-fin-soup-is-losing-its-fashion-8894495.html; accessed 27 October 2013).

Duckor, M. (2012) 'Here's What $10,000 in Smuggled White Truffles Looks Like', *Bon Appetit* (19 November 2012; www.bonappetit.com/blogsandforums/blogs/badaily/2012/11/smuggled-white-truffles.html, accessed 9 June 2014).

Fletcher, A. (2006) 'Global Caviar Trade Suspended', *foodnavigator.com* (5 January 2006; www.foodnavigator.com/Legislation/Global-caviar-trade-suspended, accessed 24 May 2013).

Four Seasons (2012) *The Luxury Consumer in the New Digital World: Then & Now. 2012 Four Seasons Luxury Trend Report* (January 2012; www.fourseasons.com/content/dam/fourseasons/web/pdfs/landing_page_pdfs/2012_TRD_Report_FINAL.pdf; accessed 29 May 2014).

Galluzzo, N. (2013) 'Italian Truffle Cultivation and Its Commercial Trend in the European Union Market', *International Journal of Agricultural Science and Research* 3.2: 47-58.

Hardyment, R. (2013) *Future Business: The Four Mega-Trends That Every Company Needs To Prepare For* (London: Corporate Citizenship).

Heine, K. (2011) *The Concept of Luxury Brands: Luxury Brand Management* (Berlin: Technische Universität Berlin).

Hoyt, J. (1994) *Animals in Peril: How 'Sustainable Use' is Wiping Out the World's Wildlife* (Honesdale, PA: The Humane Society of the United States).

India Today (2012) 'Shahtoosh: Can the Prized Industry Be Revived Again?' *India Today* (10 April 2012; http://indiatoday.intoday.in/story/shahtoosh-can-the-prised-industry-be-revived-again/1/183749.html, accessed 22 June 2014).

IUCN (International Union for Conservation of Nature) (2014) *The IUCN Red List of Threatened Species. Version 2014.1* (www.iucnredlist.org, accessed 12 June 2014.

Jorio, L. (2013) 'How the Law Protects Rare Species—Or Not', *swissinfo.ch* (4 January 2013; www.swissinfo.ch/eng/science_technology/How_the_law_protects_rare_species_-_or_not.html?cid=34642058, accessed 23 April 2013).

Kapferer, J-N. (2010) 'All That Glitters is Not Green: The Challenge of Sustainable Luxury', *European Business Review*, November–December 2010: 40-45.

Kasterine, A., R. Arbeid, O. Caillabet and D. Natusch (2012) *The Trade in South-East Asian Python Skins* (Geneva: International Trade Centre).

Kumar, S., S. Teichman and T. Timpernagel (2012) 'A Green Supply Chain is a Requirement for Profitability', *International Journal of Production Research* 50.5: 1278-96.

Mason, C., E. Bulte and R. Horan (2012) 'Banking on Extinction: Endangered Species and Speculation', *Oxford Review of Economic Policy* 28.1: 180-92.

Mostov, A., and H. El Hadad (2013) 'Infographic: The Journey of a Rhino Horn', *Al Jazeera* (7 October 2013; www.aljazeera.com/programmes/wildlife-warzone/2013/10/infographic-journey-a-rhino-horn-2013107143045828890.html; accessed 26 September 2013).

Natusch, D. (2013) 'The Trade in South-East Asian Python Skins', *SULiNews* I.4 (March).

Persoon, G. (2007) 'Agarwood: The Life of a Wounded Tree', *IIAS Newsletter* 45 (https://openaccess.leidenuniv.nl/bitstream/handle/1887/12820/IIAS_NL45_2425.pdf?sequence=1, accessed 8 June 2014).

PWC (2013) *Going Beyond Philanthropy? Pulse-Check on Sustainability* (Kuala Lumpur, Malaysia: PWC).

Rex, E. (2010) 'Is This How You Save the Crocodile?', *The Times Eureka*, September 2010: 42-43.

TRAFFIC (2008) *What's Driving the Wildlife Trade? A Review of Expert Opinion on Economic and Social Drivers of the Wildlife Trade and Trade Control Efforts in Cambodia, Indonesia, Lao PDR and Vietnam* (Washington, DC: World Bank).

Warner, B. (2012) 'White Gold: A Look at the 2012 Truffle Trade', *Grub Street* (14 November 2012; http://newyork.grubstreet.com/2012/11/inside-the-truffle-business.html, accessed 31 May 2013).

WCED (World Commission on Environment and Development) (1987) *Our Common Future* (Oxford, UK: Oxford University Press).Weird Asia News (2007) '$210,000 White Truffle' (12 November 2007; www.weirdasianews.com/2007/11/12/210000-white-truffle/, accessed 22 June 2014).

Young, R. (2013) 'Stripped Bare: Brands Move Toward Transparency and Traceability', *The Business of Fashion* (23 July 2013; www.businessoffashion.com/2013/07/nike-nudie-honest-by-bruno-pieters-stripped-bare-brands-move-toward-transparency-and-traceability.html, accessed 16 June 2014).
Zegna, P. (2011) 'Protecting Vicuñas and Producing High End Fashion', *Business.2020*, June 2011: 10-11.

Xenya Cherny-Scanlon is a sustainability professional with over ten years of experience across three continents with major international organisations, where she gained insights into global wildlife trade. She is the founder and author of *greenstilettos.com* blog and serves as a sustainable luxury and fashion expert. Email: xenya.cherny-scanlon@iucn.org

Disclaimer

The views expressed in this article are those of the author and do not necessarily represent the views of, and should not be attributed to, the International Union for Conservation of Nature.

About the editors

Dr **Miguel Angel Gardetti** has been the head of the Center for Study of Corporate Sustainability (IESC) since its foundation in 2002, and he also holds the same position at the Center for Studies on Sustainable Luxury. He is head professor in the MBA and Master's programmes both in Argentina and elsewhere. He has provided training within frameworks of executive education and in-house programmes to CEOs and corporate managers both from domestic and multinational companies in Argentina and Latin America. With regard to luxury and sustainability topics, he has lectured at the Instituto de Empresa (Madrid, Spain), one of the top business schools in Europe. Moreover, he was a speaker at Identidad Uruguay, an event organised by the Universidad de Empresa (Montevideo), with a lecture on fashion, luxury and sustainability. He was the creator of the Best Performance in Sustainable Luxury in Latin America Award (at present evolving towards the Award in Sustainable Premium and Luxury at a global level). He has developed several publications in the area of sustainable luxury. He was a member of the UN Global Compact Promoting Group in Argentina and a member of its governance body—the Board of the Argentine Chapter of the Global Compact—for two consecutive terms. He was co-founder of the Global Compact Chair in Argentina, and he was also part of the task force that developed the Management Responsible Education Principles of the UN Global Compact. He has also co-ordinated tasks for the Inter-American Development Bank, International Finance Corporation (the private sector arm of the World Bank), Netherlands Development Organisation, United Nations (New York) and the World Resources Institute (USA.)

Ana Laura Torres has a BSc in ecology from the Universidad Nacional de La Plata. She specialises in corporate sustainability at the Center for Study of Corporate Sustainability. She contributed to the creation and development of the Center for Studies on Sustainable Luxury and the Sustainable Textile Center, which she has been co-ordinating since March 2011. Up until 2012 she has been an active member of the Base of the Pyramid Learning Laboratory in Argentina since its foundation in 2005. She has also carried out environmental consulting work for the German Institute for Investment and Development (DEG) in Cologne (Germany). She has worked as both researcher and professor at Universidad Nacional de La Plata. She has co-edited many international publications in the field of sustainable textiles and fashion, such as the special issue of *The Journal of Corporate Citizenship* (UK) on fashion, textiles and sustainability (September 2012) and a book on the same subject entitled *Sustainability in Fashion and Textiles: Values, Design, Production and Consumption* (March 2013; Greenleaf Publishing, Sheffield, UK). Together with Miguel Angel Gardetti, she co-edited the special issue of *The Journal of Corporate Citizenship* (UK) on sustainable luxury (December 2013).